I0819424

HOW TO READ
(*and write*)
LIKE A CATHOLIC

HOW TO READ (*and write*) LIKE A CATHOLIC

JOSHUA HREN

TAN Books
Gastonia, North Carolina

Cover design by Chris Pelicano

Library of Congress Control Number: 2021931507

ISBN: 978-1-5051-1866-7
Kindle ISBN: 978-1-5051-1867-4
ePUB ISBN: 978-1-5051-1868-1

Published in the United States by
TAN Books
PO Box 269
Gastonia, NC 28053
www.TANBooks.com
Printed in the United States of America

For Dana Gioia,
who has given this verse a real presence:

"Be not therefore solicitous for tomorrow; for the morrow will be solicitous for itself. Sufficient for the day is the evil thereof."

—Matthew 6:34, DRA

"Joshua Hren's How to Read (and Write) Like A Catholic pays tribute to a wide range of notable authors from the Catholic literary tradition. But what follows Hren's exquisite and original exploration of literary texts is a quiet challenge: a Catholic writer whose work finds deep relevance in our age will be one who shrugs off easy platitudes and instead pursues an unflinching moral, intellectual, and artistic engagement."

—Christine Flanagan, author / editor *The Letters of Flannery O'Connor and Caroline Gordon*

"Joshua Hren shows us how to read well by delving deeply into the well of living meaning to be found in great literature. Learning to read (and write) like a Catholic is to leave the shallows to swim in the depths and to step out of the shadows into the light. It is life changing."

—Joseph Pearce, author of *Catholic Literary Giants: A Field Guide to the Catholic Literary Landscape*, and many more

Joshua Hren's How to Read (and Write) like a Catholic is not just another thick, square book. It is a catechism that will guide you through the long Catholic literary tradition, stopping along the way to introduce you to its best authors and to examine the great questions of judgment and craft that every reader and every writer must consider. This is not just a new book by an important young author; it is the fruit of an entire tradition. It is no mere survey; it is an introduction to a way of living well within the human drama of Christianity.

—James Matthew Wilson, Poet-in-Residence, Benedict XVI Institute for Sacred Music and Divine Liturgy

Contents

Acknowledgements
XIII

Introduction
1

Part I
Reading (and Writing) Like a Catholic

Chapter 1
Between a Record of Man in Rebellion and the Beatific Vision: Conversion in Catholic Literature
13

Chapter 2
Beauty Will Not Save the World but the Literature You Save May Be Your Own
45

Chapter 3
The Ends of the Novel
61

Chapter 4
Whispers *and* Shouts of Faith in Fiction: Léon Bloy and the Catholic Writer Today
71

Part II
Reading Christ-Haunted Fictions

Chapter 5
A Dank, Dimly-Lighted Place: Hemingway on Affliction, Beauty, and Being at Home in the World
97

Chapter 6
Christ-Haunted George Saunders
103

Chapter 7
Jack Kerouac's Beatific Visions
117

Chapter 8
Peace in a Plastic World: Evelyn Waugh's Nativity
123

Chapter 9
Thank You for the Light, F. Scott Fitzgerald
129

Chapter 10
The Pallor of Our Plagues: Katherine Anne Porter's *Pale Horse, Pale Rider*
133

Chapter 11
Marriage Prospects with David Foster Wallace
139

Chapter 12
Portrait of a Paralyzed Priesthood:
James Joyce's "The Sisters"
149

Chapter 13
For Whom Chekhov's Bell Tolls
157

Chapter 14
Flaubert's Fictional Faith
163

Part III
Reading Human Nature

Chapter 15
Acolyte of Ambition: Balzac's *Lost Illusions* and *Lost Souls*
177

Chapter 16
Reading the Riddle of Human Nature,
from Homer to Dostoevsky
191

Part IV
Reading Catholic Fictions

Chapter 17
The Problem of Pity: Misguided Mercy
& Dante's Infernal Purgation
227

Chapter 18
What Waugh Saw in America: An Anglo-American Romance
241

Chapter 19
The Sound and the Fury, Symbolizing Something: Walker Percy and Jacques Maritain on the Paradoxical Miracle at the Limits of Language
259

Chapter 20
Stay in Your Lane or You'll Get into 'The Trouble'": J. F. Powers and the First Commandment of Fiction
283

Chapter 21
Caroline Gordon Lost and Found: *The Malefactors*
291

Chapter 22
Mistakes Were Made: The Apocalypse of Truth in *A Canticle for Leibowitz*
313

Chapter 23
Christopher Beha's Capacity for God: *What Happened to Sophie Wilder* Revisited
319

Chapter 24
What the Catholic Novel Might Become: Randy Boyagoda's *Original Prin*
327

Part V
How to Write (Like a Catholic)

Chapter 25
Introduction
341

Chapter 26
The Trouble with Technique and the Artistic Habit
345

Chapter 27
Most Grievous Faults and Fictional Reparations
349

Chapter 28
The Problem of Proper Proportion
359

Chapter 29
Dialogue, Dead or Alive
365

Chapter 30
The Heresy of Formlessness and Old Faithful Unity
381

Chapter 31
A Handful of Dust (Drop the Rest on the Floor), and a Half-Sketched Story with an Essay Woven Through it
383

Chapter 32
The Duties of Details
387

Chapter 33
Don't Make a Scene: Consciousness and Three Sensuous Strokes
393

Chapter 34
Central Intelligence and Peripheral Points of View
415

Chapter 35
Complication and Resolution: Tragic, Eucatastrophic, Comic
429

Chapter 36
Only a Mystic Can Be a Complete Novelist
447

Appendix A
101 Books to Read Like a Catholic
451

Appendix B
Reading and Writing Like a Catholic: Further Forays
457

Acknowledgments

"Between a Record of Man in Rebellion and the Beatific Vision: Conversion in Catholic Literature": a much different, less complete version of this essay originally appeared as a chapter in *Renewal of Catholic Higher Education: Essays on Catholic Studies in Honor of Don J. Briel*, 2017. A portion of the chapter appeared as "The Artifice of Race and the Art of Grace" in *Dappled Things: A Quarterly of Ideas, Art, and Faith.* I have also delivered the essay in lecture form on numerous occasions, and am most grateful for good and clarifying counterpoints as well as encouragements from many—all of which made it better than it would have been worked out alone.

"Beauty Will Not Save the World But the Literature You Save May Be Your Own" originally appeared in *America Magazine*, 2018.

"The Ends of the Novel" originally appeared in *Dappled Things*, 2020.

"Whispers *and* Shouts of Faith in Fiction: Léon Bloy and the Catholic Writer Today," Second Place in *Dappled Things'* 2018 Jacques Maritain Prize for Nonfiction.

"A Dank, Dimly-Lighted Place: Affliction, Beauty, and Being at Home in the World" originally appeared in *Dappled Things*, 2018.

"Christ-Haunted George Saunders" originally appeared in *First Things,* 2019.

"Saunders on Story" originally appeared in *First Things,* 2021.

"Jack Kerouac's Beatific Visions" originally appeared in *First Things,* 2020.

"Peace in a Plastic World: Evelyn Waugh's Nativity" originally appeared in *First Things,* 2019.

"Thank You For the Light, F. Scott Fitzgerald" originally appeared in *First Things,* 2019.

"The Pallor of Our Plagues: Katherine Anne Porter's *Pale Horse, Pale Rider*" originally appeared in *Crisis,* 2020.

"Marriage Prospects with David Foster Wallace" originally appeared in Notre Dame's *Church Life Journal,* 2021.

"For Whom Chekhov's Bell Tolls," in *Catholic World Report,* 2020.

"Portrait of a Paralyzed Priesthood: James Joyce's 'The Sisters,'" in *Dappled Things,* 2020.

"Acolyte of Ambition: Balzac's *Lost Illusions* and *Lost Souls,*" originally appeared in *Law and Liberty,* 2021.

"Stay in Your Lane or You'll Get into 'The Trouble'" originally appeared in *First Things,* 2020.

"The Problem of Pity: Misguided Mercy & Dante's Infernal Purgation," originally appeared in *Touchstone,* 2019.

"The Sound and the Fury, Symbolizing Something: Walker Percy and Jacques Maritain on the Paradoxical Miracle at the Limits of Language" originally appeared as a chapter in *Redeeming Philosophy: From Metaphysics to Aesthetics,* 2014.

"What Waugh Saw in America: An Anglo-American Romance" originally appeared in *America* magazine in 2020.

"Humanitarianism, *Ressentiment,* and 'Love of Mankind': From Homer to Dostoevsky" originally appeared in *LOGOS: A Journal of Catholic Thought and Culture,* 2014.

"Caroline Gordon Lost and Found: *The Malefactors*" originally appeared in *America,* 2021.

"Mistakes Were Made: The Apocalypse of Truth in *A Canticle for Leibowitz*" originally appeared in *Catholic World Report,* 2021.

"Christopher Beha's Capacity for God: *What Happened to Sophie Wilder* Revisited," originally appeared in *The University Bookman,* 2020.

"What the Catholic Novel Might Become: Randy Boyagoda's *Original Prin*" originally appeared in *The University Bookman,* 2019.

"Flaubert's Fictional Faith" originally appeared in The Imaginative Conservative, 2020

"Beauty comes from the fair and the fit, Augustine says."

"I don't follow."

"In other words, it's a kind of byproduct of the elegance with which an object meets its purpose. A work whose purpose is to be beautiful gets trapped in circularity. It can't ever succeed in that goal. Beauty can only be arrived at while meeting some real need. So what's the point? What's the thing writing is supposed to do, the aim it's after that along the way produces its beauty?"

—from *What Happened to Sophie Wilder*
by Christopher Beha

Introduction

It seems that the imagination, when it obtains the depths of Catholicity, seeks to save. If we translate this into fiction, the Christic imagination incarnates human nature as having its final end not in the characters' self-actualization but in salvation. We need fiction to render for us manifold souls enframed by this end in part because we are inclined to capitulate to the shallowness of secular selves. Good fiction cracks the glass ceilings of secularism and invites us into an expansive world alight with the transcendent.

As Christopher Beha contends, the novelist is a person "for whom secularism presents a problem." Say we inhabit a mundane living room scene, in a secular age—in the Midwest, no less. Say that in this miniscule room, a couple is quarreling. Even *here,* however subtly, the Catholic imagination senses and suggests a vast and eternal stage that extends far beyond the seen scene: like the protagonist of Goethe's *Faust*, this couple tips the eternal scales, albeit by sometimes miniscule degrees. Their talk may be hot with petty frustrations over a grocery bill or cooled by a crippling disagreement, but never absent is the debt of love (Rom 13:18) both will—finally—fulfill or fail to pay. As St. Thomas says, "No deliberate act is morally indifferent." Father Garrigou-Lagrange explains why: "Every deliberate act in a rational being should itself be . . . directed to a morally good end and in the Christian every deliberate act should be directed at least virtually to God."

Good fiction helps us better grasp the fact that everything we deliberately do—from amusements to our acts of mercy—assumes moral significance. If someone "gives a poor man a penny grudgingly," the Catholic writer Léon Bloy assures us, "that penny pierces the poor man's hand, falls, pierces the earth, bores holes in suns, crosses the firmament and compromises the universe. If he begets an impure act, he perhaps darkens thousands of hearts whom he does not know, who are mysteriously linked to him." Amen.

As though hailing from the opposite antipode of the Christic imagination, St. John Henry Newman warns us against taking man "for what he is not, for something more divine and sacred, for man regenerate." He insists that literature is largely a record "of man in rebellion." "You cannot have a sinless Literature of sinful man," he adds. "Take things as they are, not as you could wish them," he counsels, with a kind of English sobriety that sounds cold-blooded, almost as though Hobbes is hovering over the shoulder of the holy man. One hankers for a sip of hot Anglo tea, or maybe some Anglo-Saxon mead; bring us a round, dear, we're taking things as they are, here, in Beowulf's mead hall, contemplating the archaic torso of the armless monster Grendel.

Newman's proclamations upon literature are insufficient in themselves, but he is right that literature—broadly taken—is mainly a record of man in rebellion. Unwittingly, he makes it evident that in order to give an occasion for salvation or damnation, the literary imagination must also render characters as in rebellion. This is one reason why many of us have a difficult time reading fiction; so much of it seems unedifying at best, at worst a minefield of occasions for sin.

Literature has long pricked the pointer fingers of prudish (as distinct from virtuously prudent) souls. The species of Catholic literature fares little better. "Catholic writing tends to be comic, rowdy, rude, and even violent," Dana Gioia confesses, and this troubles a whole committee worth of readers. Page after page of sinners, who "generally make more interesting protagonists" and whose "failings more vividly demonstrate humanity's fallen state."

For not a few, the safety of allegorical Vices are a welcome refuge to the vulgar and suggestive that seem inescapable ingredients of a literature that takes on humanness in its fullness. "I have an aunt who disapproves of adultery," says Caroline Gordon, Catholic novelist and friend to both Flannery O'Connor and Walker Percy. Mayhem and murder and incest—these things also she disapproves. Gordon admires her aunt's decorum, that "thin ice" on which we all skate as carefully as we can so as to avoid falling into "the abyss that yawns for each of us." Her aunt peers into that abyss with eyes both "sharp and compassionate," regularly startling the novelist, whose "profession" is to plumb the mysteries of the human heart, both dark and light. Auntie is keen to cavernous depths Gordon has never considered. Acute as her aunt is, she despises novels that both contain sin and lack overt moralizing that repudiates that sin. She trusts that her niece has not committed such misdeeds. But how, she asks, will other people know that? Auntie can read human nature and human relationships with startling exactitude, "*but she does not know how to read a novel.*"

Consider Gordon's most explicitly Catholic novel, *The Malefactors*; as the title justly discloses, the story does not lack deviants, lowlifes, and reprobates. An adulterous affair charges much of the action. But as Harold C. Gardiner, SJ, the onetime literary editor of *America*, explains in his *Norms for the Novel,* the reader ought not to isolate suggestive or vulgar scenes, ought not mistake them for *wholes.* "The effect of these passages has to be judged against the background of the whole moral import of the work." If truth is to be told, some scenes demand graphic treatment. Pornographic perversion and explicit titillation have no place, of course, in art worthy of the name, Catholic or otherwise. So long as "there is no allure to it, no incitement," and it fits into characters' developments and devolutions, we ought not dismiss or underappreciate the importance of well-rendered sin in good literature. Objectionable parts ought not to undermine our appreciation of their total effect when weighed within the entirety of the work.

Still, so far we've been blinded by the apparent blemishes of literature. Guided by Newman, we've been fixated on man's fallenness; like G. K. Chesterton's Father Brown, we're honed in on sin. "Has it never struck you," asks the priest detective, "that a man who does next to nothing but hear men's real sins is not likely to be wholly unaware of human evil?" Surely some second reason for reading fiction is at hand? Verily, verily, but we must duly deal with Newman's refrain: "You cannot have a sinless literature of sinful man." One might expect that the saint's rather bleak appraisal of literature would lead to his banishing it from his prescription of what makes man humane. Like a great artist, though, he concludes his take on fiction with an unexpected plot twist: Catholic thinkers should and even must analyze and teach, appreciate and criticize the sinful literature of sinful man. Why? Because most men are not destined for the cloister:

> We cannot possibly keep them from plunging into the world, with all its ways and principles and maxims, when their time comes; but we can prepare them against what is inevitable; and it is not the way to learn to swim in troubled waters, never to have gone into them. Proscribe (I do not merely say particular authors, particular works, particular passages) but Secular Literature as such; cut out from your class books all broad manifestations of the natural man; and those manifestations are waiting for your pupil's benefit at the very doors of your lecture room in living and breathing substance.

The greatness of Newman's formulation lies in its universality; the conscientious Catholic can glean truths and spy beauties regardless of the work—whether we are reading Homer's *Odyssey* or Shakespeare's *King Lear*, Joyce's *Ulysses* or Flannery O'Connor's *Wise Blood*—Newman argues that the Catholic thinker must "do for Literature in one way what she does for Science in another; each has its imperfection, and she has her remedy for each. She fears no knowledge, but she purifies all; she represses no element of our nature, but cultivates the whole."

Here Newman asserts that the study of literature must aim toward a purification and a remedy. Still, although he defines the qualities specific to literary form—it persuades, it seduces, it is multiform and versatile—he leaves much work to be done in terms of how Catholic writers and readers are to achieve this purification. In Pope St. John Paul II's "Letter to Artists," Pope Emeritus Benedict XVI's "Address to Artists," and Dana Gioia's "The Catholic Writer Today," we find a common insistence that literature infused with a Catholic vision contains distinct characteristics such as the dramatization of (at least some) suffering as redemptive and the conscious articulation of the natural world's sacramental character.

Whereas science is methodical, logical, and grave, and can convey these truths also, literature, Newman notes, "declaims and insinuates; it is multiform and versatile; it persuades instead of convincing, it seduces, it carries captive; it appeals to the sense of honour, or to the imagination." It has the advantage of appealing through humble materials, working on our intellects, sure, but only after passing through our senses. "It takes at least three activated sensuous strokes to make an object real," O'Connor writes. The good writer can poeticize dirt into stardust; but first he has to get us dusty.

Although Newman is an important touchstone, then, as we strive to read and write like a Catholic, his definition of literature is too reductive, too dusty, too earthbound. In "The End of the Novel," Osip Mandelstam suggests that modern fiction has its origins in a "secular" response to both the lives of the saints and the moralizing sketch, a transformation that included a shift from biography to greater emphasis on narrative and plot and "psychological motivation." Mandelstam's observation is very important, but he misses the ways the Christic literary imagination absorbs the action of grace that is taken for granted in the lives of the saints and crafts it back into fiction. Catholic writers take a form that has historically shed or demystified that transcendent, and they steep it in sacredness. The best of them do this in a manner that makes the sacred's permeation arrestingly persuasive. Catholic literature typically absorbs the very real gains of the form—good and evil shifting from clearly delineated hero vs. villain to vice and virtue warring within single characters, for instance. The fiction writer is preoccupied with conversion (what is sometimes called "character development") in a broader sense: perfection of the natural virtues, alteration via epiphanies, characterological maturation, etc. The Catholic writer often widens her work by narrowing this "development" of characters back to conversion in Christian sense. The stakes are high: though salvation and damnation are often merely hinted at as the final ends of a given work's characters, this reenchanting reading of reality makes the canvas of Catholic art uncannily wide: to hell and back, the Hound of Heaven is always there, however subtly, charging the cosmos with grandeur.

Reading of explicitly Christian works, however, should comprise but one part of a Catholic creature's reading list. We will consider three modes of reading literature like a Catholic:

I. Study of literature as the study of human nature, which is to say the study of ancient texts in order to obtain a greater understanding of human passions and ends, possibilities and limits, to witness man's innate social nature, to hear the whispers of natural law as it chastens man in rebellion, and to consider how the human story unfolds outside of a direct encounter with Christian revelation. (This does not exclude reading the deep meanings of these works according to the light of Christ.)

II. Study of literature that is intrinsically Catholic. This can be undertaken: through an examination of the presence of metanoia (conversion) in great literary texts; through a consideration of the way in which writers *dramatize the workings of grace upon nature*, and through a sacramental approach that sees the ways in which seen images point to unseen realities; a cultivation of the capacity to, in Flannery O'Connor's words, see evil as "a mystery to be endured" and "not a problem to be solved."

III. Study of the persistence, often in traces or in veiled form, of Catholic ideas, images, and tradition in purportedly secular or postmodern poetry and stories; additionally, literature grappling with faith within an increasingly secularized literary canon.

Toward the end of James Joyce's *A Portrait of the Artist as a Young Man,* a conversation turns upon the question of beauty. Stephen, the novel's hero, cites Aquinas: "*Ad pulcritudinem tria requiruntur integritas, consonantia, claritas.*" I translate it so: "*Three things are needed for beauty: wholeness, harmony, and radiance.*" The noble simplicity of Aquinas's definition is remarkable. As the Angelic Doctor indicates in the prologue of his *Summa Theologiae,* he prizes clarity of language. Many approaches to theology, he says, have proven to be "an enormous hindrance to those who are new to this teaching."

Keen to avoid others' errors, St. Thomas vows to circumvent three perils of learning: useless multiplication of questions, treatment of essential matters out of sequence, and inane repetition which "has tended to produce weariness and confusion in the minds of his listeners." In spite of his stated aim, his prized simplicity, his predilection for succinctness and clarity, Aquinas has a reputation for impenetrable intricacies and subtleties. So many of his intellectual children did not heed his advice. They delved into the useless questions he sought to avoid, so much so that the "scholastic" approach to philosophy and theology has come to be a synonym for needless obscurity. In Joyce's *Portrait,* this is precisely the allegation that Stephen's interlocutor levels at him:

> "*If a man hacking in fury at a block of wood,*" Stephen continued, "*make there an image of a cow, is that image a work of art? If not, why not?*"
>
> "That's a lovely one," said Lynch, laughing again. "That has the true scholastic stink."

During what leisure I could scrounge, I scoured through the pages to come, striving to rid their sentences of monotonous repetition and tedious phrasings—anything steeped in that "true scholastic stink." Being ever a foreigner in the halls of Academia, I have nonetheless acquired some of its showy jargon and pointless obliqueness. When literature's goodness is hedged by arcane professors, when specialized "explainers" corrupt its influence, the consequences for humankind are considerable. As Ezra Pound argues in his essay "How to Read," no one can think or communicate his thought, no governor or legislator can "act effectively or frame his laws, without words, and the solidity and validity of these words is in the care of the damned and despised *literati.* When their work goes rotten," when "the application of word to thing goes rotten, i.e. becomes slushy and inexact, or excessive or bloated, the whole machinery of social and of individual thought goes to pot."

Cognizant of the poverty of my words, working like a gleaner in the vineyards of the Word, I wished to honor beauty's wholeness, harmony, and radiance. But what is this penned harvest except straw next to the sublimity of its object? All I can do now is lay this book down atop the flickering votive candles in the nook nearest the *altare Dei* and pray the straw might catch fire. Please God, its burning pages will peter out until only Light in the darkness is left, "and the darkness did not comprehend it" (Jn 1:5, DRA).

Part I

READING (AND WRITING) LIKE A CATHOLIC

1

Between a Record of Man in Rebellion and the Beatific Vision: Imitating Conversion in Catholic Literature

All my stories are about the action of grace on a character who is not very willing to support it, but most people think of these stories as hard, hopeless, brutal, etc.

—Flannery O'Connor

Seeing the Situation of Catholic Literature

When St. John Henry Newman sat down to write his lectures that would become *The Idea of a University*, the newly christened St. Stephen's Green buildings showed nothing of the "deep dilapidation" that poet and fellow convert Gerard Manley Hopkins would describe to the aging cardinal thirty years later. Beautiful ideas are not like beautiful buildings.

In spite of this natural decay, this inevitable withering of stones and wood, Newman's ideas lived in and guided Hopkins's mind. They obtained that "life" of which he writes in *An Essay on the Development of Christian Doctrine*: "When some great enunciation, whether true or false, about human nature . . . is carried forward into the public throng of men and draws attention," the minds who encounter it do not do so passively. Rather, "it becomes an active principle within them, leading them to an ever-new contemplation of itself, to an application of it in various directions, and a propagation of it on every side."

It is my hope that Newman's *idea* of literature as the study of human nature, and largely of man in rebellion, can enter into a marriage with approaches to literature that overemphasize and misrepresent its relation to the beautiful; through his insistence upon the limits of literature, Newman helps us refine our understanding of literature's nature and its dangers, its possibilities and its graces. His idea, though insufficient in itself, becomes an "active principle," leading us to both purify the source of our stories (that is, ourselves) and stand soberly before the problem of compelling conversions that both build on nature and originate beyond it.

Newman wrote long before the twentieth century's Catholic literary boom, which brought to the fore such great authors as Leon Bloy, Georges Bernanos, Paul Claudel, and Francois Mauriac in France; Muriel Spark, Evelyn Waugh, J. R. R. Tolkien, and G. K. Chesterton in the United Kingdom; and Flannery O'Connor, J. F. Powers, and Walker Percy in the United States. He therefore did not have at hand a broad body of modern literary works written by Catholics, a body of works charged with what Father Andrew Greeley would come to call the "Catholic imagination." The modern Catholic literary tradition simply did not exist—although its first shoots were blooming not far from Newman himself.

Twenty-seven years before Newman's idea of literature, the once Voltairian anti-Catholic Italian author Alessandro Manzoni had composed the first great modern "Catholic novel," *I Promessi Sposi* (*The Betrothed*). In 1859, Francis Thompson, son of a doctor who converted to the Catholic faith under the indirect influence of Cardinal Manning, would be born; Thompson's age of innocence would soon fade into one of overmuch experience when, as a longtime homeless opium addict, pockets stuffed with William Blake and Aeschylus, he would come to dramatize the "labyrinthine ways" of his wrestling with God in the great Catholic long poem "The Hound of Heaven." And of course, in the 1860s, several years after Thompson's birth, both Coventry Patmore and that singular Catholic priest-poet Gerard Manley Hopkins converted to the Catholic faith. Buckling a bit under his parents' wrath over his recent conversion, the soon-to-be Jesuit would receive words of consolation from Newman himself: "It is not wonderful that you should not be able to take so great a step without trouble and pain."

Hopkins's own poetry is often cited for its exemplification of the Catholic "sacramental" comprehension of the world. Poems such as "God's Grandeur" or "Pied Beauty" speak of a natural world "charged with the grandeur of God," even as they contain tacit critiques of untethered industrialization that would find more explicit condemnation in Pope Leo XIII's *Rerum Novarum*. But Hopkins's work contains another vein, one whose tributaries share a source much closer to the theory of literature Newman develops in *Idea of a University.* In "Carrion, Comfort," for instance, Hopkins writes of "the mind, mind [that] has mountains; cliffs of fall/ Frightful, sheer." Here literature plumbs the horrifying abysses of our human nature.

And yet, again, Newman does not directly consider a "Catholic" literary canon. His scope is vast. His consideration of literature's place in the world at large and in the republic of letters in particular begins with that "Apostle of Civilization" Homer, a "blind old man" who "wandered over the islands of the Ægean and the Asian coasts." Newman assumes an unflinchingly universal aim; his characterization of literature is itself guided by Christian concerns, but he needs his judgment to hold for *all* works of the literary imagination. Literature, he writes, is a study of human nature, and therefore a "Christian literature" is impossible. By "literature," Newman, writing with the university curricula in mind, means primarily the great classical works of *literature,* those works that preceded or were written in tense relation to Christian revelation: Homer, the Greek tragedians, Shakespeare, etc. Still, his judgment concerning literature will rightfully unsettle those familiar with the Christian virtue of hope: "You cannot have a sinless Literature of sinful man."

The modern Catholic literary tradition's dominant interpretive approach is rooted in the *via pulchritudinis*; according to "the way of beauty," literature is justified and even considered good because in its sacramental dimension, it contains a foretaste of the Beatific Vision, and in its beauty, it is also full of truth. In its 2006 concluding document, *The* Via Pulchritudinis, *Privileged Pathway for Evangelisation and Dialogue,* the Pontifical Council for Culture (PCC) proclaims, "The *Way of Beauty* seems to be a privileged itinerary to get in touch with many of those who face great difficulties in receiving the Church's teachings, particularly regarding morals. Too often in recent years, the *truth* has been instrumentalised by ideologies, and the *good* horizontalised into a merely social act as though charity towards neighbour alone sufficed without being rooted in love of God. Relativism, which finds one of its clearest expressions in the *pensiero debole*, continues to spread, encouraging a climate of miscomprehension, and making real, serious and reasoned encounters rare."

The PCC goes on to position Christ as the paradigmatic incarnation of Beauty. Christ the Beautiful "invites contemporary Augustines, unquenchable seekers of love, truth and beauty," to come to eternal Beauty by way of perceptible beauty.

In the first volume of Hans Urs von Balthasar's multivolume *The Glory of the Lord,* the author argues that beauty, unlike the other two transcendentals, is "disinterested." Whereas truth and goodness give rise to innumerable self-interested debates, he claims, beauty is disinterested. In a central passage, he writes, "Our situation today shows that beauty demands for itself at least as much courage and decision as do truth and goodness, and she will not allow herself to be separated and banned from her two sisters without taking them along with herself in an act of mysterious vengeance. We can be sure that whoever sneers at her name, as if she were the ornament of a bourgeois past, whether he admits it or not, can no longer pray and soon will no longer be able to love."

Von Balthasar's argument is partially compelling: Lives, conversations, social orders shaped by truth and goodness but bereft of beauty will end up shrill, falsely pious, unpersuasively moralistic. But beauty will not save the world. Even Dostoevsky, who coined the phrase, "beauty will save the world," demonstrates the insufficiency of beauty throughout the novel *The Idiot.* Such an idea is oftentimes a hyperbolic assertion, uttered on behalf of practitioners of beauty, who mistake their good work as the only or primary means of salvation.

This enunciation of the beautiful can be traced back to Augustine's "Late have I loved you, beauty so old, beauty so new," and it finds a companionable argument in Pope Emeritus Benedict XVI's "Address to Artists," where he writes that "an essential function of genuine beauty, as emphasized by Plato, is that it gives man a healthy 'shock,' it draws him out of himself, wrenches him away from resignation and from being content with the humdrum—it even makes him suffer, piercing him like a dart, but in so doing it 'reawakens' him, opening afresh the eyes of his heart and mind, giving him wings, carrying him aloft."

Note, though, that for Pope Emeritus Benedict the beautiful is—at least not first and foremost, and in a sense not even *intrinsically*—evangelical, Christian, or doctrinal. Even as, toward the end of his address, the Holy Father references literary giants such as Dostoevsky and Hesse in order to establish the way in which literature can lead the reader to God, he nevertheless introduces a caution concerning the beautiful, noting that "too often . . . the beauty that is thrust upon us is illusory and deceitful, superficial and blinding, leaving the onlooker dazed." Rather than bringing man out of himself, failing to open him up "to horizons of true freedom as it draws him aloft, it imprisons him within himself and further enslaves him, depriving him of hope and joy." Nonetheless, Pope Benedict preserves beauty as the fundamental mark of good art.

But beauty ought not to be the sole end which we seek to apprehend and co-create in art. The great Catholic poet Dante Alighieri advanced our application of a "four-fold method" or "allegory of the theologians," which he famously outlines in a letter to his patron and protector Cangrande I, Lord of Verona. Dante explains how his work ought to be read; it is not *merely* beautiful or *merely* moral or *merely* spiritual:

> Rather, it may be called "polysemous," that is, of many senses. A first sense derives from the letters themselves, and a second from the things signified by the letters. We call the first sense "literal" sense, the second the "allegorical," or "moral" or "anagogical." To clarify this method of treatment, consider this verse: *When Israel went out of Egypt, the house of Jacob from a barbarous people: Judaea was made his sanctuary, Israel his dominion* [Psalm 113]. Now if we examine the letters alone, the exodus of the children of Israel from Egypt in the time of Moses is signified; in the allegory, our redemption accomplished through Christ; in the moral sense, the conversion of the soul from

> the grief and misery of sin to the state of grace; in the anagogical sense, the exodus of the holy soul from slavery of this corruption to the freedom of eternal glory . . . they can all be called allegorical.

This interpretive framework, inherited from medieval biblical exegesis, trains the mind to see a given literary work as *saturated* with meanings—literal, allegorical, moral, and anagogical. As Umberto Eco jocularly remarks, here Dante "tak[es] a way of reading the bible as an example of how to read his own mundane poem!" Revolutionary as Dante's move may have been, his insistence that "mundane" or non-sacred literature can contain an *anagogical* sense continues to ripple through Catholic readers, writers, and educational institutions today.

Still further, although beauty may be a part, a means, even *one* of the ends of literary art, literature—especially the modern novel—does not take beauty as its object in the same manner as the plastic or visual arts. As Jacques Maritain makes plain, "The novel differs from other forms of literature in having for object not the manufacture of something with its own special beauty in the world of *arte/acta*, deriving only its elements from human life, but the conduct of human life itself in fiction, like providential art in reality. The object it has to create is human life itself; it has to mould, scrutinise and govern humanity. Such seems to me to be the distinctive characteristic of the art of the novel. (I mean the modern novel of which Balzac is the father.)"

In much poetry, in the novel, in fiction, beauty is *neither subject nor object;* rather, it located at the level of the line—in well-made sentences—and in the unity that forms the whole, and in the clarities and epiphanies that radiate forth.

In *The Arts of the Beautiful,* Etienne Gilson insists that the first cause of poesy is not beauty but "that man is an imitating animal. Mimicry is part of his nature, as we observe it in children. . . . The second cause is that everybody enjoys imitations. This is verified by the fact that we like even ugly things to be well represented." Although literary art is not defined exclusively by representations of ugly things, literature—and especially modern fiction, Catholic or otherwise, but in Dante's *Inferno* also—typically contains beautiful representation of ugly things.

Although a novel may contain beautiful souls, in the words of Francois Mauriac, "It's a long way from hagiography to the novel. We can write the life of a saint . . . but it is impossible to imagine writing a novel about a saint, that is, creating a saint. Grace is not invented. Bernanos is the only man who has known how to create all those martyrized priests of his from his own substance, without borrowing anything from hagiography. But precisely because he is a novelist and not a biographer, their cross is always rooted in muck."

If a novelist is to take saintliness as his theme, "He nails his country priest to a scaffold outlined against shadows swollen with crime." Why? Because "sin is the writer's element; the passions of the heart are the bread and wine he savors daily." Here Mauriac brings us from the "beauty will save the world" of the *via pulchritudinis* to Newman's *idea* of literature, in which the latter is defined as an inevitably problematic record of man's sinfulness.

If, in defining poetry as a record of human sinfulness, Newman is not defending it merely as a record of human sinfulness for its own sake, it is necessary that we probe the ways in which that record of human sinfulness has been interpreted and that we consider what end toward which a study of this record ought to strive.

A Record of Rebellion and Grace

In his *Confessions*, Augustine momentarily conducts a poetics of concupiscence: "I was captivated by theatrical shows . . . [because] they were full of representations of my own miseries and fueled my fire. Why is it that a person should wish to experience suffering by watching grievous and tragic events which he himself would not wish to endure? Nevertheless, he wants to suffer the pain given by being a spectator of these sufferings, and the pain itself is his pleasure."

Augustine does not mention the delight in mimesis that Gilson emphasizes. Instead, he considers theatergoing an "amazing folly" in that when one is moved by such scenes, she enslaves herself to similar passions. For Augustine, fiction (specifically theatrical, but—and I am not here unduly taking his *particular* experience of Roman theater for the *whole* of fiction—we can expand his consideration) is problematic precisely *because* it represents sins and because it is an invented dramatization of passions and others' sufferings; the fallen human heart will imitate the very sinfulness portrayed, if not in action then at least through the impassioned imagination. When one suffers *in reality* this is called misery, and when one feels compassion for others this is called mercy. Beholding fictions of tragic human existence, however, the audience's own sinful appetites are piqued and fostered, and, crucially, *the audience is not excited to offer help,* for the object of their attention is fictional, but is simply *invited to grieve.* Augustine seems to close the door to the possibility of purgation of these passions, and thus departs from Aristotle, who, in his *Poetics,* infamously posits that fictional representation of tragedy, "through pity and fear," effects "the proper purgation [*catharsis*] of these emotions."

Although John Henry Newman finds kinship with Augustine insofar as both articulate the problematic character of fictionalized representations, he sees more in its messiness than an occasion of sin. In *The Idea of a University,* he posits literature as related to man in the same way that science is related to nature. Literature, he argues, is man's *history*. He "thinks and he acts; he has appetites, passions, affections, motives, designs; he has within him the lifelong struggle of duty with inclination; he has an intellect fertile and capacious; he is formed for society, and society multiplies and diversifies in endless combinations his personal characteristics, moral and intellectual."

Literature is the expression of all of this, a sort of autobiography of man. Newman's definition of literature keeps the literary distinct from the theological; it is a study of *man,* not God. Although Hebrew literature is "simply theological," having, as it does, a character impressed upon it that is above nature, remember that Newman is striving to account for *all* literature, not, say, works of fiction written by authors who are Catholic or Christian, or whose rendered characters and plots are steeped in the Judeo-Christian vision. As literature is the record of man, and man is intelligent, sentient, creative, and operative independent of supernatural aid from heaven, independent of any religious belief or sanctifying grace, literature represents him as such. Literatures are "the voices of the natural man."

Newman establishes the aforementioned account of literature *in part* to lay out its *disadvantages.* Because literature is the reflection of nature both moral and social, and because nature moral and social is endowed with a will, is self-governed and never abides in a "mere state of innocence," he is "sure to sin, and his literature will be the expression of his sin, and this whether he is heathen or Christian." Christianity has only converted certain specimens of man, Newman contends, and thus has not altered the character of his history or of his mind. Here we see most clearly that in developing his theory of literature, Newman is not referencing solely those works written before revelation or written in traditions outside of or in tension with the influence of Revelation. Because literature can only reflect man as he is "in proportion as there has been an abuse of knowledge granted and a rejection of truth," literature is the science or history "partly of man in rebellion." Whereas physical science is dangerous because it is intrinsically indifferent to the idea of moral evil, literature is even more perilous because it is inclined to understand and recognize evil too well, to become excessively focused upon the abyss, and, as

Nietzsche observes in *Beyond Good and Evil*, "when you gaze long into an abyss the abyss also gazes into you."

Newman contends that as literature is a study of human nature, a "Christian literature" is impossible: In his famous formulation, "you cannot have a sinless Literature of sinful man." This is not to say that it is impossible for a maker of literature to represent something grand, something great, but that when one achieves such a thing, this thing, whatever it may be, is not literature. Such an author or artist will have departed from the delineation of man *as such* in favor of *possible man* or *purer man*, in favor of man as he might be under particular vantages. Newman asks that one who undertakes such a task should "not say that you are studying him, his history, his mind and his heart," but something else. "If you would in fact have a literature of saints, first of all have a nation of them." Implicit in this ordering of literature and political-historical reality is a stubborn insistence that literature, as literature, cannot and should not articulate the *possible;* no, literature is more mimetic than prescriptive; it can only imitate what already exists in reality. If a nation of saints should arise, *then* literature could record this redeemed Man spoken of in eschatological Scripture.

One might expect that Newman's rather bleak appraisal of literature would lead to his banishing it from the Republic of the Liberal Arts University's Letters, but, like a great artist, he concludes with a somewhat unexpected plot twist. Indeed, he insists that a Catholic university *should* and even *must* teach the sinful literature of sinful man. Why? Because most men are not destined for the cloister:

> We cannot possibly keep them from plunging into the world, with all its ways and principles and maxims, when their time comes; but we can prepare them against what is inevitable; and it is not the way to learn to swim in troubled waters, never to have gone into them. Proscribe (I do not merely say particular authors, particular works, particular passages) but Secular Literature as such; cut out from your class books all broad manifestations of the natural man; and those manifestations are waiting for your pupil's benefit at the very doors of your lecture room in living and breathing substance.

Here, though, Newman does not seem to do justice to the degree of depravity that artificial sin can incarnate. Some literary waters are so troubled that no swimming instructor could prevent the pupil from drowning. Such is implied in the thoughts of Jacques Maritain, who too wrestles with the problem of sinful literature. Unlike Newman, his emphasis is on the artist, not the reader, and, unlike Newman, he makes a distinction between the different ways in which a Christian will grapple with evil and sin. In *Art and Scholasticism,* he portrays the question as not whether a fiction writer can or cannot represent this or that aspect of evil, but rather "*at what altitude* he is prepared to depict it and whether his art and his heart are pure enough and strong enough for him to depict it without complicity or connivance."

Should the novelist wish to probe the abyss of human misery and wish the work to avoid scandalous sinfulness, she would require superhuman virtues. This is what Mauriac means when he contends that though "Maritain urges us to describe [sins] but not to connive in them," strict detachment from sin is for the imaginative writer "not possible," as his "whole art consists in making visible, tangible, and odorous a world as fraught with criminal delights as saintliness." This is especially true because the fiction writer has as its object not a thing-to-be-made that, as an *artifact*, would have as its end a sort of beauty-in-itself, and for which human life would comprise only the elements, but—and this distinction is terribly important, as here Maritain intersects with Newman—*life*, *human life in itself*, molded into fiction.

Maritain then reaches the crescendo of his qualifications when he insists that "only a Christian, nay more, a mystic because he has some idea of *what is in man,* can be a complete novelist." Even this is problematic because the novelist needs some measure of *experimental* knowledge of the creature, and such knowledge can only come from the gift of understanding (which comes from the Holy Spirit) and man's experience of the sins of which he writes, and one must wonder whether the Holy Spirit would give the writer a knowledge of sin both complete and pure—and that this gift would provide sufficient substance for compelling characterizations of fallenness in poetry and fiction. I am not here questioning the capacity of the Holy Spirit, but rather the nature of sin. It would seem that we could only have a sinless knowledge of sinfulness in paradise when, as St. Augustine explains at the end of *City of God,* "the memory of our previous miseries will be a matter of purely mental contemplation, with no renewal of any feelings connected with these experiences—much as learned doctors know by science many of those bodily maladies which, by suffering, they have no sensible experience." Such a state can only come to be when we have "freedom even from the power to sin," for our wills will be as "ineradicably rooted in rectitude and love as in beatitude." But here we have wandered into Newman's "nation of saints," a land so far from and foreign to the world of literature.

Unlike Augustine, whose life epitomizes experiential engagement with *real* human sinfulness, and unlike Maritain, who defends literature on the grounds that *at a certain altitude* fiction can truthfully render human sin in all of its awfulness and the perfecting of (sometimes hell-bent) human nature via grace, Newman finds in literary sinfulness and suffering a means of mediating the harsh world to the student. If good can come from literature, he seems to say, much depends upon the teacher's capacity to impart those virtues necessary for right reading of sinful literature—namely, "wit and humour" and imagination, "fastidiousness of taste," "rule[s] . . . for discriminating 'the precious from the vile,' beauty from sin, the truth from the sophistry of nature, what is innocent from what is poison." If the teacher does not, through literature, mediate the sinful world, the student will meet this world with all of the charm of novelty, "all the fascination of amiableness."

Newman warns us against taking man "for what he is not, for something more divine and sacred, for man regenerate." He cautions us to "beware of showing God's grace and its work at such disadvantage as to make the few whom it has thoroughly influenced compete in intellect with the vast multitude who either have it not, or use it ill." Perhaps this is where Newman's limitation comes forth most clearly. *Brideshead Revisited*—and we could say this about the fiction of Flannery O'Connor's short stories, Muriel Spark's *The Prime of Miss Jean Brodie*, J. F. Powers' *Morte D'Urban* and so many others in the Catholic literary tradition—does not show God's grace in a manner that distorts the incomplete, impoverished condition of human beings. For would not the "Record of Man" of which Newman speaks be amiss if it lacked some representation of grace? If grace is beyond literary representation, surely its effects are not? "Take things as they are, not as you could wish them," he counsels, with a kind of cold English sobriety.

But in accounting for things as they are, we need not do so in the manner of the political philosopher Hobbes, who, in the *Leviathan*, states that "there is no such *Finis ultimus* (utmost ayme), nor *Summum Bonum* (greatest Good), as is spoken of in the Books of the old Morall Philosophers." In place of this *summum bonum,* Hobbes puts "for a general inclination of mankind, a perpetuall and restlesse desire of Power after power, that ceaseth only in Death." Does not the record of man's sinfulness, lest it remain a Hobbesian or Calvinistic documentation not merely of sinfulness but of an unreal, hyperbolic depravity, also beg to become at least in part the record of grace built upon that sinful being? It seems that when Newman espouses "[taking] things as they are, not as you could wish them," he means to discourage what Mauriac calls the "worst kinds" of literature, those *safe* works of fiction that proffer a "falsification of reality, an untrue portrait of man." This falsification is "absolutely bad and serves only the demon of witless stupidity, the fiend who sometimes opens the half-latched door to all his fellow devils." Still, if we can't redeem these devils, even the meanest rebellious character can meet, in the right artist's hands, artful conversion via the actions of grace.

Conversion

A realistic literary account of man's history, of human nature, should not lack the possibility of *conversion,* conversion of both characters and readers. Because he strove for a universal definition of literature, Newman could not posit one of literature's possible subjects—conversion—as a subject of major import in the Catholic approach to literature. However, as the possibility is embodied in Newman's own novels *Loss and Gain* and *Callista,* he would not discard it either. It seems, then, that he does not discard such a possibility either in theory or fiction, but because the story of nature building upon grace would concern a comparatively small contingent of the overall literary corpus, he does not incorporate the workings of grace into his firmly general definition.

Newman's idea of literature is a sound corrective to accounts of literature that misrepresent and justify it insofar as it walks the way of beauty. We should take seriously his warning against taking man for "what he is not, for something more divine and sacred, for man regenerate." But we ought not, in our efforts to avoid one error, commit another: showing the action of grace rightly, we will be in no danger of misrepresenting man as more regenerate than he is; rather, the artful rendering of grace both *reveals* man's rebellious nature and narrates conversion as coming about not through this nature alone but through the actions of grace upon him. However, as we shall see, "saving" literature with grace in this way seems to take us to the limits of what artistry can achieve.

Although Mauriac agrees with Newman when he admits that "the passions of the heart are the bread and wine" the writer "savors daily," he holds that "Grace [may] none the less abide in our work; may the reader everywhere seek the subterranean flow, communion of love, even when it is seemingly derided or denied." His emphasis, however, is not on the ways in which Grace abides in the fictionist's work but rather the apparent truth "that Grace sometimes makes use of this trouble-stuff, these quite feeble poisons." He cites a person who "confided to a novelist that his books had given her the knowledge of evil she needed to reach some sinners and to understand the secret of their wretched lives. . . . The novelist, without rubbing her nose in human depravity, guided her through the shadowy world inhabited by the ravaged and the possessed. The people she had seen flounder through fictitious lives she recognized by a cry or a glance in their counterparts in the world of actuality." Thus the "saintly spirit" could bring good from the sad experience of a tale teller. Mauriac knows that "even if Grace makes use of evil for a greater good, the evil is not excused or made legitimate thereby." The Christian examines his passions only insofar as he needs to in order to conquer them. Still more, "passion being what it is, has the unveiling of its shame and unhappy consequences ever persuaded anyone to give it up?" Terrifyingly, "the unpitying delineation of grave human aberrations" may—may it not?—make us "accomplices in evil," and "may even incite us to more concrete experience, because the image itself can become an enticement, drawing us from the familiar to the habitual." Although he tries, then, to defend literature as inhabiting territory accessible to grace, Mauriac's conclusion corrals it in a dark corner shadowed by depravity. Literature is no mere *record* of rebellion; it may well authorize and incite evil. Here we are, back with St. Augustine.

It is left to Flannery O'Connor to defend as at least one of fiction's aims the rendering of grace upon nature. In "The Church and the Fiction Writer," O'Connor, too, is filled with Augustinian anxiety over fictionalized representation. What leads the writer to the fruition of her work and even her salvation may, O'Connor contends, "lead the reader into sin, and the Catholic writer who looks at this possibility directly looks the Medusa in the face and is turned to stone."

Try as she might to purify the source, the writer will find that her work may still scandalize. Even though such scandal may be the fault of an ill-equipped or scrupulous reader more than her own, she may decide that such works are somehow sinful. This is complicated in that at least in most modern minds and thus in most modern representations, nature and grace have been separated with severity. Grace, the supernatural, is often reduced to pious cliché, and nature is represented in two distorted forms: the obscene and the sentimental. Sentimentality is born of an excess emphasis on innocence and a cheap and emotive shortcut to the good.

Some readers may be scandalized simply because the work is not pious enough, is not filled with a nation of saints, because it is not what O'Connor would call "pious trash."

In order to avoid paralysis, sentimentality, or an indiscriminate embrace of depravity, the Catholic writer needs to represent "the presence of grace as it appears in nature," and it is this possibility that legitimates the creation and contemplation of literary works. Whereas Mauriac tries to locate a link between grace and literature by enunciating the good that grace can make out of fiction's foul elements, O'Connor refuses to leave us lost before the either/or of literature as a record of man in rebellion and literature as justified by the beautiful. For all of her grotesque extremities, O'Connor inhabits a mean between literature as a record of man in rebellion and the *via pulchritudinis*. We might even call beautiful those works of literature that represent well the way in which grace halts and redirects rebellion.

In one of her letters to "A," O'Connor addresses "the problem of religious conversion" in fiction, noting:

> You can't have a stable character being converted. . . . It seems to me that all good stories are about conversion, about a character's changing. If it is the Church he's converted to, the Church remains stable and he has to change. . . . The action of grace changes a character. Grace can't be experienced in itself. An example: when you go to Communion, you receive grace, but you experience nothing; or if you do experience something, what you experience is not the grace but an emotion caused by it. Therefore in a story all you

> can do with grace is to show that it is changing the character. Mr. Head [in "The Artificial Nigger"] is changed by his experience even though he remains Mr. Head. He is stable but not the same man at the end of the story. Stable in the sense that he bears his same physical contours and peculiarities but they are all ordered to a new vision. Part of the difficulty of all this is that you write for an audience who doesn't know what grace is and don't recognize it when they see it. All my stories are about the action of grace on a character who is not very willing to support it, but most people think of these stories as hard, hopeless, brutal, etc.

"All my stories are about the action of grace on a character who is not very willing to support it," O'Connor writes. This narration of grace's motion, as the Jesuit Father William F. Lynch contends in *Christ and Apollo: The Dimensions of the Literary Imagination,* is rooted in the great fact of Christology: that Christ descended and passed *through* the particular in order to redeem. This movement is a model for the Christic imagination: the poet or fiction writer needs to pass through the concrete (the way down) in order to arrive at insight (the way up). Any storyteller worth her low-iodine Pink Himalayan sea salt does this by discovering particulars—sensory details, images, actions, bits of dialogue—that signify more than themselves "without becoming less actual in so doing." These symbols "make the imagination *rise* indeed, and yet keep the tang and density of that actuality into which imagination descends." Other imaginations get hellishly stuck in the passage from one particular to another, as when Proust's protagonist "wished to see a person again without realizing that it was simply because that person recalled to me a hedge or a hawthorn in blossom." Such "exploiters of the real" (Lynch's phrase) rush through the finite in order to "send the soul shooting up into some kind of absolute." But the Christic imaginer passes through the tang and density of actuality in order to work out the characters' salvation—or damnation. Lynch lifts up Dostoevsky as the ultimate novelistic embodiment of this Christic movement but the stories of O'Connor, who insisted that the fictionist must be contented with the humbleness of her materials and who read Lynch carefully, demonstrate the difficulties that attend the passage through particularity to epiphany. In spite of this insistence, the end of her story "The Artificial Nigger" apparently instantiates the fictionist's temptation toward explanation over action—insight at the expense of sufficient definiteness.

In the stir of sincere agonies, ideological convolution, and virtue signaling of our national conversation—when our ability to converse is itself called into question—and given the origins and innumerable abuses wielded through the word "nigger," the mere title of Flannery O'Connor's "The Artificial Nigger" would seem sufficient cause for the story's consignment to the dustbin of history: on account of the titular statue, O'Connor's own stature would seem to merit immediate removal.

An argument in favor of its depth, a thoughtful voice drawing out the "honesty" and "profound perception" of O'Connor's vision, comes from the late Toni Morrison, whose appreciation of the story should halt the superficial, reactionary righteousness that would commit such fiction to the bonfire of white vanities.

In her book *The Origin of Others,* Morrison takes the story as "representative of [a] deliberate education in escaping rather than becoming the stranger." In this controversial conversion narrative, "the word 'nigger' is used constantly, even when and especially when it is unnecessary," which is precisely the point: O'Connor demonstrates the importance of excessive racial expletives for the "self-regard" of the poor white protagonist Mr. Head.

Head's self-assigned mission in the story is to pass onto his grandson Nelson this inheritance of white supremacy. For Nelson to fully learn his lesson, grandfather must take him to the city, because the last black resident of their county had been "run out" twelve years earlier. The racial character of their field trip to Atlanta sharpens when a palpably prosperous black character passes them. Mr. Head quizzes Nelson: "'What was that?' he asked," substituting *what* for *who,* framing the question with a dehumanization that invites disgust. Nelson, oblivious to Head's heavy-handed misdirection, answers "A man," and when this is insufficient, he adds other accidentals such as "fat" and "old" before Head intervenes with the authoritative answer: "That was a nigger," he huffs, slouching back into his seat.

Morrison hones in on another crucial scene, when grandfather and son wander, alarmed, through a neighborhood marked by "black eyes in black faces . . . watching them from every direction." Lost, the two pause to ask directions from a "large colored woman." Interacting with an incarnate black woman for the first time, Nelson is stirred by "a feeling" he "had never had" before: "He suddenly wanted her to reach down and pick him up and draw him against her and then he wanted to feel her breath on his face." Head sees Nelson's attraction as pernicious. As the black stranger loses her *thatness,* Morrison explains, "without the glue of racial superiority there seems to be no possibility of forgiveness or re-union" between Nelson and his grandfather, who continue to grope their way helplessly through the city's foreign core.

Mr. Head lets his grandson Nelson get lost in order to teach him a lesson—to, it would seem, recover the mock grace of racial glue. When the frantic Nelson literally runs into an elderly lady, scattering her groceries and possibly causing an injury, Mr. Head denies Nelson in front of the crowd, imitating St. Peter in an act so gross that "the women dropped back, staring at him with horror, as if they were so repulsed by a man who could deny his own image and likeness that they could not bear to lay hands on him."

Here, as O'Connor's Catholic imagination reads small particulars in light of the Great Particularity of Christ, we grasp that Head's racist disposition is an insidious species that is part of a deeper problem: his solipsism, his ruthless penchant for resisting all reality that differs from himself, even to the point of a masochistic trick played on a grandson whose physical similarity is supposedly undermined by his failure to pass the prejudice test.

At last, Mr. Head and his protégé enter an all-white neighborhood, where, Morrison argues, "their fear of not belonging, of becoming, themselves, the stranger, destabilizes them." Head's educative aspirations are frustrated by these "safe" streets until they are (to use Morrison's phrasing) "calmed and rescued" by a black jockey lawn ornament who, O'Connor writes, "was meant to look happy because his mouth was stretched up at the corners but the chipped eye and the angle he was cocked at gave him a wild look of misery instead." Grandfather and grandson experience what William Lynch calls "insight."

O'Connor does not make plain the *why*, but as Mr. Head and Nelson gaze upon the plaster figure (which is about the same size as the grandson), it is "as if they were faced with some great mystery, some monument to another's victory that brought them together in their common defeat," to the point that they "could both feel it dissolving their differences like an action of mercy." O'Connor's attention to the singularities and ironies of the statue is superb: the chipped eye and the stretched mouth, which is meant to smile but obviously miserable. Still, her work evinces how hard it is to obtain the right proportionality between what William Lynch calls "the definite" (concrete particulars) and the "insights" that we can gain by passing *through them*, for the Christic imaginer must be led not into the temptation of trying "to get as much as possible of heaven out of as little as possible of earth."

Her invocation of the similarity between racial Othering and divine mercy is especially unsettling. Morrison contends that the manufactured "mercy" is Nelson's salvation from the city's racial heteronomy and his acquisition of racism, which bestows on the young student "the illusion of power through the process of inventing an Other." And

Morrison's argument—that the boy "has been successfully and artfully taught racism"—is compelling so far as it goes. But the story does not end with this mock mercy: it concludes with a conversion wherein Head's self-justification is (at least seemingly) interrupted by actual grace.

The end of O'Connor's story exemplifies the difficulties that plague the artist's efforts to artfully render the action of grace—to capture conversion—in fiction; in *The Habit of Being*, she argues that her protagonist Mr. Head is "not the same man at the end of the story." Though "stable in the sense that he bears his same physical contours and peculiarities . . . they are all ordered to a new vision." In the letter pertaining to this story, O'Connor indicates that "what you experience is not the grace but an emotion caused by it," and this passage fulfills her characterization: the words *feel* and *felt* recur. However, we don't really see the feeling of mercy *dramatized* and made palpable and persuasive as a feeling of mercy: we are instead *told* that mercy is operative, told that *he* feels mercy. We are as it were on the outside, denied the effects of grace in all of their concreteness even as we are told that the character is undergoing a considerable conversion. When O'Connor narrates Head's purgation, she violates the unspoken oath taken by all contemporary fictionists: show, don't tell. "Mr. Head had never known before what mercy felt like because he had been too good to deserve any, but he felt he knew now." And, a little later, he "stood very still and let the action of mercy touch him again but this time he knew that there were no words in the world that could name it."

Here the piece pulses with the heart of the problem: there are no words in the world that can name it, but O'Connor does so still: *mercy,* it is called. On the other hand, her outright mention of mercy could be a counterpoint and corrective to that which only felt "like an action of mercy"—the racially-tinged bond experienced by the two white men as they stand before the statue. Crucially, Head had "never known before what mercy felt like," and in part because of this, he may have sought to manufacture it. If she were to stop there, at this explicit explanation that he is experiencing mercy, the story would be considerably weakened. But then we witness the effects of the mercy on Mr. Head's *thoughts* (which is of course apropos, given his name):

> He understood that it grew out of agony, which is not denied to any man and which is given in strange ways to children. He understood it was all a man could carry into death to give his Maker and he suddenly burned with shame that he had so little of it to take with him. He stood appalled, judging himself with the thoroughness of God, while the action of mercy covered his pride like a flame and consumed it.

Importantly, given Newman's insistence on literature's study of man's sinfulness, the effect of the effects of mercy is to give him a vision of his own rebellion: "He had never thought of himself a great sinner before but he saw now that his true depravity had been hidden from him lest it cause him to despair." O'Connor considers Mr. Head as "ordered to a new vision," a vision that includes his and humankind's history of depravity but finishes in forgiveness: "He realized that he was forgiven for sins from the beginning of time, when he had conceived in his own heart the sin of Adam, until the present, when he had denied poor Nelson."

W. F. Monroe contends that the prospect of actual "conversion" is undermined by Mr. Head's "overconfidence in the rational mind," arguing that Head's reliance on his own knowledge at the conclusion of the story is "static, pat, and even hackneyed." The story's final lines lend some credence to this misgiving.

While his grandfather's neat conversion leaves the old man "ready at that instant to enter Paradise," Nelson watches him "with a mixture of fatigue and suspicion." Just before this point the pair's fear, their anxiety that they may again get lost, is so great that they "stood ready to jump off" if the train did not stop at their desired suburban station. As the same train "disappeared like a frightened serpent into the woods," Nelson's face "lightened" and he vows never to go to the city again.

Why? Has the serpentine train been a vehicle of his grandfather's fearful bigotry? Is he here refusing to find faux reconciliation through grotesque racist statuary?

"There is nothing that screams out the tragedy of the South," O'Connor wrote, "like what my uncle calls 'nigger statuary.'" Here, says Jeanne Perreault, "she makes one of the few comments that demonstrate that she sees the South as tragic, and that the tragedy is specifically based in racial injustice." Before the story was published, when her editor John Crowe Ransom objected to its title, O'Connor countered that "to have sanitized the title would have robbed the story of its real power, the power to invert racist intention into anti-racist redemption." Toni Morrison applauds O'Connor for exhibiting "with honesty and profound perception her understanding of the stranger, the outcast, the Other"—the "construction of the stranger and its benefits."

At first glance, though, these "benefits" seem to include Mr. Head's purported redemption. But if the statue can be read as both a disfigured representation of blackness *and* disfiguring those who gaze upon it, this freakish "figure for our essential displacement" obtains two levels of meanings. As they gazed upon the statue, Head scrounged for something to say to the child to "show that he was still wise," and Nelson, too, is "hungry" for that "reassurance." When he opens his mouth to "make a lofty statement," all he can say is, "They ain't got enough real ones here. They got to have an artificial one," accentuating whites' "need" for the Otherness of blackness for the construction of their own identity.

Head's conversion, for all of its religious explicitness, occupies an indeterminate space: is it "an artificial one"—or is it real? Wrestling with this question, we register the ramifications of redemption. The end of eternal salvation is larger than the purgation of racism, but prejudice—a species of deadly pride—must be rooted out of the wholly saved soul. The only specific sin Head names is his denial of "poor Nelson." If the just severity of mercy's true action has only *now* touched him, if he here—for the first time—recognizes his capacity for depravity and "monstrous" sins, only a ruthless, reductive reading would deny the possibility he might go home to reckon with his racist bent, even if this prospect remains wholly in potency as the curtains close.

O'Connor argues that insofar as a literary symbol succeeds, it should "transcend any neat allegory that might have been intended or any pat moral categories a reader could make." "The Artificial Nigger," frustrating all attempts at oversimplified "epiphanies" in the face of such saturated racism and such deep-seated *superbia*, instantiates her fiction's necessary thickness—its innate invitation to reckon profoundly, simultaneously, with our nation's "original sin" and with our own descent from Adam.

O'Connor considers "part of the difficulty of [dramatizing grace] is that you write for an audience who doesn't know what grace is and don't recognize it when they see it." Her solution, in "The Artificial Nigger," is to *name mercy as mercy* and show that one of the effects of mercy is that man can *name sin as sin.* The question remains: Mr. Head's insights come through the utterly concrete face of the statue that "gave him a wild look of misery": does O'Connor try to milk "as much as possible of heaven out of as little as possible of earth"?

In "The Artificial Nigger," O'Connor, conscious of her audience's incapacity to recognize grace, concludes her story with a kind of explanatory shout. It is as though she were saying, "In case you don't understand how grace operates upon nature, or in case, to cite Newman, you were about to take man 'for what he is not, for something more divine and sacred, for man regenerate,' I will state the source of regeneration with utter clarity." O'Connor's shouts are an indispensable occasion of grace on the literary landscape, but they raise a question prompted by Newman: if whispering grace and sins means not naming them as such, how do we show that the source of regeneration is outside of man? How, if we are to whisper the actions of grace, do we narrate the source without naming it?

2

Beauty Will Not Save the World but the Literature You Save May Be Your Own

The last decade has seen a lively debate over whether Catholic literature is dead or alive. Without denigrating or diminishing the import of Flannery O'Connor and Co. (makers of the twentieth-century Catholic literary boom), conversations about faith and culture (especially faith and fiction) have seemingly paid them more than due homage; devotees of Catholic letters have often wound dizzying circles around their novels and stories in part because many do not know where else to turn.

Catholic novelist Randy Boyagoda began his contribution to the conversation in a *First Things* piece with an unforgettable lede: "I'm sick of Flannery O'Connor. I'm also sick of Walker Percy, G. K. Chesterton, J. R. R. Tolkien, C. S. Lewis, T. S. Eliot, Gerard Manley Hopkins, and Dostoevsky. Actually, I'm sick of hearing about them from religiously minded readers. These tend to be the only authors that come up when I ask them what they read for literature."

The national debate over Catholic literary art was first spurred by Paul Elie's *New York Times* article "Has Fiction

Lost its Faith?" in which he asks, "Where has the novel of belief gone? The obvious answer is that it has gone where Belief itself has gone. In America today Christianity is highly visible in public life but marginal or of no consequence in a great many individual lives. For the first time in our history it is possible to speak of Christianity matter-of-factly as one religion among many; for the first time it is possible to leave it out of the conversation altogether."

Elie contends that the believing Christian writer, like the Christian, is placed "on the frontier again, at the beginning of a new adventure; it means that the Christian who was born here is a stranger in a strange land." It is no surprise, he says, that few people see it as an adventurous opening: "People of faith see decline and fall. Their detractors see a people threatening rear-guard political action, or a people left behind."

In 2013, Dana Gioia published *The Catholic Writer Today*, an influential essay that diagnosed the state of Catholic letters. He began with a paradox: although Catholics comprise roughly 25 percent of the American population, nearly no living Catholic writers occupy visible, noteworthy places in national literary culture. We have the tremendously talented Alice McDermott, whose *Charming Billy* won the American Book Award; she has written many a story about (Irish) Catholics, but whose relation to what O'Connor called "the mind of the Church" is openly tense. We have the very capable Donna Tartt, whose Dickensian *The Goldfinch* won the Pulitzer Prize. But Tartt takes the posture of John F. Kennedy: *"As a novelist who happens to be a Roman Catholic," she confesses, "there is a constant tension between my faith on the one hand, and my vocation as a novelist on the other, since the novel in its history and genesis is an emphatically secular art form."*

The contemporary dearth of visible Catholic writers is a pendulum-swing from fifty years ago, when Catholic writers from J. F. Powers and Edwin O'Connor to Walker Percy and Walter M. Miller wrote stories that found a broad-reaching readership. Gioia called all Catholics committed to literature to rehabilitate their waning tradition. The last lines of that piece likens the state of contemporary Catholic literary culture to "a crumbling, old immigrant neighborhood." It is time, Gioia said, to "renovate these remarkable districts that have such grace and personality, such strength and tradition. . . . Renovation is hard work, but what a small price to pay to have the right home."

In *America* magazine, Kaya Oakes observed that "Catholic literary culture today might best be described as a funeral for multiple corpses. This, for living Catholic writers, makes for a rather depressing set of circumstances to enter into."

Perhaps in part as a reaction against these obituaries, some proctors and proponents of the Catholic literary tradition have proclaimed that "beauty will save the world," a sort of clarion call beckoning us away from the culture wars and into the "disinterested" pages of beautiful things. Another strand of contemporary writers has introduced into the conversation the rubrics and aims of identity politics, a recent phenomenon that calls attention to various stigmatized, neglected, or victimized demographics. By this they intend to challenge narratives of Catholic literary decline and rewrite the terms of the argument, rallying us around various stigmatized authors with sometimes thin connections to Catholicity, revisiting dead or "canonized" writers in order to reestablish their present-tense relevance as affiliates of disenfranchisement or diverse sorts of "deviance" rather than because of the character of their contributions to literature.

I suggest that, provocative as these stances have been, we need to avoid the reductive compromise of "Catholic identity politics." There is a less factional, a less fractional—a more Catholic—way.

As I've mentioned elsewhere, the Catholic literary tradition has been marked by writers who understood that human nature finds its final cause not in mere beauty, not in mere inclusion, but in salvation. The idiosyncrasies of a given writer and the singularities of his or her times determine the tenor of this implicit or explicit preoccupation. Consider Evelyn Waugh's *Brideshead Revisited*, which shows us just how difficult it is for grace to hound the decadent, destructive souls of the dying English aristocracy. The task of giving good form and truthful content to grace building upon nature is perhaps the greatest difficulty of fictional art. It is all too easy for such writing to collapse into pious sentimentality and disputatious moralism. But a Catholic literary culture that works in continuity with its rich heritage will give us a contemporary literature that both gazes unflinchingly at the messiness of our present moment and artfully works out its characters' salvation or damnation. In his apocalyptic thriller *Father Elijah,* living Catholic novelist Michael O'Brien effectively captures the trials—harrowing and supersubtle—of a soul being sanctified, and living Catholic poet Dana Gioia gives shape to a soul's inhabitation of hell-on-earth in his haunting long poem "The Homecoming."

In his 1926 essay "The Negro Artist and the Racial Mountain," Langston Hughes deprecates African-American artists who fail to support writers of their race until mainstream or "white" publishers have granted such authors the stamp of "success." Hughes scoffs at an unnamed writer who declares his aim to be "a poet—not a Negro poet," contending that what this poet is saying is that he wishes to be white—that therefore he will not be a poet at all until he can embrace his identity as an African-American.

Bernardo Aparicio García, founder of the Catholic literary magazine *Dappled Things*, countenanced the question of whether the Catholic artist's dilemma is similar to that of the African-American artist at a conference at Fordham University in 2017. Aparicio García said, "Many Catholic writers can identify with what the poet Hughes talks about, but there's a difference because our universal identity as Catholics is of a different kind than an identity rooted in race, sex, nationality and so on. And this is what people mean when they talk about 'identity politics.' While being male or female, French or South African or the like can give a certain accent, as it were, to our experience of being human, being Catholic means having a certain perspective on what being human is all about, regardless of accent."

Aparicio García is arguing that Catholic literature will be more good, more true, and more beautiful than alternatives defined by the narrowness of identity politics. This is not to say that Catholic authors ought not to grapple with, say, racial prejudice in their poetry or prose. J. F. Powers does so masterfully in "The Trouble," in which a priest prays over a dying woman during race riots; in "The Black Madonna," Muriel Spark gives shape to the banal evil of white liberal racism; Glenn Arbery's *Bearings and Distances* draws out deep tensions buried in the "post-racial" moment of President Obama's election; Harlem Renaissance writer Claude McKay climbs the racial mountain in many of his early poems, even as he looks beyond its summit in his "Cycle Manuscript," composed after his conversion.

But the most enduring Catholic writers of the past did not tear down the constellations by which the Catholic vision sees reality in order to assert their identity as, say, feminist or "poor white" or homosexual. The Catholic writers we remember did not mistake the Church for themselves or themselves for the Church; they were not so foolish as to think their own personal traits were universal, even if they necessarily passed through the particulars to the communal—and, ultimately, the eternal. Flannery O'Connor was a hillbilly. But she was also a Thomist. Did the priest and poet Gerard Manley Hopkins, SJ, wrestle with homosexual desires? It is fashionable to focus on this question, but a sacramental vision would see that he definitely wrestled with God. Shūsaku Endō's *Silence* is positively Japanese. But it is absolutely Jesuit, probing the problem of martyrdom with an Ignatian imagination. (I should add that the novel's Japanese authorities are remarkably jesuitical!)

In "Tradition and the Individual Talent," T. S. Eliot notes that when we praise a literary artist, we tend to praise the parts of the work that are most singular, bits that we can isolate out as original. Eliot encourages us to shed this prejudice. In doing so, "we shall often find that not only the best, but the most individual parts of his work may be those in which the dead poets, his ancestors, assert their immortality most vigorously." Of course this apprenticeship to dead must not result in cheap imitation. Nor need it mean the obliteration of the living writer. As Caroline Gordon says, one of the reader's great delights "is the sight of one master borrowing an effect from another master and yet not losing a whit of his own originality." Capacious writers, she explains, "will take a device which has been used by other writers and extend it or transmute it to suit his own purposes."

Perhaps younger writers fret over influence with the greatest frequency. As Zadie Smith notes, they often feel that "reading while you write is unhealthy," because other voices will corrupt their own. For people who think this way, she says, "the sovereignty of one's individuality is the vital thing, and it must be protected at any price," even at the expense of salutary lessons from the masters—lessons as cheap as the cost of a paperback.

As writers, then, Catholics ought not be anxious about their influences. When they forget their traditions, Catholics, like any other creatures, become intoxicated on the fumes of the present moment—trapped in the "relevance" fallacy and exposed to the experiments of historicist novelties. If a contemporary Catholic writer has borrowed from

Dante the device of comedic devilish character, Godspeed! If a contemporary Catholic writer has absorbed some of O'Connor's Christ-haunted characters who experience grace violently, this is not necessarily a sign of "unoriginality." To be traditional is, in part, to be unoriginal. Today's Catholic literary artists should familiarize themselves with the notable array of Catholic authors who have preceded them, from frequently cited exemplars like Muriel Spark or François Mauriac to authors like Sigrid Undset or John Finlay, who are often left out of the limelight. All great Catholic literature is a footnote to Dante, but to many living Catholic writers who have lost their inheritance, Dante may be the deadest of all.

In *Whose Justice, Which Rationality?* the Catholic philosopher Alasdair MacIntyre argues that a tradition is defined in part by "those internal interpretive debates through which the meaning and rationale of the fundamental agreements came to be expressed." Sometimes, MacIntyre observes, two or more thinkers within the same tradition become external critics of one another. For instance, if, as John Henry Newman contends, literature is largely "a study of human nature," Catholics, like any other writers, can begin to master their subject by becoming astute students of other people and themselves. But, like O'Connor, a writer of Catholic fiction or poetry could also develop her understanding of human nature by mulling over certain sections of the *Summa Theologiae*, which she "read for about twenty minutes every night" before bed. Seeking a Catholicity of continuity, O'Connor also became cognizant of the very different picture of human nature advanced in *The*

Phenomenon of Man, by Pierre Teilhard de Chardin, SJ. Initially contending that "this is a scientific age and Teilhard's direction is to face it toward Christ," she concluded that "if [his books] are good, they are dangerous"; O'Connor, who named *Everything That Rises Must Converge* after an optimistic passage in Teilhard that contrasts starkly with her dark and tragic story, exemplifies MacIntyre's characterization of tradition as "an argument extended through time," one in which disagreements and agreements are "defined and refined."

A tradition, MacIntyre continues, can also be sharpened when its adherents reckon with forces external to it. In terms of her fiction, O'Connor herself was not influenced exclusively or even mostly by Catholic writers. Though the bourgeois and nihilistic villains of Léon Bloy and Dostoevsky ghost through her stories, she claimed as literary forebears Nathaniel Hawthorne, Henry James, and Franz Kafka. The Catholic writer can and must engage the broad literary culture of her times, learning from the experiments, thematic turns, and sheer acumen of, say, Balzac and Woolf, Jorge Luis Borges and Ralph Ellison, David Foster Wallace and Lorrie Moore.

Still, sincerely Catholic literature will always foster fictions that populate a definitively Catholic cosmos. Consider, for instance, Myles Connolly's *Mr. Blue.* Like F. Scott Fitzgerald's *The Great Gatsby,* the novel tackles the tensions between a frenetic capitalist culture and what we might call the Catholic conscience. Nevertheless, Connolly sees salvific possibilities that are lost to Fitzgerald's universe. And O'Connor's characters may have borrowed Kafka's overcoat, but because the Catholic understanding of freedom is distinct from the existentialist one, the overcoat does not always, as it does for Kafka's characters, become a straightjacket. As she says in her preface to *Wise Blood,* for some readers of an existentialist bent:

> Hazel Motes's integrity lies in his trying with such vigor to get rid of the ragged figure who moves from tree to tree in the back of his mind. For the author, Hazel's integrity lies in his not being able to do so. Does one's integrity ever lie in what he is not able to do? I think that usually it does, for free will does not mean one will, but many wills conflicting in one man. Freedom cannot be conceived simply. It is a mystery and one which a novel, even a comic novel, can only be asked to deepen.

The Catholic novel should strive to *deepen* what it borrows from the "gentiles."

In *The Theory of the Novel*, the Marxist philosopher György Lukács claims that "the novel is the epic of a world that has been abandoned by God." There is a great deal of truth to this, especially if we look at the genre's origins and the flourishing of the novelistic form in the "enlightened" nineteenth century. But insofar as it is populated with human beings and insofar as human beings are the very image of God, literature is intrinsically theological and, by extension, is undergirded by philosophical premises. As Dana Gioia writes in *The Catholic Writer Today*, while there is no staunchly uniform Catholic worldview, "it is possible to describe some general characteristics that encompass both the faithful and the renegade among the literati. Catholic writers tend to see humanity struggling in a fallen world. They combine a longing for grace and redemption with a deep sense of human imperfection and sin. Evil exists, but the physical world is not evil. Nature is sacramental, shimmering with signs of sacred things. Indeed, all reality is mysteriously charged with the invisible presence of God. Catholics perceive suffering as redemptive, at least when borne in emulation of Christ's passion and death."

We need to add to this descriptive list a concern with conversion in light of the first and last things: as I've said now with a frequency that is consciously obsessive, Catholic writers tend, even in spite of themselves, to be obsessed with their characters' salvation. This is as true of Dante in his dark woods as it is of Endo and his defecting priests. Insofar as all of the above is true, from this juncture we can see the insufficiency of the aforementioned approaches to making and reading literature.

The works of contemporary Catholic writers are always best wrestled out, written, and criticized within the broader Catholic literary tradition, just as Catholic life is best lived in communion with the long Catholic tradition of councils and encyclicals, friends who give encouragement and fraternal correction, liturgy and "social teachings" that can serve as deepening alternatives to obsessions with originality (the regime of novelty) and identity politics.

When I founded Wiseblood Books in 2013, on the feast day of Blessed James Duckett, patron of book publishers (at the time I did not know it was his feast), I flung Wiseblood Books out the window of a small apartment in a bohemian neighborhood of Milwaukee. The apartment was located—as is everything in Milwaukee—between a bar and a church. It was little more than a blueprint. I was sober. And I was praying. No windows broke, and I didn't hear it hit the ground. In the days that followed, it was clear that a fair wind had caught the thing and scattered pieces of it across the States. I suppose you could say that I founded the press singlehandedly, alone, but you could say a lot of silly things. With startling frequency others began to join in.

Before then, I'd been combing through the editorial slush pile of *Dappled Things* literary magazine and coming across truly well-made, beautiful, truthful stories that seemed to contain inklings of a new idiom in the Catholic literary tradition. When I corresponded with these authors, I came across a familiar refrain: we can't find a publisher.

Many claimed that the faith-charged vision that governed and grew from the very hearts of their stories set them at a disadvantage against a publishing industry that is immodestly secular. I started scouring the neon pages of the World Wide Web, and just as they said, so it seemed. When conversations surrounding this problem of secularization and of the seeming decline of Catholic literature emerged in the pages of the *New York Times*, or in the *Wall Street Journal,* some began to contend that religious questions had disappeared from literature, others that secularism is a myth. Still others openly wondered whether Catholic writers who failed to get their "great" novels published weren't merely nursing the wounds of their bad artistry in the comforting arms of the Mother of God—blaming their failure to write good literature on the wolf of secularism at the door of the Cathedral.

I situated the press within the Catholic literary tradition by the very name, as Flannery O'Connor's *Wise Blood* signifies a work that embodies a Catholic vision but also strives after literary excellence that can move any reader. I am not dogmatic about her or her work. She was a good but not a great writer. Yet she raised some crucial problems: In literary works written in a world that lives as though God were dead, do we need to shout so that the deaf can hear, draw large and startling figures so that the blind can see? Does not grace feel like violence, sometimes, and is not fiction particularly capable of dramatizing the awful conversions that can come of the disruptions that reorient us toward our last end?

Many things have changed a great deal since O'Connor's time. Nonetheless, the modern human condition has (when it is not replaced by robotic automata) remained the same. When we try to say "God" in contemporary fiction, should we fake a sneeze at the same time, lest it actually sound as though we were narrating some of the eternal questions of religion—of the nature of grace acting upon human life, of the problem of suffering, of the sacramental dimensions of nature, of conversion—even here in this Year of Our Lord?

Gioia beckoned Catholic writers and intellectuals to "leave the homogenous, characterless suburbs of the imagination and move back to the big city—where we can renovate these remarkable districts that have such grace and personality, such strength and tradition. . . . Renovation is hard work, but what a small price to pay to have the right home."

Wiseblood is just one troupe of several committed for life to the national Catholic literary revival. *Dappled Things* began before the real ignition, and *Presence* has emerged as another notable journal. Soon after I started renovating in our little corner of Milwaukee, others came by and said that they'd like to help do a bit of editing on the side—the way you tell your friend you'd be happy to help him sand those floors that are stained where mold spots block gorgeous hard wood. Down the street I saw others spilling gorgeous paint and asked if I might help. While Gioia traveled the country, mulling what would become "The Catholic Writer Today," he heard a common complaint: Catholic writers felt alienated and alone, as though each were the only of her kind. Thanks be to God that is no longer the case; many have labored and now we have a home. Even if it is more ghettoized than we'd like, it's good to dwell poetically on the earth with a band of Catholic co-conspirators.

Bernardo Aparicio García rounded out his remarks on Catholic literature by saying that when he looks "at the task of Catholic literary journals or presses today, [he] tends to think less in terms of speaking from or about a particular identity but rather from a tradition or worldview and through a multiplicity of identities. This tradition needs to find a way to speak in our time."

There are practical means by which we can scatter literary seeds and help others who are laboring at this particular task:

1. Incorporating Catholic literature—old and new—into high school and college curricula, thereby expanding the canon and teaching students to recognize both the debts and the distinctions of the Catholic literary tradition.
2. Sustaining distinctly Catholic publications and presses through subscriptions, middle-brow book reviews, and patronage.
3. Forming book clubs at the parish level and elsewhere. Such clubs regularly form somewhat organically. However, they often take cues on what to read from, say, Oprah, rather than the exhaustive lists of Catholic writers and works compiled by Paul Elie, Dana Gioia, and others or the catalogs of presses continuing the tradition.
4. Encouraging bright-eyed undergraduates to pursue work in publishing, thereby situating editors who have "eyes to see" in places where works charged with Catholic vision can reach a broader readership.

Beauty will not save the world, dear reader, but the literature you save may be your own.

3

The Ends of the Novel

In the Comedy . . . *an awareness had been born that a man's concrete earthly life is encompassed in his ultimate fate and that the event in its authentic, concrete, complete uniqueness is important for the part it plays in God's judgment.*

—Erich Auerbach, *Dante: Poet of the Secular World*

IN "THE END of the Novel", Osip Mandelstam suggests that modern fiction has its origins in a "secular" response to both hagiographical lives of the saints and the moralizing sketch, a transformation that included a shift from biography to greater emphasis on narrative and plot and "psychological motivation." As Joseph Bottum makes evident in his new book *The Decline of the Novel,* the form asserts that "all human beings *are* interior selves." This shift inward, into the psyches of the protagonists, typically teaches us to look down, to look within man, into his tangled motivations, measuring them, as Evelyn Birge Vitz would have it, against the ultimately unknowable depths which may or may not contain explanations for our actions. Contrast this to the narratives of saints, where the deepest mysteries are not within the self but up, outside man, in "the equally mysterious workings and will of God," all of which *affect individuals.*

Consider the searching inquiries of St. Augustine's *Confessions,* which press into the interior with great verve: "Do heaven and earth contain you because you have filled them? Or do you fill them and overflow them because they do not contain you? Where do you put the overflow of yourself after heaven and earth are filled? . . . Why do I request you to come to me when, unless you were within me, I would have no being at all?" The transcendent God constantly interferes in and takes precedence over human intentions and acts. In much of modern literature, Vitz argues, the reader is lulled into losing the sense that our "selves" are necessarily formed by "transcendent forces," whereas the lives of the saints constantly remind the reader that its personages, though impressively ardent and at times apparently untouchable "in the pursuit of their desires, are set in a reality that transcends and overarches them."

Vitz's account is superficially accurate, but it ignores Bottum's argument that the novelistic form moves us beyond mere imitation of these interior beings into a description of "the crisis of those modern selves"; still more, at its "highest and most serious level," the novel offers solutions to the crisis. This is why the novel's decline matters. However, given that sacred mysteries are the highest realities, what promise can we find in a form that (for Bottum) only awkwardly fits a vision of things that swells beyond the modern self's assured sovereignty?

Now, as James Wood notes, "the religious tendency remained strong in the novel throughout the eighteenth and nineteenth centuries." By Joseph Bottum's account, the novel "was wrapped in very Protestant clothing," an argument he addresses at greater length in his essay "The Novel as Protestant Art." Seen through the Protestant monocle, the self's journey is "the deepest, truest thing in the universe, and the individual soul's salvation is the great metaphysical drama played out on the world's stage." When this concern with the self is unhinged from salvation, we may find ourselves, as in the finely-tuned, hyper-conscious novels of Virginia Woolf or Marcel Proust, stuck in a "relentless search inside the psyche, the endless dwelling on internal reality" to such a degree that thoughts and feelings about the self become "as important and interesting as actions and thoughts about the external universe." Thus, Bottum concludes his provocative "The Novel as Protestant Art," when a "Catholic-aiming" novel fails, it does so because it is "at war with its own form." Bottum's propositions merit much mulling; even where it seems to misfire or exaggerate, it is difficult to locate a dispensation that eliminates his diagnoses entirely.

First, witness the Catholic and Christian novelists who inherit the action of grace that is taken for granted in the lives of the saints and craft it into a form that has historically shed or demystified that transcendent. Dostoevsky, for instance, who though not Catholic, establishes a decidedly catholic core for his fiction through his character Zossima's aphorism, "Everyone is really responsible to all men for all men and for everything." His mature works are marked by a profound synthesis of hagiography and the modern novel, mixing the mysteries of sanctity with increased interiority: this synthesis is most complete in *Brothers Karamazov,* but though the saint-apprentice, Alyosha, and Dmitri, the romantic hero, are sewn together into the same story, this conjunction does at times strain the unity of the novel.

Second, and more importantly, as Rene Girard has demonstrated in *Deceit, Desire, and the Novel,* it is precisely the "victory over self-centeredness," the "renunciation of fascination and hatred," which is the "crowning moment of novelistic creation," and it can therefore be found in all great novelists. It is true that victory over the self is achieved through a suspended penetration of "the Self." However, as Proust proclaims through *The Past Recaptured,* "self-centeredness is a barrier to novelistic creation." Crippling self-absorption initially incites an imitation of others that manifests a desperate desire to "live outside ourselves," and as novelists as different as Flaubert and Dostoevsky and Proust narrate, the self often ends up being torn apart before its autonomous arrogance is shed through a painful renunciation of pride. All novelistic conclusions, Girard insists, are conversions, and in these conversions, the novel "reaches the heights of Western literature; he merges with the great religious ethics and the most elevated forms of humanism."

Bottum is not wrong, then, when he argues that in the novel, "the inner life, self-consciousness and self-understanding, become the manifestation of virtue and the path for grasping salvation." He errs, however, in assuming that because an author begins and builds the novelistic world upon an essentially modern, Protestant understanding of the self, that he also ends with that same understanding. Many novels seem to defy this. Consider J. K. Huysman's *Against Nature,* written just before his conversion to Catholicism occasioned a tetralogy of thickly Catholic novels chronicling the protagonist's passage from the Satanism of the Parisian underworld to the oblation of the Benedictines. In *Against Nature,* the anti-hero Des Esseintes, driven by a professed "contempt for humanity," retreats into a remote villa and escapes his painful self-centeredness by becoming a connoisseur of colors and tastes and smells; he tries to drown his own faults and failings in refined and decadent consumption—seeking solace, finally, in the sorrowful maxims of Schopenhauer and Pascal.

But finding that "the arguments of pessimism were powerless to comfort him," that only the "impossible" belief in eternal life could do, he becomes filled with a "fit of rage" which rattles through his resignation and indifference. Des Esseintes's epiphany is that nothing can be done, that men who have molded modernity according to their small-minded selves "were guzzling like picknickers from paper bags among the imposing ruins of the Church—ruins which had become . . . a pile of debris defiled by unspeakable jokes and scandalous jests." Perhaps, he wonders, the "pale martyr of Golgatha" and the God of Genesis will rekindle the rain of fire that once consumed the cities of the plain.

In the final lines of the novel, this misanthrope prays for pity on the Christian who doubts and the unbeliever who believes. Petering out on the page, he conceives of himself as a "galley-slave of life who puts out to sea alone, in the night, beneath a firmament no longer lit by the consoling beacon fires of the ancient hope."

Bottum terminates his initial analysis with a question that could have cropped up from the consciousness of Des Esseintes: "And as the atmosphere grows thinner and thinner in the West, as confidence fails, where shall we seek our future arts, our future selves?" Insofar as new novels themselves can answer this question, Catholic writers need to render the thinness of the atmosphere in the West.

How?

In two ways: following Huysmans, through rendering tenacious modern selves who, finding that the answers they seek so desperately could not, finally, come from further psychologizations and therapeutic self-actualizations, arrive at the threshold of the transcendent. And, following Fyodor, through novels structured around families and cities and whole nations rather than sovereign selves, novels inhabited by dependent, rational creatures rather than autonomous desiring protagonists, novels whose characters' self-determined trajectories are interrupted by the transcending providence of God.

Paradigms of this fool's errand do not abound—but they are to be found. Though the "protagonist" of Rumer Godden's *In This House of Brede* is purportedly the novice Philippa Foot, a widow of high stature in government service who bets on the Benedictine option. Even if she is a protagonist, of sorts, she is, as Phyllis Tickle has written, more so a novelistic "icon" of that "bright sadness which informs every Byzantine painting that has ever been hallowed, and every iconostasis that has ever been venerated."

Still more, once we are immersed in the interior of Brede Abbey, we find not descent into self but, on any given page, a profoundly communal form of narration: Godden moves us through the consciousness of Abbess Hester into the associated soul of Dame Clare, along with a whole host of sisters who possess a piercing admixture of humility and "the deadly knowledge of old family servants." The disparate sufferings and sanctities of the sisters are woven into a pattern of their motto, which is "'Pax,' but the word was set in a circle of thorns."

From the other side of the rose window we have J. K. Huysman's *Saint Lydwine of Schiedam*, which chronicles the victim soul in a manner discontent with *mere* hagiography. Huysmans criticizes Lydwine's prior biographers for having constructed "women who are not women, heroines impeccable but false, beings who have nothing living, nothing human, about them. We must not impose upon Lydwine those badly made portraits who possess, as though from birth, "all the virtues without the trouble of acquiring them." Huysmans, a novelist at heart, gives us a slow and painful repudiation of self that is analogous—though in an entirely different key—to those of any number of the novel's haughty heroes of good will. Elizabeth Bennet, for instance. And then, as though waiting in the narthex, a welcome replacement to kitschy pamphlets, we find Evelyn Waugh's *Helena*, the author's own favorite. When the poet John Betjeman confessed to being confused over the fact that the novel's Helena "doesn't seem like a saint," the great satirist responded that he "liked Helena's sanctity because it is in contrast with all the moderns think of as sanctity.

She wasn't thrown to the lions, she wasn't a contemplative, she didn't look like an El Greco. She just discovered what it was that God wanted her to do and did it. And she snubbed Aldous Huxley, with his perennial fog, by going straight to the essential physical historical fact of the redemption."

In taking his heroine through the discovery of the true cross, Waugh took himself there, too. As George Weigel has noted, in his later years the novelist undertook a purgative "spiritual quest for compassion and contrition. As for many of us, the contrition likely came easier than the compassion." *Helena,* Weigel maintains, was a piece of Waugh crucible; though the protagonist lacks the hagiographer's aureoles, focusing on her namesake helped the author move away from the raw meanness displayed in some of his farce, and into, "for all its chiaroscuro shadings, a divine comedy indeed." Still, there is something apparently unsettling about the writer who makes claims to locate the stirrings of sanctity—in novelists as in their characters. Who are we to imagine we can imagine God's visitation to us, his wayward bride, and, still worse, to do so through fiction's supposedly noble lies?

Enter Fear and Trembling dressed like Don Quixote. It would seem that those who narrate providence are transgressing the limits of imitation: how can grace, the precise workings of which none of us can pinpoint, be *shown*? Christic imaginers would, at first glance, seem to be committing a crass immoderation, feigning a kind of "mastery of God" and His work by deciphering His workings too surely. "We may be able to grasp," says Josef Pieper, "in faith the actuality and the ultimate meaning of God's working in history. But no man can presume on his own to point to any providential happening of the here and now, and to say: 'God has manifested His intention in this or that reward or punishment, confirmation or rejection.'"

There is a major difference between our presuming to pinpoint the providential happenings in history, or the composer of the lives of the saints specifying the workings of grace in a particular soul, and the fiction writer fitting divine things to his form. In the former case, the writer is saying what God *did*, whereas the fictionist is showing us, to paraphrase Aristotle's *Poetics,* "the kind of thing that God *would* do." Importantly, in the latter case, we are dealing with hypothetical probabilities, with plausibility, which, as James Wood says, "involves the defense of the credible *imagination* against the incredible. This is surely why Aristotle writes that a convincing impossibility in mimesis is always preferable to an unconvincing possibility."

The Catholic novelist does not deal in slavish "realistic" imitation but with mimetic persuasion. Let him test the novel's conventions and constraints, meld mystery—in a measured manner—into a literature hell-bent on secularity and individuality. Let him convince us this end could come, that the impossible could happen, has happened, will happen *in saecula saeculorum.* Amen.

4

Whispers and Shouts of Faith in Fiction: Léon Bloy and the Catholic Writer Today

The 'Door of the Humble,' which is the door of the Apocalypse itself, is so narrow and so fearfully padlocked that I do not know how I will ever be able to get through it. Ask of Her who weeps to turn me into one of those tiny lizards of the colour of hope which can slip through the crevices of the wall of doves mentioned in the Canticle.

—Léon Bloy

THOSE PIGHEADED FOOLS still bent on fostering the Catholic literary tradition are badly in need of a patron saint capable of delivering on behalf of lost causes. I hereby announce my quixotic campaign to have Léon Bloy canonized for just such a case as this. Now, in what Walker Percy called "these dread latter days of the old violent beloved U.S.A. and of the Christ-forgetting Christ-haunted death-dealing Western world," when the Trade Union of Catholic Artists has seen a sharp decline in card-carrying members, the leonine Parisian and reactionary Catholic writer is just the outsider candidate we need advocating for us on the Other Side.

Kairos calls. We must ransom the time. Of late, Bloy's works, long out of print, have been resurrected from their untended graves, shuffling off their mortal coils and proving themselves perennial. St. Augustine's Press reprinted his novel *La Femme Pauvre* (*The Woman Who Was Poor*) in 2015. In the 365 days that followed, Wakefield Press became the unlikely champion of Bloy's short story collections *Disagreeable Tales* and *Sweating Blood,* both freshly translated by Erik Butler. Then in 2017, equipped with a new introduction by David Bentley Hart, Cluny Media pushed Raïssa Maritain's translation of Bloy's *The Pilgrim of the Absolute* (collected writings) back through the presses. In 2020, Snuggly Books brought out a publication of *The Desperate Man,* his first novel, heretofore never translated into English. And finally, in 2021, Wiseblood Books plans to publish *Exegesis of Bourgeois Expressions,* also rendered into English for the first time. A self-described "voluntary fanatic" all the days of his life, long after he left us to occupy the afterlife, Bloy is returning with a vengeance, reminding us that genuinely Catholic fiction needs to avoid both punitive puritanism and pathetic political correctness. The frankness of this Frenchman reminds us that fiction is not meant to tell us prophylactic lies that help us sleep at night. Rather, fiction helps us tell the truth about human beings: the pendulum swings between clowns and kings, pusillanimous ass and capital-S Saint. H.ere C.omes E.verybody.

"Today the faith found in literature is more whispered than shouted," claims Gregory Wolfe, founder of *Image: Art, Faith, and Mystery.* Here he alludes to Flannery O'Connor's manifesto: "For the hard of hearing you shout, and for the almost-blind you draw large and startling figures." Wolfe wants us to recede from fiction that finds grace through violent grotesqueries. "That made sense in the context of her time, when the old Judeo-Christian narrative was locked in a struggle with the new secular narratives of Marx, Freud and Darwin," he wrote. "However, we live in a postmodern world, where any grand narrative is suspect, where institutions are seen as oppressive." As Paul Elie notes in "Has Fiction Lost its Faith?" O'Connor forged a way to "make belief believable." She called for fiction that dramatized "the central religious experience," which she characterized as a person's encounter with "a supreme being recognized through faith." She wrote that kind of fiction herself, shaped by her understanding that in the modern age, such an encounter often takes place outside of organized religion—that in matters of belief we find ourselves on our own, practicing "do-it-yourself religion." Today, the United States is a vast Home Depot of "do-it-yourself religion." But you wouldn't know it from the stories we tell. The religious encounter of the kind O'Connor described forces a person to ask how belief figures into his or her own life and how to decide just what is true in it, what is worth acting on.

While the whisperings Wolfe advocates certainly contain some frequencies of Catholicity, and the "still, silent" metaphor describes well any number of contemporary novels written by writers who happen to be Catholic, I fear that his approach is far too historicist, and far too enslaved to verisimilitude. More plainly, the Catholic literary tradition is not mimetic so much as it is sacramental: although we need stories marked by the fact that trust in the Grand Narrative of Catholicism has been badly shaken, the superabundance of grace still thrills through our lives, and an approach to literature that calls for a categorical quieting of God's grandeur is likely to mutter indecipherably instead of whispering gracefully.

Further, Wolfe's account of the "small voice that is all around us" does not do justice to the whole of the Elijah narrative to which it appeals. In 1 Kings 19, God commands the prophet Elijah to "'go forth, and stand upon the mount before the LORD.' And, behold, the LORD passed by, and a great and strong wind rent the mountains, and broke in pieces the rocks before the LORD; but the LORD was not in the wind: and after the wind an earthquake; but the LORD was not in the earthquake; and after the earthquake a fire; but the LORD was not in the fire, and after the fire a still small voice" (11–12).

Note that God does not only orchestrate a whisper; he precedes this whisper with thunderous bombast that rivals the Zeus of *Prometheus Bound.* Do the earthquake, strong wind, and fire serve merely as points of contrast, enunciating God's quiet manifestation, or does God, too, appeal to "shouts" in order to arrest Elijah's attention, before he more gracefully reveals His nature?

If we follow the trail left by Wolfe's sensibility, we may find greater affinity with the literary trends of our times, and more acceptance into the literati's gnostic MFA mysteries, but we will lose the hermeneutic of continuity that the Catholic literary tradition demands. Tracking his scent, we will remain haunted by longings for artistic incense incapable of rousing the noses of our immortal souls.

Although historically Bloy lived in Paris, metaphorically—and metaphysically—he dwelt in the unchanging. Of the writer's eternal residence, Erik Butler writes, in "the realm of Truth, no exaggeration is possible, no ink too black, no hue too bold. *Being,* not *seeming,* stands at issue. The sun falls from a right angle on high. . . . '*Our souls could see each other.* There was the sensation of standing face to face at the edge of a cliff,'" one of Bloy's characters cries, incarnating the Catholic writer's insistence that, even in mere literature, what belongs to the world of flux and finitude must be recast according to Revelation's artful lights. As Remy de Gourmont put it, "Monsieur Bloy's genius is theological and Rabelaisian. His books are as if written by Saint Thomas Aquinas in collaboration with Gargantua. They are scholastic and gigantic, Eucharistic and scatological."

Instead of assuming a chameleonic approach to the artistic trends of his times, Bloy committed a paradigmatically Catholic theft. Having perfected his literary chops, capable of going toe-to-toe with his collegiate *artistes*, "he took the 'Art for art's sake' of his Symbolist contemporaries and restore[d] it to the Deity whom unbelievers claim to have dethroned. It is impossible to trump this rhetorical gesture, for it occurs in the name of ages and generations reaching back to the very foundation of the world." As I noted earlier, and as James Wood argues in *How Fiction Works,* the novel "has its origins in a secular response to the religious lives and biographies of saints and holy men." Which brings us to Bloy's first miracle: while he appropriated and advanced upon the frontiers of Decadence, Naturalism, and Symbolism—his experimental and exploratory form winning him praise from Franz Kafka and Jorge Luis Borges—he simultaneously restored to fiction its preoccupation with salvation found in the hagiographies from whence it came. Wolfe might argue that, given the "freethinking" literary free-for-all that dominated France's arts at the time, Bloy ought to have taken greater care to smuggle his sacramental vision into his stories. Instead of muzzling his savage soteriological yelp into a cowed whine, Bloy "does not mince words," but, to use Butler's words, "offers the portrait of realities that people who are not gifted with second sight cannot even discern," a dynamic that returns us to O'Connor. "When you can assume that your audience holds the same beliefs you do," she writes, "you can relax and use more normal means of talking to it; when you have to assume that it does not, then you have to make your vision apparent by shock—to the hard of hearing you shout, and for the almost-blind you draw large and startling figures."

The whispering way of Wolfe will reach some wayfarers who yet have ears to hear in this Waste Land of postmodernity. As with most things Catholic, we should avoid the dualistic mistake of turning the "shout" / "whisper" debate into an either or; we should opt instead for one more (in a long line of) both / and (that includes grace and nature / Scripture and Tradition, and other venerable pairings). Still, it would seem imprudent to stake too much on altering Catholic art until it receives the stamp of a pastiche aesthetic defined by anxious skepticism and *jouissance* cynicism. For, as Butler explains, "lulled (and often medicated) into dull contentment, the occupants of the postmodern aquarium drift in the tepid waters of 'the best of all possible worlds.' Nothing guarantees this state will last." Further, especially in consideration of the fact that the fragmented narratives of our postmodern condition are increasingly haunted by the grandly apocalyptic character of our times, we cannot do justice to the Catholic literary tradition without asking the intercession of the grandiose Léon Bloy, who once wrote a work entitled *Au seuil de l'Apocalypse* (*On the Threshold of the Apocalypse*); whom Barbey d'Aurevilly described as "a cathedral gargoyle who pours the waters of heaven down on the good and on the wicked." Léon Bloy, patron of lost cause Catholic literati, *ora pro nobis!*

I first met Bloy fifteen years ago, waiting for the bus in that same bohemian neighborhood of Milwaukee where I would go on to found Wiseblood Books. There a friend gave me a paperback copy of Raïssa Maritain's books *We Have Been Friends Together/Adventures in Grace*. (I still have the book, which, though in critical condition, is kept alive by duck-tape over the binding.) The year before, I had just barely snuck into the Catholic Church through its creaky back door. I didn't know the Maritains and their chronicles from Ray Bradbury's science fiction *Martian Chronicles*. In this spiritual biography, Raïssa recounts how she and Jacques encountered Léon Bloy. Steeped in the intellectual nihilism of their times, troubled specifically by a scientific determinism the tenets of which they deeply understood and by which they were left in existential anguish, the two young geniuses, who were then courting, made a pact to commit suicide together on a given impending date, unless they should come in contact with absolute truth. If the world lacks absolute truth, as they had been taught—if, in other words, truth is arbitrary—then, they concluded, existence is too cruel to countenance any longer. There is a remarkable sincerity to this proposition, even as it is extreme and dark. As their search for this truth ticked away, they happened to read a review of *La Femme Pauvre* that touted the novel as one of the only French works of the age that flashed with genuine metaphysical insights.

Upon reading *The Woman Who was Poor*, they found themselves "for the first time . . . before the reality of Christianity." They did have some reservations about Bloy's "endless endeavors to note minute ugliness or mediocrity, that fixed predilection for violence and force, the perpetual hyperbole," still, they concluded that the novel was "saved by a shining sincerity, an unswerving uprightness, a genuine, deep, inexhaustible lyricism, by the exquisite tenderness of a heart made to love absolutely, to cling entirely to what it loved."

To our desensitized minds, *La Femme Pauvre* is not exactly shocking in its presentation of ugliness, violence, and force. Taken as a whole, the story follows Clotilde Marechal as she is led by providence and eager teachers out of the world of her mother's prostitution and her stepfather's oppressive callousness and into the life of a saint. Throughout the novel, Clotilde is taught about the Church by a painter named Gacougnol, a writer named Marchenoir, and Leopold, who illuminates manuscripts. In winding and wonderful digressions, these three men discuss modern art and argue over whether there can be such a thing as "Christian art." They also give some sobering portraits of their fellow artists' disillusionment with the Church.

Clotilde, innocent, although not naïve, and hungering for holiness, is eager to be relieved of her poverty and affliction. The novelistic logic proclaims that some suffering is actually sanctifying her even as a species of arbitrary suffering is simply grinding away at her soul. By means of his narrator, Bloy grants his prospective audience a harsh warning: "Take it all round, in fact, and those gracious readers might do even better by not opening the present volume at all, for it is itself a long digression on the evil of living, the infernal misfortune of existence, hogs lacking any snout to root for tit-bits, in a society without God."

In *La Femme Pauvre,* even those "with" God will have nothing of his holy poverty, although "those who will have none of such a mate die sometimes from terror or despair, at her kiss." And yet, as in the case of Flannery O'Connor's *Wise Blood,* this dark tale is, finally, filled with hope, if even it is a hope that lacks any sense of the sentimental and saccharine. These writers do justice to Christ's revelation that numerous souls dwell at the gates of hopelessness: wide is the path that leads to perdition; "Again I say to you, it is easier for a camel to go through the eye of a needle, than for a rich man to enter the kingdom of God." The novel navigates this needle. Its two-part division is a map that moves us from the "Flotsam of the Shadows" to the "Flotsam of the Light." Jettisoning gems as though jetsam across the page, Bloy writes, "When the chaos of this fallen world is sorted out, when the stars are begging their bread, and only the most despised dust of the earth is permitted to reflect the Glory; when men know that *nothing was in its place,* and that the rational species lived only on enigmas and illusions; it may well be that the torments of the unhappy, unfortunate man, may reveal and display the wretched poverty of soul of a millionaire, corresponding with his rags, on the mysterious Register of Redistribution of Universal Solidarity."

Masked hope led the Maritains to send a letter requesting a meeting with the begging star. They stuffed some money into the envelope and waited. Soon, the couple crossed the writer's brink. As Jacques notes, "Once the threshold of this house was crossed, all values were dislocated, as though by an invisible switch. One knew, or one guessed, that only one sorrow existed here—not to be of the saints. And all the rest receded into the twilight."

The Maritains' pact to kill themselves in the absence of the absolute also receded into the twilight, and soon they were welcomed into the Catholic Church, with Bloy as their godfather. And it was through this conversion that Jacques made voluminous contributions to the revival of Thomistic philosophy in our time. Also through Bloy, Jacques met the painter Georges Rouault, whose conversion had also been incited by *La Femme Pauvre.*

Some years back, during my sole stint in Paris, I used Raïssa's *We Have Been Friends Together* to search out Bloy's old home in Montmartre, situated at the base of Sacré-Cœur—the Basilica of the Sacred Heart. During the search, I was blessed by a meeting with Rouault's grandchildren, who told me of the connection between Bloy,

Maritain, and Rouault. Although the leonine writer called God's "Providence . . . a Pactolus of tears," he was nonetheless an instrument of great grace. Bloy was godfather to Rouault's child, and the Maritains and Rouaults would frequently find themselves around the Bloy's table—engaging in intense debates, playing dominoes with the children, and praying. In fact, Rouault was a major source of inspiration to the now classic *Art and Scholasticism*, Jacques Maritain's influential Thomistic take on the nature of art.

Bloy gave himself two nicknames which nicely capture his grandiosity and self-deprecating sincerity: "The Ungrateful Beggar," a reference to his unremitting dependence on friends and his perpetual indebtedness, and "The Pilgrim of the Absolute," an encapsulation of the totalizing quality that pervades his wayfaring life and works. We see both of these strands at work when, on the dime of an anonymous benefactor, Bloy "went out to get a syphon of Seltzer water in the neighborhood," and "the old man who waited on me gave me a spray of lilies taken from a bunch he had just cut in his garden. The flowers were half faded, but what does that matter? It was hard for me to keep back my tears because I had the illusion or the evidence of an impulse of goodness."

Enraptured with the absolute, other things in life, ordinary things—but, more to the point, mediocre aspects, mediocre people—he did not handle well. I am unable to say whether the more insidious side of this attitude contributed to the death of his two eldest children. One of them died due to an excess of toxic dust from a nearby construction site just down the road from their dilapidated

Parisian Rue. I am not sure whether it was entirely outside his manic power to get out of the poverty he and his family lived under. It may have been a weakness, even a sin. But he wrestled with it always. In his journal, alongside entries such as, "We thought we were dying of hunger when ten francs arrived from a poor priest from whom I have asked nothing," he records many prayers to God, pleading to be able to become a regular worker. A characteristic passage reads: "Will God at last want me to live by my work like other laborers? This is a grace which I have so long begged with tears!" These words indicate that the impoverishment was much deeper than an accident of his striving after the absolute. A strong strand of his soul yearned to be stripped of the writer's hairshirt. He yearned, he noted elsewhere, to support his family in a different way, in a "normal" way. When one of his children died very much unexpectedly, he made a solitary pilgrimage to the mountain in La Salette where Our Lady appeared in the mid-nineteenth century. His passages on this pilgrimage, on the experience of losing a child, are overwhelmingly intense. "In the face of a child's death, art and poetry come to resemble a great destitution."

From a distance, I long stood in awe of Bloy's apparently providential appointment as Catholic writer of the Parisian slums. From a distance, I long admired the apparent potency of *La Femme Pauvre,* which had affected the French Catholic Renaissance so directly. For years I searched for an affordable copy of the novel. One could find it dangling online like forbidden fruit, selling for a staggering hundred dollars per copy, and the libraries lacked a single edition.

Around this time, I was beginning to write under the influence of the Catholic literary tradition, and many framed the work as the first modern Catholic novel, so though I felt I had to find it, I could not justify spending so much money. So, well, I prayed. Léon Bloy surrendered his entire being to Divine Providence; why could I not also make such a surrender?

Some years later, on Christmas Day 2005, a friend of mine presented me with a thrift store copy of *The Woman Who Was Poor,* translated in 1939 by I. J. Collins. The yellowed pages exuded that sweet "odor of literary sanctity" so rare among old tomes that typically reek of moldy, dank, acidic paper. The inside cover bore the blurred stamp of "The Franciscan Library." In the upper left corner, in mockery of Bloy's poverty, someone somewhere had penciled $50.00, evidence that the novel had fallen victim to those ironies of the market by which the starving artist, denied substantive monies in life, earns a killing as a ghost. I read it through by New Year's Day, and distinctly recall that, though the bombastic, sometimes unbelievably hyperbolic style was at times abrasive, in the upper room of a smoky Milwaukee coffee house (an actual, not-metaphorical house that, as a teenager, I ran away from home to inhabit), in the wee hours before the 2006 New Year, I had the only mystical experience that I have ever had while reading a work of fiction.

Marchenoir, one of the main characters who is modeled after Bloy himself, ascends the mountain in La Salette, supplicating Our Lady and Our Lord for succor, for his child has died due largely to the awful sanitation in their region of Paris. I cannot recount the scene here, for as it is stunning as it stands I will not rewrite it—you've got to read the book—but suffice it to say, Bloy blew through the smoke of that coffee house like a comet struck by the *Primum Mobile.* That night, he was acquitted of those little gargoyles that had been appearing on my shoulder, accusing Bloy of being one more Parisian *poseur* playing the tortured *artiste* to accommodate his habitual irresponsibility.

In *We Have Been Friends Together,* Jacques and Raïssa Maritain also give evidence of a dubious disposition toward their godfather. Tongue-in-cheek, speaking in a metaphorical key, Bloy himself "admits that it lies outside my power to remain calm. When I'm not killing, I must *injure.*" The Maritans tackle the question of his charity directly: did Bloy's faith and actions possess a core of real *caritas*? Did he not degenerate into a gadfly dressed in Franciscan garb? The Maritains note that when they met Bloy for the first time, he "uncovered for them . . . the tenderness of Christian brotherhood, that trembling both of mercy and of fear with which a soul marked with the love of God is seized when it faces another soul. Bloy appeared to us as the contrary of other men, who hide grave failings in the things of the spirit and so many invisible crimes under a carefully maintained whitewash of the virtues of sociability. Instead of being a whitewashed sepulcher, like the Pharisees of every time, he was a fire-stained and blackened cathedral. The whiteness was within, in the depth of the tabernacle."

A world filled with Léon Bloys, copies of Léon Bloys, clones of Léon Bloys—Léon Bloy as a sort of absolute ideal for all humanity: this is indeed an unsettling picture to imagine. It is something like imagining a zoo filled with nothing but lions. Cage after cage, nothing but lions. But then a world absolutely lacking the one Léon Bloy it knew: this is also unsettling—a vacuum! Nonetheless, his provocative prose raises questions concerning its—how can I put it politely?—"rhetorical efficacy." Jacques Maritain offers at least one possible answer to this question:

> I understand quite well that for certain minds, fortunate in having been spared the dizziness of any abyss, whether from its brink or from its depth, the case of Léon Bloy is a singularly obscure puzzle. But I must repeat: there are perishing souls who seek beauty in darkness, and on whom quiet apologetics would be without avail. Nor would pure theology act on them, for their reason is too weakened by error; they imagine that obedience to faith is incompatible with boldness of intellect, or with the play and freedom of art and beauty; in short, the mediocrity of a great number of Christians frightens them off. Bloy, in crying out his disgust at all lukewarmness, in shouting on rooftops his thirst for the absolute, inspires these famished ones with a presentiment of the glory of God. But nothing, in the last analysis, would have any effect without the secret of this magnificent beggar and vociferator, I mean without his charity: it is his love of God and souls that does everything.

Still, outside philosophically-minded-former-card-carrying-nihilistic-socialists like Maritain, who hears the Léonine Bloy's roar? Does the Ungrateful Beggar's rowdy rhetoric and "irresponsible," "unrespectable" existence exclude him from influencing the lukewarm at whom he gnawed with a prophet's discontent? Those "neither hot nor cold" whom the Lord speaks of in *the book of Revelation:* does someone like Bloy actually stand a chance of stoking the coals of their smoldering faith? How could he come off as anything but a lunatic, a fanatic, a threat? This question burns like a wildfire through Salvation History, a strange chronicle that again and again orders us to avoid gauging a prophet's success on the people's conversion. Outside Jonah, most prophets met fates that make them appear to have achieved little more than Failure.

To be fair, as souls have seen since Plato at least, a thin line divides prophecy and madness. Although I am not a gambling man, I would bet that, were he to have lived today, and were he to have made his way into one of our innumerable psychological clinics, Bloy would perhaps have been diagnosed with severe depression, bi-polar disorder—something for which the doctors would advise anti-psychotics. His mind was not entirely sound. But mental sanity is not always the best measure of sanctity. Grace does build upon nature, and this dictum is proven with utter clarity in Bloy. A man who was recklessly abused as a child, who, even after his conversion, bore the marks of sin that came from his former life among prostitutes—a man such as this will not assume the quiet professorial life of, say, Tolkien; he will not write the same species of satire as, say, Evelyn Waugh. But grace will build even upon prose that lingers sometimes a little too long in the gutter, in the underbelly of the world.

Bloy's prose can hardly be read as anything but the linguistic equivalent of camel-skin clothes and a diet of honey and locusts. He writes with large lines, and here is where we return to his crossover with Flannery O'Connor. O'Connor's fiction is often perceived as being overly violent, extreme. Upstanding Citizens of Christendom everywhere are shocked beyond comment by, say, the Misfit, or Manley Pointer, or Hazel Motes. "Could this really come from a Christian?" some wonder. Of course we know that she did not create violent characters simply to revel in their violence. But to make the link between O'Connor and Bloy, I have to take two steps back before taking a step forward.

Bloy, the unmannerly finger-pointer, began as a violently atheistic painter. He converted in 1870, a massive shift that resulted from friendships with, he notes, "various priests." Later, he met and engaged in a relationship with a prostitute, Anne-Marie Roule, for whom he experienced immense sexual passion. Bloy served as a blunt instrument in Roule's conversion to Catholicism, and soon after this, she began seeing visions and heard what he described as "celestial utterances" which she communicated to him. After some time, however, Roule lost her mind and was committed to an asylum, where she remained until her death in 1907.

I hope this doesn't merely serve the interests of Flannery specialists, but the drafts of *Wise Blood* contain remarkable echoes of Anne-Marie Roule's life, in the form of the character Sabbath Lily Hawkes. Both are visionaries who end up being locked up in mental institutions—Anne-Marie being taken under locks by the "social services" and Sabbath

Lily, who in the drafts is the wife of Hazel Motes, by Hazel himself.

At any rate, in 1886, Bloy published his first major novel, *Le Désperéré.* In 1890, he married Jeanne Molbeck, daughter of a Danish poet. She brought him much peace, served as a source of great stability in his life, much in the manner of Dostoevsky's second wife Anna, without whom we may never have seen *The Brothers Karamazov* and the other late, great novels. Several months before the marriage, Molbeck had been baptized into the Church. The year 1897 brought the publication of *La Femme Pauvre,* Bloy's philosophical and literary masterpiece.

O'Connor had a copy of *The Woman who was Poor* in her library. She also had a copy of Albert Beguin's *Léon Bloy: a Study in Impatience.* But the circle in the fire that circumscribes affinities between Bloy and O'Connor goes beyond the latter's library and her early, discarded drafts of *Wise Blood.*

As Sarah Gordon notes, "Maritain's defense or rationale of Bloy's subject matter and technique sounds as though it could be a defense of O'Connor's shock tactics: Bloy, Maritain argues, was writing to 'men who most of the time live in the senses, and who need to be led to the intelligible by means of the tangible.' . . . Bloy liked to repeat that he wrote not for the righteous—neither for the perfect, nor for those who are progressing, nor for those who are beginning—but for the sleeping ones who needed his sufferings and his outbursts, for publicans and scoundrels." At a time when many French saw the Catholic Church as the institution of the wealthy and powerful, Maritain notes that Bloy was intent on "opening the eyes of many a strayed person who foolishly believed the Church of Christ occupies itself more with safeguarding the possessions of the rich than with consoling the poor."

La Femme Pauvre is, then, not merely the pose of a literary man who is supposedly concerned with "the poor." Poverty was holy for Bloy because Christ was poor. Here we have not the Parisian bohemian who lives an anti-bourgeois life for specious reasons, not the debauchery shrouded behind sentiments of romantic artistry that Hemingway depicts in *A Moveable Feast.* Here we have a holy, if sometimes problematic poverty (that he lost two children remains gut wrenching and soul haunting), one that resides side by side with a grotesque literary style. O'Connor, too, knew pecuniary impoverishment. Though less ungrateful, she would not have been able to write had she not lived as a veritable beggar in the house of Sally and Robert Fitzgerald. And, in spite of any literary success, her Lupus bills led her to review books in order to build her library (she could not afford to buy books), to travel while sick in order to earn much needed monies.

Again, O'Connor's body of stories sustain a hermeneutic of continuity in that Catholic grotesque that finds its most potent modern precedent in Bloy, even as both writers express their indebtedness to E. A. Poe, whose horrific overcoat each tailors until it fits. Both do violence to the everyday, bourgeois nihilism lurking behind platitudes such as, "It takes all kinds to make the world," "Rome wasn't built in a day," "Well, other people have their opinions too" (from O'Connor's "Good Country People"). In fact, it seems likely that O'Connor, by having her "good people" characters utter trite truisms and clichéd maxims, makes new Bloy's own mockery as found in "The Wisdom of the Bourgeoisie" (alternately translated "Exegesis of the Commonplaces"). This book is filled wholly with vignettes satirizing various bourgeois sayings, ranging from "Business is business" to "It is the truth only which gives offense," to "Every man for himself and the Good Lord for all," to "Religion is so consoling." Consider Bloy's analysis of the latter: "It implies that you have just enough religion not to resemble those publicans who sorrowfully fast from one end of the year to the other, while you all the while polish off exquisite meals in great peace of conscience. You owe nothing to people who are dying of destitution, since they have religion to console them."

The violence of O'Connor's stories, the invectives of Bloy's meditations, their joint ownership of the grotesque: these things are not undertaken merely to abolish mediocrity. True, like her Catholic compatriot Christopher Dawson, O'Connor insisted that "Catholicism is opposed to the bourgeois mind"; she praised her favorite art form, the grotesque, as the "true anti-bourgeois style." But the works of O'Connor and Bloy are more than mere *anti-*, mere negations. In both authors' fictions this violence first and foremost makes way for the terrible speed of God's mercy, for that grace which is experienced, at least subjectively, as painful, even violent. In both cases, these Catholic writers mock pretensions and spit out the pabulum of the bourgeois in order to reveal that, as Bloy writes at the end of

La Femme Pauvre, "There is but one sadness—not to be a saint."

"Art," Bloy proclaims in a celebrated (celebrated by whom?) passage, "is an aboriginal parasite of the skin of the first serpent." From this origin it derives its "overweening pride and power of suggestion. It is self-sufficient like a god, and the flowered crowns of princes, compared with its headdress of lightning, are like iron-collars of torture. It will no more submit to worship than to obedience, and no man's will can make it bow before any altar. It may consent to give alms out of the superfluity of its pomp, to temples or palaces—when it is more or less to its advantage; but you must ask it for a thimbleful over and above what is strictly required."

Here again, as always, Bloy walks the plank and falls overboard to make his point. But the essential antimony between art and humility is crucial, especially for those who have worked to revive the Catholic literary tradition with renewed vigor since Paul Elie published his "Has Fiction Lost its Faith?" and Dana Gioia followed on Elie's heels with "The Catholic Writer Today." Strong is the tendency for art to become a "product" consumed only by other artists, strong is the temptation to weave artistic accolades around your head like a glittering aureole. Literary magazines and literary culture that is incestuous, writers who write only for other writers, the dreadful MFA solipsism: these, no less than the bourgeois mind, are ready to undermine even the most earnest efforts toward a Catholic literary revival. As Gioia writes in his controversial "Can Poetry Matter?" literature (poetry in particular) is "no longer part of the mainstream of artistic and intellectual life, it has become the specialized occupation of a relatively small and isolated group. Little of the frenetic activity it generates ever reaches outside that closed group. As a class, poets are not without cultural status. Like priests in a town of agnostics, they still command a certain residual prestige. But as individual artists they are almost invisible."

If we were to hire a high-profile data consultant to help us artificially manufacture a situation of sin designed to stew artistic pride, she could do no better. How badly we need Bloy as a sort of "patron saint" of the Catholic literary revival, for, *artiste* though he was, he knew well the limitations of art, and thus has much to teach us in terms of artistic humility. He knew too that, far from fostering an escape from reality, an Art for Art's sake museum of self-contained beautiful things, literature's highest aim should be to reveal the heart of the real around us.

Bereft of Bloy's witness to Christianity's absolute character, bereft of fictions such as Bloy's, we are left to cultivate privatized gardens comprised of our own most cherished "pleasant fictions," coy and convenient lies that line our everyday lives. Bereft of the Bloys of this world, we are even more inclined to cover over the valley of tears, to surrogate the grandiosity of self for God's grandeur. "Bloy has come my way," O'Connor wrote. "He is an iceberg hurled at me to break up my Titanic, and I hope my Titanic will be smashed." May he smash ours also, leaving us like shipwrecked passengers clinging to those drifting shards of wood his words leave behind. Treading there in the dark, on the deep, we may chafe against the exposed nails of the sinking ship's split wood, but the iceberg will lift water level all the same, floating us heavenward alongside all the other Flotsam of the Light.

Part II

READING CHRIST-HAUNTED FICTIONS

5

A Dank, Dimly-Lighted Place: Hemingway on Affliction, Beauty, and Being at Home in the World

"Yet in nearly all of them you can rewrite what you have already written, seeing what is not true and seeing the true that you have not put in and it is always much clearer and easier to rewrite something in one of these places than when it was first written."

—Ernest Hemingway, from his unpublished essay "On Cathedrals"

It seems that claims about beauty are given to extremes, swinging between swoons and cynicism. Beauty is Cinderella or celebrity, portion of the privileged or savior of the world. In his recent essay "Beauty and Desecration," Roger Scruton contends that "our human need for beauty is not simply a redundant addition to the list of human appetites. It is not something that we could lack and still be fulfilled as people. It is a need arising from our metaphysical condition as free individuals, seeking our place in an objective world." He takes as evidence our occasional ceremonial dinner, in preparation for which we "set the table with a clean embroidered cloth, arranging plates, glasses, bread in a basket, and some carafes of water and wine." We do this, he writes, "lovingly, delighting in the appearance, striving for an effect of cleanliness, simplicity, symmetry, and warmth."

Ernest Hemingway engages the mystery of our need for beauty in his short story "A Clean, Well-Lighted Place." Two waiters watch as an elderly, deaf man sits in the shadow of the brightly lit café, sipping his drink. "Last week he tried to kill himself," one waiter relates, but his niece cut him down out of "fear for his soul." Impatient to go home and be with his wife, the young waiter refuses to grant the elderly man another brandy. When the older waiter presses the younger, asking him why he did not let the deaf man stay, the young man asserts his bombastic confidence, which in the story has that feel of slippery arrogance. "Each night I am reluctant to close up," the older confides, "because there may be some one who needs the café." When the youth retorts that "there are bodegas open all night long," the elder sees even further the chasm that divides them: "You do not understand. This is a clean and pleasant café. It is well lighted." Further, bodegas offer only bars before which you cannot stand with dignity, while the café is dotted with tables set out for "all those who need a light for the night."

Scruton argues that the table is a symbol of homecoming, that there is "an abundance of meaning and good cheer . . . somehow contained in the appearance of the table." The table tells us that we are home because it is beautiful, which is deeply significant, in that "our greatest need is for home."

Still further, at the table we are not alone, an importance that even the younger waiter admits when he ponders the difference between drinking in a café and buying a bottle and drinking at home. The beauty of a clean, well-lighted place "tells us that we are at home in the world," allowing us to cease our alienated, resentful wanderings, draining our suspicion and distrust. All of this is lost on the young waiter because he is drunk on the pseudo-beauty of youthful confidence. He has "everything," the older waiter says, irony stirred into his statement, his effort to reveal to the young man a certain sourness beneath his wistfulness.

But then Hemingway's story takes a distinct turn. After the younger man departs, the older tells himself, "It was all a nothing and a man was nothing too. It was only that and light was all it needed and a certain cleanness and order." From the darkness, meditating on the light, the old waiter at last utters a prayer, but it is a strange and subversive one: "Our nada who art in nada, nada be thy name thy kingdom nada thy will be nada in nada as it is in nada."

Paul Smith sees in this prayer the story's embrace of "the moral landscape of a world with no ground for faith, *nada,* to which the only possible response is despair," Hemingway's narrative musing on "whatever meagre fare there may be for those who hunger for certainties." If this is the case, the story contains a tension between its clear "contention" that the cleanliness, light, and order of beauty tell us that we are at home in the world, and, well, that beyond this well-lit place encroaches the awful *nada* in which we art. Scruton observes that during modernism, we see "art increasingly aimed to disturb, subvert, or transgress moral certainties," and we can certainly read in the old man's *nada* a subversion, transgression, and desecration of the beautiful prayer which Our Lord taught to us. But the old waiter doesn't stop with this, nor is his "Hail nothing, full of nothing, nothing is with thee" the end of the story. He himself goes to a bar, the waiter becoming the waited-upon. When he responds "Nada" to the barman's request for his drink order, the latter considers him "Otro loco más." But though the old waiter momentarily capitulates to desecration, he continues to speak of his certainties regarding beauty. "The light is very bright and pleasant but the bar is unpolished," he says to the barman, who refuses to engage, asking only if the old man wants another drink. Beauty, we might say, has been banished from the bar of the bodega.

"The current habit of desecrating beauty," Scruton concludes, "suggests that people are as aware as they ever were of the presence of sacred things. Desecration is a kind of defense against the sacred, an attempt to destroy its claims." The old man defends himself against the sacred prayer, just as the bartender defends himself against the *imago dei* in man. Although the bar is bereft of beauty, it is adorned with a "shining steam pressure coffee maker." "Do not adorn the church and ignore your afflicted brother, for he is the most precious temple of all," writes St. John Chrysostom. Hemingway seems to laicize Chrysostom's command. The older waiter recognizes the afflicted deaf man as a precious temple, but he can only recognize the beauty of the human temple by the light of the clean café. It is this light against the night which moves him to love. "We can be sure," Von Balthasar insists, "that whoever sneers at [beauty], as if she were the ornament of a bourgeois past, whether he admits it or not, can no longer pray and soon will no longer be able to love."

However, we cannot deny the fact that beauty does not save the old man, just as it did not keep Hemingway from committing himself to *nada.* Pope Benedict XVI pointed out in his meeting with artists that "too often . . . the beauty that is thrust upon us is illusory and deceitful, superficial and blinding, leaving the onlooker dazed." Rather than bringing man out of himself, failing to open him up "to horizons of true freedom as it draws him aloft, it imprisons him within himself and further enslaves him, depriving him of hope and joy." Beauty, too, can be degraded into an instrument or a sham; all good things are capable of corruption. But the clean, well-lighted place is not a sham. It radiates with the goodness of true beauty. The waiter's prayer to *nada,* and his desperate desire for light in the night, however, betray the fact that beauty will not save the world.

While Scruton tells the truth when he writes that beauty "tells us that we are at home in the world, that the world is already ordered in our perceptions as a place fit for the lives of beings like us," he does not here tell us the whole truth.

The final lines of Hemingway's short story read thus: "He disliked bars and bodegas. A clean, well-lighted cafe was a very different thing. Now, without thinking further, he would go home to his room. He would lie in the bed and finally, with daylight, he would go to sleep. After all, he said to himself, it's probably only insomnia. Many must have it."

Perhaps what the old waiter most needed was not, then, a clean, well-lighted place, or even whatever scanty comfort his own room might bring, but rather a dank, dimly-lit Church. Jesus reminds us that "foxes have holes, and birds of the air have nests; but the Son of man has nowhere to lay his head" (Mt 8:20). Strangely, it is perhaps through the gloriously ornate Churches that our tradition has given us that, more than anywhere else, we know this homelessness as a good. In 1949, the Reverend Theodore Klausser argued that "it would be a mistake to arrange and decorate the interior of a church in such a way as to create the atmosphere of a comfortable and cozy bourgeois residence.... It should bespeak forcibly the grandeur of God which surpasses all earthly measure." Had the waiter slipped into, say, an old cathedral, the last lines might have read like so: He disliked bourgeois, domesticated churches. A dank, dimly-lighted cathedral was a very different thing. Now, without thinking further, he would go home to his pew. He would kneel on the board and finally, with daylight, he would go to Mass. After all, he said to himself, it's probably only homesickness. Many must have it.

6

Christ-Haunted George Saunders

In his 2013 essay "The Catholic Writer Today," Dana Gioia argued that the term "Catholic writer" no longer applies only to card-carrying members of the Church. Among the "three degrees of literary Catholicism," he wrote, are "cultural Catholics, writers who were raised in the faith and often educated in Catholic schools [and] gradually drifted away." Though their worldview is markedly Catholic, "their religious beliefs, if they still have any, are often unorthodox."

One such "cultural Catholic" is George Saunders, author of four collections of short stories and the novel *Lincoln in the Bardo,* which won the 2017 Man Booker Prize. Saunders, who left the Church in 1972 and became a proponent of Tibetan Buddhism, once said in an interview that he does not "see Christianity and Buddhism as separate; in fact, for me, one picked up where the other left off." He is one of many former Catholics whose spiritual trajectory gives credence to Pope Benedict's diagnosis that "the undoing of the Catholic church in the 20th century wouldn't come from Marxism but from Buddhism."

Insofar as he espouses syncretic "harmony" between Christianity and Buddhism, Saunders smudges the fundamental principles that define each. He once said he "feel[s] that our purpose here on earth is to move from a position of strong belief in self (strong ego, anxiety, fear, a sense of permanence) to a Christ- or Buddha-like position of unconditional love and erasure of self and acceptance of the conditionality of all things." At first, this sounds similar to St. John of the Cross's depiction of "two ways of going after God: one consists of a departure from all things, effected through a contempt for them; the other, in going out from oneself through self-forgetfulness, which is achieved by the love of God." But while we might detect hints of Christian mysticism in Saunders's words, the combination of Buddhism and Christianity ultimately short-circuits: Buddhist self-forgetting is not synonymous with Christian self-forgetfulness. In Buddhism, self-authored self-annihilation ends in blissfully detached acceptance of impermanence. In Christianity, the disciple finds the love of a God whose revealed commandments he must fulfill in faith.

Still, though Saunders may have formally left the Church, its forms didn't leave him. Raised in parochial Catholic schools in the 1960s, to this day he traces his need for "mystery, and metaphor, and beauty" to "the power of the Catholic Mass" he encountered in childhood:

> The Mass was still done in Latin. . . . Artistic things were going on there. Every day the altar would be decorated differently, in different colors, for different holy days and so on, and I remember being really interested in that—in the care that was taken in the visual display. And there were things about the Mass itself

> that were powerful training for a would-be artist. The Mass is a beautiful, big metaphor, and one thing a kid could learn by going to Mass over and over was that meaning can be conveyed . . . through metaphor and repetition and what is not said.

Unfortunately, Saunders falsely equivocates Mass and metaphor. As Flannery O'Connor once said of the Eucharist, "If it's a symbol, to hell with it!" Nonetheless, Saunders has captured the sense in which the Holy Sacrifice of the Mass—the liturgy—can become the "source and summit" of artistic life, a truth that deepens and does not contradict the Mass as the source and summit of eternal life.

Saunders's cultural Catholicism often appears in his love for his characters, and his capacity to engender the same love in his readers. George Eliot once said, "The greatest benefit we owe to the artist . . . is the extension of our sympathies." Saunders sees fiction as capable of a still higher end: "Modeling, in the prose, a form of Christian love . . . sort of training us in what it might feel like to really (really) believe that we are all brothers and sisters." In his writing, such as in his short story "Isabelle," Saunders sharpens his characters' sympathy via suffering and satire until it assumes the shape of sacrificial love.

"Isabelle" is written in a manner that makes the reader *love* the characters, through a nuanced blend of ethical sincerity and grotesque irony that resists sentimentality. This quality is evident from the story's opening lines: "The first great act of love I ever witnessed was Split Lip bathing his handicapped daughter. We were young, ignorant of mercy, and called her Boneless or Balled-Up Gumby for the way her limbs were twisted and useless." When Split Lip dies, Boneless (whose real name is Isabelle) is left to what Dorothy Day called "Holy Mother State" and is devoured by "the maw of the state home," where "invalids were frost-bitten in their beds and lunatic women became pregnant without known lovers." Throughout the story, the narrator goes from merely sympathizing with Boneless to showing her sacrificial love. At the end of the tale, he can't quiet his conscience. "Jesus Christ, enough is enough," he says in a kind of swear-prayer, and moves Boneless in with him: "It's not perfect," he concludes. "Sometimes it's damn hard. But I look after her and she squeals with delight when I come home, and the sum total of sadness in the world is less than it would have been."

"Isabelle" also contains hints of Saunders's Catholic upbringing. In the story, one source of the narrator's movement from mere sympathy to *caritas* is a side character whose rough fate and firm faith leave a lasting impression: "[Norris] was an altar boy whose skin tore like paper. The nuns said that because of his affliction he didn't have to kneel through Stations but he did anyway and offered it up to the Lord whenever he bled through his pants." As a child, Saunders himself had a skin condition "where I'd get cuts really easily," so that his "knees and ankles were always open wounds." During Stations of the Cross, when "you'd have to kneel for a long time . . . these sores would open up and start to ooze and sting." Finally, he confided in a nun. "Offer it up to the Lord," she advised. Saunders admits he initially "thought it was a bunch of bull, but I did it, and afterward I found I had discovered a way to sort of play through pain, so to speak. I remember thinking, 'This hurts, yes . . . but what *is* hurt?' . . . That ungentle style of Catholicism led me to certain meditative insights I wouldn't have had otherwise."

Unwittingly, Saunders offers up a crucial question that Catholic art—in implicit imitation of the practice of penance—would do well to evoke: "This hurts, yes . . . but what *is* hurt?" In the gospel story, the cross darkens the disciples with these same grotesque questions; through the bloody wounds of Christ, the queries continue to pierce, pulsing past even the divine comedy of the resurrection.

Despite his pluralistic syncretism, then, Saunders's life and works remain Christ-haunted. Which other living writer of such stature speaks reverently of the Latin Mass and the traditional Catholic practice of "offering it up"? As Saunders demonstrates, it is worth watching out for writers of repute who, even if they might not be able to recite the Nicene Creed in good conscience, are marked by their inherited, cultural Catholicity.

Saunders's devotion to story, then, is irredeemably religious. Fiction, far from being "a hobby, pastime or indulgence," reminds us that "everything remains to be seen. It is a sacrament devoted to this end." On the other hand, he's wary of "a certain way of talking about stories that treats them as a kind of salvation," as if the world would be made whole if only more folks would read the right literature. "We shouldn't overestimate or unduly glorify what fiction does." The seven stories at the center of his new book—by Chekhov, Turgenev, Gogol, and Tolstoy—were written during a

Russian literary renaissance that lasted seventy years . . . and was "followed by one of the bloodiest most irrational periods in human history." The beauty of that "artistic bounty" wasn't enough to save the world.

MFA-culture can be flagrantly presentist, chasing after the utterly-contemporary and letting the patriarchs of the past rest in peace. *Sed contra,* Saunders assumes an approach reminiscent of *The House of Fiction: An Anthology of the Short Story,* wherein Allen Tate and Caroline Gordon alternate paradigmatic short stories with analyses of these exemplars which teach us how to "read like writers." In *A Swim in a Pond in the Rain: In Which Four Russians Give a Master Class on Writing, Reading, and Life*, Saunders interprets these giants of the short story through an unassuming idiom, dispensing indispensable, story-saving stuff in the voice of a (well-read) Midwestern mechanic. He culls from Chekhov ways to achieve "ritual banality avoidance" for instance. Say we "want to make a good structure." Easy: "we just have to be aware of what question we are causing the reader to ask, then answer that question." Sure we can bite our lips, restraining answers ("Art doesn't have to solve problems," said Chekhov, "it only has to formulate them correctly"), but such avoidances must be artful. Saunders applies his well-tuned diagnostics to "In the Cart," "The Nose," and other short stories, charting for us what that might mean.

On the other side of subtle and intentional exclusion is excess and apparently distracting inclusions. The "swim in the pond in the rain," which happens in Chekhov's "Gooseberries," is itself a purported deviation, seemingly purposeless in terms of the story's main focus—until we learn that the man who "kept on swimming and diving," exclaiming "By God! Lord have mercy on me!" later poses as a dour moralist, bereft of the joy we saw him embody.

Another kindred conundrum appears in "The Singers" by Turgenev, wherein "action and description seem to take turns stepping up to the microphone, one falling silent while the other speaks." The action of the singing contest, which is set in a country tavern (transformed, through these songs, into an almost-sacred space), is constantly cut short by "excessive" asides "in which the people keep freezing" in mid-motion to allow whole paragraphs of lengthy descriptions. "Yep," Saunders imagines Turgenev's rejoinder, "Mr. Nabokov is right as usual, even though he hasn't even been born yet: my literary genius *does* fall short on the score of naturally discovering ways of telling the story which would equal the originality of my descriptive art. But what am I supposed to do?"

Weaker writers might defend their digressions as authentic self-expression, but in fiction a limitation can become a blessed borderline. A writer who cultivates his heirloom talents within the wiry fence of his weakness need not come a cropper. As Willa Cather put it, "To note an artist's limitations is but to define his talent." A detour can become "part of the plan," as in Turgenev": "what seemed a failure of craft turns out to be integral to the story's meaning . . . [and then] all is forgiven" to the point that "we might even understand the profitable exploitation of that apparent excess as a form of virtuosity." In several cases Saunders renders alternate actions, directions the Russian stories could have taken, epiphanies we may wrongfully wish had been added; his exercise in contrasting roads not taken clarifies the genius of the originals, shocks us into a sense of why they so move and mystify us.

Take Tolstoy's "Alyosha the Pot," a short tale whose titular character acquiesces to (almost) everything with "cheerful obedience." After many years of subservience, Alyosha is surprised to find a woman for whom he is "in no real way necessary" but who still, inexplicably, needs him. Soon after his master and his father forbid the marriage, Alyosha falls from a snow covered roof. As he lays dying, Alyosha stays silent, though he "looked like he was amazed at something. Then something seemed to startle him and he stretched out his legs and died." Why, Saunders wonders, would Tolstoy "omit those final thoughts, thoughts which would have told us exactly how to read the story"—whether Alyosha is, say, a woefully-passive soul, duped by his habitual cheek-turning, or a "saint" who "enacted radical Christian humility"? Saunders convincingly argues both sides, spelling out why Alyosha seems "more evasive than saintly" and musing that Tolstoy meant to deny us narratological clarity in order to "surprise/rankle/discomfit a secular reader, to make him see how conventional and reflexive and ultimately ineffective our habitual way of reacting to a tormentor (ie. fighting back) is." Sometimes, says Saunders, there is wisdom in omission; "the most artful and truthful thing is sometimes simply that which allows us to avoid being false." Refusing to raid a character's thoughts at a crucial moment might for the amateur be a "defect" which "leads to unclearness," but for the literary master it can be a "virtue," clouding the reader into a rich unknowing.

Saunders bends two planks that typically don't touch, arcing them into a strange bridge that may not seem safe to cross; his readings are attentive to the ethical-religious while also tethered to the organizational and practical. Only a former engineer / cradle Catholic could invent the "Ruthless Efficiency Principle" and explain it by means of the liturgy: "We might think of a story as a kind of ceremony, like the Catholic Mass." Because "we understand the heart of the Mass to be communion," all "those other parts (the processionals, the songs, the recitations, and so on) will be felt as beautiful and necessary to the extent that they serve the heart of the ceremony." Note that word *felt*.

The book is filled with *feels*. Yes it would be folly to relegate art's effects and its essence to the rational. Art has reasons that reason cannot understand. We "turn to art" precisely because "we 'know' something (we feel it) but can't articulate it because it's too complex and multiple." Art reveals that this "knowing," more than "real," is "superior to our usual . . . (reductive) way." Still, the main weaknesses of *A Swim* stem mainly from an underlying emotivism, which (in *After Virtue*) Alasdair MacIntyre describes as "the doctrine that all evaluative judgments and more specifically all moral judgments are nothing but expressions of preference, expressions of attitude or feeling." On the surface, Saunders frequently says he "feels," but often he rescues his own analyses from the unpleasant sentence of emotive assertion by giving reasoned discussions of things hard to descry.

Sometimes, though, the book devolves into facile moral dispensations and maxims that mix self-help and sentimentalism, as when he tells writers to "go forth and do what you please," adverse advice that seems especially bland when served next to sharpened craft talk that tastes like decades-fermented Kvass. (The analogy, dear reader, is not without veracity: Saunders has been teaching these stories at Syracuse for years, and now all those classes are contained in a mason jar.) While, with Hemingway, Saunders hopes that writing and reading well can "refine into sharpness" the "built-in, shockproof" truth-teller within us, his depiction of the mind is riddled with contradictions, lessening the force. Mind is bearer of "deep truth" we access and can verify I know not how, especially given that mind is also a mechanism bent on making "*all the time* . . . with words, a world that doesn't, quite, exist."

Saunders, the surgeon of literatures' sickness and health, is not wrong to trace the pulse of so many literary problems to the heart of the heart of our small-s strivings after moral salvation: great works contain multitudes, breeding caution in our meaning-making. Fiction that we knee-jerk label "absurd," Gogol's "The Nose" preeminent among them, offer a strange saving grace by convicting us that our many misperceptions and miscommunications might, "under duress, become catastrophic"; better attuned to the eerie harmony between the utterly impossible and the everyday plausible, more convinced of our own illusions, we might just stave off (even minor) indignities in the actual lives we lead outside the books.

Saunders calls language "a meaning approximator that sometimes gets too big for its britches and deceives us." Stories can call attention to this deception, imparting a teaching analogous to the spiritual counsel of de Caussade's

Abandonment to Divine Providence: "there is a time when . . . a soul's own ideas, intuitions, work, investigations, and inferences become sources of delusion." When ordinary human speech "realizes all its weaknesses and shortcomings and feels completely baffled," God disentangles the soul from her troubles "far more easily than novelists, working away in the peace of their rooms, extricate their heroes from all their dangers." Not being God, the storyteller sometimes does better to make our troubles palpable rather than solve them.

For Saunders, however emotive his morality may be, fiction is fundamentally moral; a badly made story lacks moral authority and a well-made one leads us to love better. Chekhov convinces us that a good story, as a story, "isn't really in a position to 'prove' anything," but an aesthetics that would deprive our literature theses would sacrifice concerns central to our humanity even as it protected us from ideology. When in "Gooseberries" Ivan lectures his friends on the harms of happiness amidst others' awful sufferings, when he interrogates their delights with a zeal that keeps them up at night (although they also can't sleep because he failed to clean his pipe, and it reeks to high heaven in the same sleepless night), Chekhov shows us that "maybe it's a question not of *if* a belief is represented in a story but of *how*—of what use is made of it." Chekhov gives his character "the power of his heartfelt opinion" even as he lets Ivan grow "heated and cranky and inexact": the story gains moral force by revealing the broadness of human nature—the noblest aspirations next to the petty degradations. Faced with this riddle of contradictions, Ivan Karamazov balks: "No, man is broad, even too broad, I would narrow him down." Reading Chekhov and Tolstoy, we might pine for such narrowing, but this very wishful thinking is cathartically cured. Saint John Henry Newman knew that literature, however filled with sin, can convict us of one sure thing: "we must take things as they are, if we take them at all."

The Russians teach us that lasting literature is not "something decorative" but is instead "a vital moral-ethical tool." Especially when ("as you may have noticed," says the tongue-in-cheek Saunders) we live in a degraded era diseased by "facile, shallow, agenda-laced" information, we can turn to these greats to recover the "aim of art" which is mainly to "ask the big questions," such as "how are we supposed to be living down here?" Although I cannot assent to a number of conclusions Saunders suggests as answers to that question, his (free) admission of the theological-ethical is especially welcomed in the work of a man who *Time* numbered in the world's most influential people. Something tells me the Influencer himself would ask us to laugh off the magazine's shellac. The man after all must be seen as distinct from those hard-won epiphanies peppering this book. As Saunders himself admits, "I like the person I am in my stories better than I like the real me. That person is smarter, wittier, more patient, funnier—his view of the world is wiser." Here he puts his finger on a perennial problem—the storied distance between artist and man.

Posing the "singular harshness" of the "problem in crude terms," Jacques Maritain insists that "by nature Art and Morality are two autonomous worlds, with no direct and intrinsic subordination between them." Art is, finally, subordinate to morality, but this relation is indirect. Whereas prudence is concerned with the good of a man, art is concerned with "the good of the work, not with the good of man." Thus we have the same Tolstoy modeling compassion in "Master and Man" and failing his wife Sonya so miserably. Saunders cites her diary entry: "He pushes everything off onto me, everything without exception. . . . His biographers will tell how he went to draw water for the porter, but no one will know how he never gave his wife one moment's rest or one drop of water to his sick child; how in thirty five years he never sat for five minutes by a bedside or let me have a rest or sleep the night through or go for a walk or simply pause for a moment to recover my strength."

Without qualms, Maritain can call Oscar Wilde "a good Thomist" for having said that "the fact of a man being a poisoner is nothing against his prose." True enough, Saunders might say, but let's not bluff the horror away. Let's not allow the "pleasure" to "have been, on the page," less pusillanimous, dupe us into divided selves—"thrill-at-truth" fictionists and hellish spouses. If we can't outdo Tolstoy and his compatriots artistically, just maybe by reading their stories for nourishment, our souls can take shapes both beautiful *and* good, forms that defy our habitual fancies.

7

Jack Kerouac's Beatific Visions

Jack Kerouac, who coined the phrase "Beat Generation," railed against those who interpreted it as meaning "beat down," "heedless," or "rootless." For him, it meant "*beato,* the Italian for beatific: to be in a state of beatitude, like St. Francis, trying to love all life, trying to be utterly sincere with everyone, practicing endurance, kindness." Whereas the Lost Generation had "believed in nothing," Kerouac claimed he never heard more talk of first and last things than when among his Beat Generation peers. The Beat poets, he said, tried to cultivate "joy of heart" in a "mad modern world of multiplicities and millions."

In a postwar world where "sinister efficiency" posed as peace, the "serious, curious" beats hungered for more soulful realities they could meet with "intense conviction." Sometimes the Beats sought the Spirit in the booming underground of bop; according to Kerouac, jazz transfigured hipsters into "12th Century monks high in winter belfries," listening "wildeyed" to "the Gothic organ." And in his essay "Origins of the Beat Generation," Kerouac swears that circa 1954, when he returned to his childhood church of Ste. Jeanne de Arc, suddenly, with tears in his eyes, he had a "vision of what I must have really meant with 'Beat.'" It came in the "holy silence" of the church, "the candles . . . flickering alone just for me."

Ti Jean (Kerouac's nickname) was baptized in Lowell, Massachusetts, to a family of "mill rats"—French Canadian Catholics who lived in the ghettos. Kerouac's favorite intercessor was St. Joseph (a "humble, self-admitting, truthful saint"), on whose feast he was born in 1922. *Ti Jean's* devotion to St. Thérèse of Lisieux continued through decades; until death, he watched for her roses from heaven. Even so, he left the Church at fourteen. Mystifying memories of Ste. Jeanne de Arc's statues returned to him regularly, though. He believed that he was able to, at times, "stop being a maniacal drunkard" on account of "the Holy Mother": "Ever since I instituted the little prayer, I've not been lushing."

Despite these litanies to saints, Kerouac never formally returned to the faith. Instead, he flirted with Buddhism. Yes, he writes in his final novel, *Vanity of Duluoz,* Christ's example is not to be taken "lightly," given that "He really meant it right down to the cross." But following Jesus would cost him his "kind of drinking, which prevents me from thinking too much." Something else prevented him, too: "There's a hole in even Jesus' bag." The "hole" is Christ telling the rich man to sell everything and give to the poor. What do we do afterward, Kerouac wondered: "Wander and beg our food off poor hard-working householders?"

And yet, at the end of *Vanity of Duluoz,* Kerouac writes, "I saw the cross just then when I closed my eyes after writing this. I can't escape its mysterious penetration into all this brutality." Earlier in his life, he had had a similar vision. Hidden in a cabin at California's Big Sur, as he fought advanced alcoholism and addiction and percolated paranoia, he wrote, "Suddenly as clear as anything I ever saw in my life, I see the Cross."

> I SEE THE CROSS, it's silent, it stays a long time, my heart goes out to it, my whole body fades away to it, I hold out my arms to be taken away to it, by God I am being taken away my body starts dying and swooning out to the cross standing in a luminous area in the darkness, I start to scream . . . let myself go into death and the Cross: as soon as that happens I slowly sink back to life—Therefore the devils are back, commissioners are sending out orders in my ear to think anew, babbling secrets that are hissed, suddenly I see the Cross again, this time smaller and far away but just as clear and I say through all the noise of the voices "I'm with you, Jesus, for always, thank you."

In *Golden Dreams: California in an Age of Abundance,* the late Catholic historian Kevin Starr contends that what the writer saw was both the literal "cross atop the newly established Camaldolese monastery-hermitage nearby" and the symbolic "cross of Kerouac's collapsing life." After this vision, Kerouac rejected his "Buddhist studies and pipe-smoking and assured meditations on emptiness." Later, he told a friend that on this "night of the end of Nirvana . . . I realized all my (years of studying) Buddhism had been words," and then "saw those masses of devils racing for me." In the final pages of *Vanity of Duluoz,* he mocks Buddha's insufficient advice, dispensed as the sage "lay there in an awful pool of dysentery."

Vanity of Duluoz is devoted to the cross. "Dedicated to Σταυρουλα," the novel's first words read, "Means 'From the Cross' in Greek, and is also my wife's first name." The final words, too, are tied to Christ's sacrifice. "*Hic calix!*" writes Kerouac, and then tells the reader to "Look that up in Latin." The words, of course, are from the Mass: "For this is the Chalice of My Blood of the new and eternal Testament."

Still, Kerouac never seemed quite able to reconcile these stirrings with what Chesterton called the romance of orthodoxy. "The only people for me," his alter-ego says in *On the Road*, "are the mad ones, the ones who are mad to live, mad to talk, mad to be saved, desirous of everything at the same time, the ones who never yawn or say a commonplace thing, but burn, burn, burn like fabulous yellow roman candles exploding like spiders across the stars." As with other searchers of our post-Christian age, this hunger for mystical experience belies a kind of spiritual gluttony—the great expectation that God dispenses consolation and personal revelation on demand. Yes, these "solitary Bartlebies staring out of the dead wall window of our civilization" had good reason to get squeamish in the mad "machine of the West." But the solution for Kerouac and the other Beat writers was often merely "taking drugs, digging bop, having flashes of insight." The father of the Beats had a hard time distancing himself from these dubious means of beatification.

God moves in mysterious ways—so goes the platitude. But Kerouac's case asks we who are "mad to be saved" to pray that God grant such mad prodigals beatitude.

8

Peace in a Plastic World: Evelyn Waugh's Nativity

Western secular culture "is a kind of hothouse growth," Christopher Dawson wrote—an artificial culture that shelters us from "the direct impact of reality." Neither birth nor death in secular societies occasions confrontation with ultimate realities. Rather, each brings us "into closer dependence on the state and its bureaucracy so that every human need can be met by filling in the appropriate form."

Evelyn Waugh's *Love Among the Ruins: A Romance of the Near Future* dramatizes this sheltering. In this novella, "junior sub-official" Miles Plastic does clerical work for the "Department of Euthanasia" in a dystopian state. Plastic, whose surname epitomizes artificiality and malleability, ensures that those in line for a happy death do "not press ahead of their turn" and adjusts "the television set for their amusement." Although "a faint whiff of cyanide sometimes gave a hint of the mysteries beyond," Plastic is content to empty the waste basket and brew tea for the patients.

Because the "services" offered by the Department of Euthanasia are "essential," Plastic has no feast on "Santa Claus Day" (December 25). After work, he walks to the hospital to visit his lover, Clara, who is with child, and finds "the hall porter . . . engrossed in the television, which was performing an old obscure folk play which past generations had performed on Santa Claus Day, and was now revived and revised as a matter of historical interest." The porter's interest, Plastic supposes, is "professional," for the show "dealt with maternity services before the days of Welfare." The porter cannot look away from "the strange spectacle of an ox and an ass, an old man with a lantern, and a young mother." "'People here are always complaining,'" the porter says. "'They ought to realize what things were like before Progress.'"

The Nativity, the great fact of Christology (Christ descended and passed through utter poverty in order to redeem) ghosts through the television screen. However, these "hothouse" inhabitants are haunted not by the mystery of Christ's humility, but by Mary and Joseph's woeful lack of medical conveniences. In the world of the novella, the Story of Christ has been shrunken and sanitized into a museum-like documentary. As Dawson wrote, "A completely secularized culture is a world of make believe in which the figures of the cinema and the cartoon-strip appear more real than the figures of the Gospel."

Plastic moves through the hospital's bowels until he finds his beloved in a ward marked "Experimental Surgery." There, he inquires after "our child"—but Clara tells him, "*That* had to go" (italics mine). She then says that Santa Claus Day marks the nativity of her new face; her former one, ruined with facial hair, has been replaced by a "'wonderful new substance, a sort of synthetic rubber that takes grease-paint perfectly.'" Clara's plasticity is more real to her than the child (the "that") which has been eliminated by a simple, state-proffered operation. Like a mother who has just given birth, she sits up in bed, "joyful and proud," but Plastic cannot countenance the "tight, slippery mask," which he experiences as "quite inhuman." Instead, he stares at the bedside TV, where "further characters had appeared" in the obscure folk play: "Food Production Workers" apparently "declare a sudden strike," for they leave their sheep in a frenzy "at the bidding of some kind of shop-steward in fantastic dress," accompanied by "an old, forgotten ditty: 'O tidings of comfort and joy.'"

Through Waugh's artfulness, the Nativity has been "made strange" in *Love Among the Ruins*. The Russian formalist Viktor Shklovsky contended that the purpose of art is to make strange that which we have forgotten on account of deadening familiarity. Although the twenty-first-century West does not yet evince the extreme secularity of the dystopian society in *Love Among the Ruins*, Waugh helps us perceive how our own world, too, is unreal, and how in our day, too, the God who is Love has been relegated to the category of "historical and cultural preservation." Waugh pairs Clara's plastic joy with the tidings of comfort that break from the "machine" beside her. This juxtaposition brings Plastic to retch "unobtrusively" before he exits the surgery ward, baffled.

Waugh's novella incubates us in a world that has abandoned God. Though the TV light extracts grace from the Christmas Story, Plastic and the porter watch with rare attention. They are arrested by the foreignness of God's

Incarnation, though they cannot put the fragmented pieces of the Story together. T. S. Eliot captures the disruptiveness of Christ's coming in his poem "Journey of the Magi." The narrator, one of the three kings, wonders whether he was "led all that way for / Birth or Death?"

> There was a Birth, certainly,
> We had evidence and no doubt. I had seen birth and
>   death,
> But had thought they were different; this Birth was
> Hard and bitter agony for us, like Death, our death.
> We returned to our places, these Kingdoms,
> But no longer at ease here, in the old dispensation,
> With an alien people clutching their gods.
> I should be glad of another death.

Although he daily helps hasten the happy terminations of unwanted lives, Miles Plastic has been kept conveniently away from the "mysteries beyond" the door. His first real encounter with death comes through the surgical slaughter of his child. And it makes him miserable. Holy Mother State has anesthetized his consciousness against the pains of reality, but the death of "our child" on Christ's birthday makes him long for another death. By the end of the novella, he has forged "a desert in his imagination which he might call peace," a poor surrogate for the Prince of Peace. It's a desert that leaves him, like the Magi, "ill at ease."

We inhabit a hothouse in many ways akin to that of Miles Plastic. Who among us can exit the hothouse and enter the enduring chill where the soul encounters the "bitter agony" and sublimity of Christ's birth? Who among us can craft a crèche that will soil our artificiality with the ultimate reality? Who can arrest us until our unease passes into peace, until we dare call the Maker's cave-set maternity ward—like his death on Friday—"good"?

9

Thank You For the Light, F. Scott Fitzgerald

THIS FUNDAMENTAL REALITY should by now be clear: the dramatic action of grace is rooted in Christology. Christ descended into the world and passed through the particular in order to redeem. This movement is the model for writers with Christic imaginations; they strive to imitate it—or at least make legible its effects. The poet or writer needs to pass through the concrete in order to arrive at insight. Any storyteller worth her salt does this by discovering particulars—telling details, arresting images, revelatory actions, snatches of dialogue—that signify more than themselves "without becoming less actual in so doing," as Father William F. Lynch contends in *Christ and Apollo: The Dimensions of the Literary Imagination*. These symbols "make the imagination *rise* indeed, and yet keep the tang and density of that actuality into which imagination descends." F. Scott Fitzgerald's posthumously published short story "Thank You for the Light" narrates an action of grace that, though comic, successfully captures how Christ transfigures the mundane and works miracles through the concrete particulars of this world.

Fitzgerald introduces the protagonist Mrs. Hanson as "a pretty, somewhat faded woman of forty, who sold corsets and girdles." We find that "smoking meant a lot to her sometimes." Mrs. Hanson is a widow without relatives, and her loneliness is exacerbated by her weak eyes' inability to endure more than one moving picture per week. Since her reassignment to the Iowa-Kansas-Missouri sales circuit, she'd had difficulty drawing a pull of tobacco. Although "nobody who was in the war would ever object to anyone smoking," most are wary of a woman taking drags.

One day, Mrs. Hanson is condemning herself as "a drug fiend" and fretting over her recent decision to quit smoking when she beholds a Catholic cathedral. Not Catholic herself, she amuses us with her musings. "If so much incense had gone up in the spires to God, a little smoke in the vestibule would make no difference," she supposes, though "the thought offended her." Reasoning that he wouldn't mind because "in His days they hadn't even discovered tobacco," Mrs. Hanson steps inside only to come up empty when she digs for matches in her bag. Carried away, she decides to "go and get a light from one of their candles." But as she enters the inner sanctum, she sees an old man striking out the last votive light.

Darkness erases all but the electric chandelier "high overhead" and "the ever-burning lamp in front of the Sacrament." (The Catholic novelist Ron Hansen has pointed out that Fitzgerald's choice of "Sacrament" instead of "tabernacle" here gives the story a deep strain of Catholicity.) When the departing sexton asks her if she came to pray, she says, "Yes, I did." The reader feels the lie stretch into truth as she kneels down in the dim. Rifling through the spare change of her spirit, she "scarcely knew what to pray for." She utters some pleas on behalf of her clients and employer, and in this moment, we are bent over by her utter loneliness.

Mrs. Hanson nods into dreams of the Virgin taking her place on the sales circuit, and when she wakes, she finds that "there was a familiar scent that was not incense in the air"—her cigarette is mysteriously alight. Too drowsy to think, she looks into the Madonna's "vague niche" and thanks her twice, the second time from "her knees, the smoke twisting up from the cigarette between her fingers."

The grace that lights Mrs. Hanson's cigarette rings true because it doesn't summon an unbelievable epiphany or a cold call conversion. How hard it is to strike the right balance between what Lynch calls "the definite" (concrete particulars) and the "insights" that we can gain by passing through them. The Christic imaginer must guard against the greedy poetics of "[getting] as much as possible of heaven out of as little as possible of earth." Mrs. Hanson has no grand transformation. Instead, during her brief sleep in the pew, she dreams of a Madonna who does things the Mother of God would never do: "In her imagination, the Virgin came down . . . and took her place and sold corsets and girdles for her and was tired, just as she was." In answering her unspoken ask for a light, the miracle absolves her from fretting over at least the sin of smoking in church, and the action of grace solicits more from this sinner than from the nine lepers Christ cleansed: "Thank you very much for the light," Mrs. Hanson says.

It can be tempting for Christian poets and writers to rush through the finite in order to "send the soul shooting up into some kind of absolute" (Lynch's phrase). But the best Christic imaginers pass through the tang and density of actuality in their stories in order to work out the characters' salvations or damnations, proceeding one insight at a time.

Fitzgerald possesses an affection for the real; he is never one to exploit particularities by making them epiphanies. Surely this comes at least in part from his Catholic sensibility; a sacramentality sometimes shimmers through his stories. *The Beautiful and Damned* begins when "irony," "the Holy Ghost of this later day," descends upon its protagonist as "the final polish of the shoe." The short story "Absolution" unravels a young Jimmy Gatz abandoning the Church in favor of sucking "the pap of life," of finding "something ineffably gorgeous somewhere that had nothing to do with God." In *The Great Gatsby,* Fitzgerald gives us tragically restless characters who rush to force as much of paradise as possible out of the humble shirts of created things. In "Thank You for the Light," by contrast, Fitzgerald gives us the widow's mite, his incarnational imagination passing lovingly through the small, definite things of this world. At the story's end, Mrs. Hanson remains earthbound, but the smoke of her lit cigarettes lifts our hearts like incense—a poor surrogate for bittersweet myrrh but what do you expect from the woman?—curling through our brains the smoky, braided praise by which we will inch toward heaven.

10

The Pallor of our Plagues: Katherine Anne Porter's "Pale Horse, Pale Rider"

Death, decries the novelist Alan Harrington, is "an imposition on the human race" from which we will be saved by "medical engineering and nothing else." Though the dark hearse of death drives fear of that moment when "everything will go black . . . our messiahs will be wearing white coats."

In "Pale Horse, Pale Rider" by sometimes-Catholic writer Katherine Anne Porter, the narrator Miranda comes to know precisely this sort of salvation—and she finds it wanting. Recovering from the 1918 Spanish Influenza, which stole at least seventeen million lives, Miranda finds herself in an enervated, fever-fueled state. "Let me go, let me go," she cries, for she knows "that the smell of death was in her own body." But just as she slips beyond recovery, medics "do the trick" with a hypodermic needle, and she startles into consciousness to find doctor and nurse looking at each other "with the glance of initiates at a mystery." The affectionate nurse pities the "salvaged creature" whom she "had snatched back from death with her own hands," even though Miranda remains silent and apparently ungrateful.

How could the twenty-four-year-old who now had "time for everything" not teem with the thrill of survival, especially when so many others are succumbing to this resistant malady? How could a saved soul be so cold? After all, when she first fell ill and her landlady summoned an ambulance, we learn that there "aren't any beds" and all the drivers are already hurrying elsewhere: "all the theaters and nearly all the ships and restaurants are closed, and the streets have been full of funerals all day and ambulances all night." Her boss, editor of the *Blue Mountain News*, has to cajole and elbow her into a hospital, wherein a "pallid white fog" disinfects the room of a dead man who, swathed from head to foot in white, is covered "tenderly and exactly" by wordless orderlies: only through death is the place's scarce space freed for the sick but still breathing.

Given that she could have passed away in her apartment, with the landlady hovering over her and harping about "the plague, my God, and I've got a houseful of people to think about!" it should seem strange that when she wakes, Miranda is made miserable by "the precise machine of the hospital" which has "conspired to pull her inseparable rack of bones and wasted flesh to its feet," only to set her in safety on the road that would again lead her to death. Bombarded by colleagues bent on buoying her up, surrounded by a pile of mail celebrating her victory over mortality, Miranda plays along, telling everyone what a "pleasant surprise" it is to find her heart beating. No, it will not do to "betray the conspiracy . . . of the living: that there is nothing better than to be alive." But, secretly, Miranda has defected from this all-too-human collusion. Mere living will never again be enough.

Prior to this "happy ending," Porter's mercurial prose has taken us deep into a half-known territory that borders transcendence and delusion. From the novella's very start we weave in and out of visions, with a sickly Miranda striving to "outrun Death and the Devil." In a dream more palpable, more substantial than many of the story's waking scenes, she swings into the saddle of her horse, Graylie, who "because he is not afraid of bridges," may be able to help her surpass the "blank still stare of mindless malice that makes no threats and can bide its time." But the stranger keeps pace, rides beside her "easily, lightly . . . his pale face smiled in an evil trance, he did not glance at her."

Miranda recognizes the rider, who is no stranger to her, though she cannot place him; she does not know it yet, but her "burning slow headache" and constant fatigue—these are the marks of a Spanish Influenza which, Miranda at one point remarks, "seems to be a plague, something out of the Middle Ages." The opening of the story captures well the confusion that comes with such sickness. She tries to communicate her concern to Adam, a young soldier to whom she has recently taken a liking. "Well let's be strong minded and not have any of it." His voice echoes with the townspeople of Camus' *The Plague,* men who "disbelieved in pestilences": "A pestilence isn't a thing made to man's measure; therefore we tell ourselves that pestilence is a mere bogy of the mind, a bad dream that will pass away. But it doesn't always pass away and, from one bad dream to another, it is men who pass away, and the humanists first of all, because they haven't taken their precautions."

When Miranda succumbs to the immeasurable, leveling sickness, Adam takes no precautions. He is falling in love with her on the verge of action: World War I awaits. Relentlessly and restlessly he tends to her, bringing medicine and ice, pressing closer as their impending parting hangs over everything.

On the night before she is hospitalized, still shorn of needed medical care, Miranda curates their conversation towards the faith. "Do you remember any prayers?" she asks suddenly, and he scrapes up "the Lord's prayer"; she replies with a "Hail Mary" and the Confiteor. They fumble through "Now I lay me," forgetting half the words before they take the reins of an old black spiritual. In a "hoarse whisper" shc sings, "Pale horse, pale rider, done taken my lover away." The couple partakes of what the narrator of Cormac McCarthy's *The Road* calls "the sacred idiom shorn of its referents and so of its reality." With death knelling all around them, they seek consolation in childhood prayers and the misremembered spiritual, but they don't exactly kneel. Rather, as they sing of death's horseman "leaving one lover to mourn," Adam presses his smooth face beside hers, moves his mouth toward her mouth, romantically contracting the germs that will kill him before he can even see battle.

Alone in the hospital, however, Miranda approaches something like the sacred with greater immediacy, more nakedly, and it is this which saves her from the reductive satisfaction of her fellow men, many of them people of good will, some of them heroic. Still, they are stubbornly contented by mere survival, definitively circumscribed by the things of this world. Approaching the end, she steels her will to live, which Porter captures as a "fiercely burning particle of being that knew itself alone." The particle begins to curve outward like a great fan, rainbow-like. Beneath the arc a great company of persons emerges, all of their faces transfigured; all of them she had known while alive. Here (where?) they are "pure identities," eyes "clear and untroubled as good weather," each figure "alone but not solitary" as they drift into a widening circle. Her paradisiacal image is interrupted when she realizes that she has forgotten "the dead"—that is, those we call "living," the people who pity and mourn those who have passed; a hypodermic needle rouses her back to "reality."

Like the embodied soul in Plato's *Phaedrus,* fresh from beholding the forms, Miranda chafes at her incarnate self. The body "is a curious monster" she says, "no place to live in, how could anyone feel at home there?" Saturated with the fears and feverish strains of consciousness that come with pandemics, Porter's "Pale Horse, Pale Rider" persuades: it is the waking dead lives lead by many, and not the plague, that ought to own the name "mortality"; true, our medics are often heroes, but not messiahs.

But Miranda's "heaven" is no place for dead men made whole; who could feel at home *there,* either, in that self-made landscape willfully forged by a particle of being that "relied upon nothing beyond itself for its strength"? The circling "pure identities" surround no God, none but the self, and the self—given to grandiosity when it becomes the center of things—is a pusillanimous god.

Nonetheless, Porter's story helps us to revise our vision during this time of dramatic reorientation. "Pale Horse, Pale Rider" reins in death's pride; through hypnotic passages that take us straight through the dark woods of delirium and bewilderment, it cathartically needles the pustules of our plague-born anxieties, which, justified or not, can be maddening—perilously so. But pity the one who does not fear death on account of a self-made heaven. Yes, "there might never be light again, compared as it must always be with the light she had seen." Dante, too, saw unsurpassable sights as Beatrice led him through the Empyrean; beatified, souls have become whirling lights. But unlike Porter's "modernized" paradise (which is indebted to Dante's but robbed of its main Mover), these little lights have a center, a source, an utmost aim:

> Before that Light one's will to turn is spent;
> one is so changed, it is impossible
> to shift the glance, for one would not consent,
>
> Because all good—the object of the will—
> is summed in it, for it alone is best:
> beyond, defective; there, whole, perfect, still.

Before that Light, pestilences of both body and soul burn into colors so pale it is hard to believe they were real.

11

Marriage Prospects with David Foster Wallace

David Foster Wallace, who "twice failed to pass the Rite of Christian Initiation for Adults" and took his own life in 2008, would seem a dubious source for insights into problems besetting marriage. The capacious fictionist was racked by intractable mental sickness. But this literary "anti-rebel" was bent on assuming "the childish gall actually to endorse and instantiate single-entendre principles" and treating "plain old untrendy human troubles and emotions in U.S. life with reverence and conviction." Wallace was wary of the "weary cynicism" so common in contemporary America, condemning it as a cheap mask worn to evade the "last true terrible sin" of our times: capitulation to unsophisticated naiveties. Marriage is an outstanding candidate for the dust bin of unsophistication. Consider the desperation with which traditional marriage is satirized as a slavish practice suitable for patriarchal Neanderthals, or worse. The author of *Infinite Jest* bids us to wonder: maybe the relentless ironies marshalled to mock marriage in the mode of "hip cynical transcendence" are actually piqued by "fear of being really human," since being human, he insists, is to be weak and dependent in ways that our cult of contractual, individual selves is loath to confess.

Beyond the concupiscence that convinced Cain to kill Abel, the causes of this catastrophic cult of the self are several. As Tocqueville tells us, the spirit of democracy "breaks the chains and frees each link," erasing our ancestries "isolating [us] even from our contemporaries. Each man is forever thrown back upon himself alone and there is a danger that he may be shut up in the solitude of his own heart." Democratic liberalism and radical individualism have always been friends, but, as Patrick Deneen points out, we must not discount the role played by capitalism ("both liberalism's handmaiden and its engine") in the displacement of bonds subjected to its logic. G. K. Chesterton argues in "The Superstition of Divorce," "Capitalism, of course, is at war with the family. . . . It desires its victims to be individuals, or (in other words) to be atoms. For the word atom, in its clearest meaning (which is none too clear) might be translated as "individual." If there be any bond, if there be any brotherhood, if there be any class loyalty or domestic discipline . . . these individualists will redistribute it in the form of individuals; or in other words smash it to atoms."

In fiction, Wallace made such atomization a consistent concern. In *Oblivion,* the abstracted office environs of late capitalism promise meaningful "creative" work in part as a surrogate for other loyalties and higher ends. Take Terry Schmidt, the fraught Focus Group facilitator of the story "Mister Squishy." Terry is supposed to be bestowing sophisticated praise upon Mister Squishy's newest product—*Felonies!*® This impossibly chocolaty snack cake is meant to "parody the modern health-conscious consumer's sense of vice / indulgence / transgression vis a vis the consumption of a high-calorie corporate snack," and the Focus Group's task is to test how tantalizing the treat truly is. Schmidt despairs over his "smallness within a grinding professional machine you can't believe you once had the temerity to think you could help change."

The degree of despondency Schmidt suffers suggests that he has made his work into a kind of "calling," the emergence of which Max Weber traces in *The Protestant Ethic and the Spirit of Capitalism.* "The *calling,*" he contends, is "a religious conception, that of a task set by God." Weber locates this concept's origins in the Reformation and its correlation with the rise of capitalism. According to the calling, "the fulfilment of duty in worldly affairs as the highest form which the moral activity of the individual could assume." Consequently, everyday "worldly" work was given "a religious significance." In truth, though, this theological handmaid of capitalism projects onto work a level of spiritual meaning that we cannot obtain, veiling the limitations of our jobs behind a religious fabrication. Yes, Christianity's influence over the West has weakened, but this theory of the calling has persisted, albeit in a manner morphed by the therapeutic turn mapped by Philip Rieff and Christopher Lasch. As the latter says in *The Culture of Narcissism,* the contemporary American's search for a self-expressive life extends into the workplace, where we seek satisfactions in the name of a "mental health," which, Lasch quips, is the "modern equivalent of salvation." Schmidt, who started out with all the zeal of one called (to change the world and achieve healthy actualization), is tempered by the dehumanizing grind he goes through to win his daily bread.

Work cannot in practice realize ideals that originate in religion. We cannot equivocate our vocations and our professions. In part because of this, Schmidt yearns for ends far more natural and—Catholic. Midway through the story, Wallace substantiates his fascination with the Church when the lure of Catholic marriage descends unbidden into the mind of Terry Schmidt. Atomized to a dangerous degree, he has not lost all attractions to former, deeper bonds. In "total subjective private" he entertains sexual fantasies with Darlene, his married co-worker. Dazed by his secret fears and prospective failures, his impotence and "terrible and thoroughgoing *smallness,*" Schmidt has a vision of the conference room constituents as icebergs, only their caps showing, unknown and not knowable, "and he imagined that it was probably only in marriage (and a good marriage, not the decorous dance of loneliness he'd watched his mother and father do for seventeen years but rather true conjugal intimacy)" that the private worries and unseen moles, yellow toenails and dependent souls, could be truly known.

Wallace divorces himself from the tired novelistic trope of "the affair"; instead, and incredibly, he hints that in a self-made world marked by suicidal loneliness, Catholic marriage emerges as a sacrament for which there is no surrogate. For Schmidt, only the sturdiest specifications will stand a chance at assuaging the "childish heartbreak" felt when, having achieved success in the workplace, he finds himself radically incomplete. He seeks "not just a ceremony and financial merger but a true communion of souls." Seeing this, Schmidt begins to grasp why the Catholic Church, all throughout his childhood and Confirmation, called it "the Holy Sacrament of Marriage." For a man who pleasures himself before sleeping alone, who is desperate on account of failing to make the "high-voltage" "difference" he thought he might at work, such a marriage seems nothing short of miraculous. But the "miraculous" character makes it, to his mind, not merely unnatural but symbolic and supernatural. In a word—impossible. Schmidt mingles a scintillating celebration of marriage with a devastating downturn: "as remote from the possibilities of actual lived life as the crucifixion and resurrection and transubstantiation . . . which is to say it appeared not as a goal to expect ever to really reach or achieve but as a kind of navigational star, as in the sky, something high and untouchable and miraculously beautiful in the sort of distant way that reminded you always of how ordinary and unbeautiful and incapable of miracles you your own self were."

Though Schmidt was raised Catholic, his parents did little more than a "decorous dance of loneliness"; the Holy Sacrament of Matrimony was never modeled or known; he therefore locates it in the stars. Like so many, he yearns for marriage but does not consummate. Wallace traces this incompletion to (in part) a lack of compelling exemplars who would make it a sacrament instead of a symbol, a visible sign of the unseen instead of an astronomic image of the untouchable. If marriage becomes a mere symbol, it will not endure. To cite Flannery O'Connor again concerning the Eucharist: "Well, if it's a symbol, to hell with it." Marriage's survival depends on its incarnate practicality, a practicality that is hard to assume if one has never been an apprentice. Oddly, the constellation of marriage still maintains a navigational pull for Schmidt; it remains a measure of relationships. Unlike many of his peers, he does not demystify the institution in favor of self-assertion helped by wholesale capitulation to passing pleasures.

In his *Spirit of the Liturgy*, Joseph Ratzinger asks, "Are we not interested in the cosmos anymore? Are we today hopelessly huddled in our own little circle?" Schmidt, overcome by what he considers the faraway character of Catholic marriage, retreats. The stellar mysteries of marriage: these are too great for such a small man, a soul who has stopped going out at night, has ceased to stare at the celestial bodies, and has shut it all out with lightproof curtains. The scene is creepy but executed to solicit our sympathies. All alone, he stares anxiously at the telephone, most nights, waiting for the courage to call Darlene. After meditating on marital realities, he finds himself seeking from her not sex but an open heart. It is as though, given the fact that *she* is married, she—unlike so many others—has the virtues necessary to know another without flinching and turning away.

But he does not call. He says his prayers and imitates the iniquities of Onan in pathetic perpetuation of his loneliness. In Wallace's hands, Schmidt's sterility is tied to his work is tied to his eventual murderousness through a marriage of poison and pleasure. Measuring the poison he plans to inject into *Felonies!*®, Schmidt uses a scale weighed down with "low-value coins combined and tied in an ordinary Trojan condom." Jeffrey Severs reads these condom-coin metaphors as reflecting "the subversion of civic responsibility's (and flowing liberty's) language throughout: an ad focus group treated as jury duty, for in-stance, with 'voir dire' procedure."

Freed from the obligations of the marital state, Schmidt knows no liberty. Still, if he succumbs to such petty titillation as masturbation, he nonetheless shuns the impoverished state of marriage. He yearns for that small, good thing—two dependent creatures carrying one another and others (often badly, always imperfectly) through this valley of tears. No alliance signed by two independent individuals will do. Having someone to care for in sickness and in health; being someone to be cared for till death: unable to approximate these old-fashioned, "single-entendre" ends, Schmidt descends into one of the story's saddest and most disturbing moments.

During his morning shaves, Schmidt has taken to calling his mirrored self *Mister Squishy,* an appellation that escapes his lips against his will. Despite his attempts to resist, "the large subsidiary's name and logo had become the dark part of him's latest taunt, so that when he thought of himself now it was as something he called *Mister Squishy,* and his own face and the plump icon's wholly innocuous face tended to blend in his mind into one face," a design that one could assign some petty use but which "could never love or hate or ever care or truly know." Although the unalloyed logo (a "childlike cartoon face of indeterminate ethnicity") possesses a facial affect that almost forces the onlooker to smile with satisfaction, Schmidt sours when he mingles it with his own face. Wallace's image does not sugar the icon's awful truth. Men who yearn for marriage but are consumed by work are innately dissatisfied: cut off from the daily demands, the "domestic discipline," the saving need to sacrifice for family, their identification with work becomes overwhelming. The atomized "self" is an extraordinarily powerful invention, and it frees us from inherited obligations and forms, institutions and norms. But there is always a catch. The self, if sometimes experienced as expansive and massive, is intrinsically small.

"What is love?" asks Nietzsche's Last Man. "'What is creation? What is longing? What is a star?' thus asks the last man, and blinks. The earth has become small, and on it hops the last man, who makes everything small. . . . One still loves one's neighbor and rubs against him, for one needs warmth." Notice the dynamic at play: the last man, who makes everything small, blinks at the biggest things, but his pusillanimous state does not leave him unsettled. Schmidt, on the contrary, recognizes and balks at his own smallness—he has eyes for the sacred and yearns to be transcended but does not know how; gazing at the distant dots of the cosmos and even using them as guides, he instantiates one of the riddling problems of our age: marriage remains a lodestar for many, but exemplary (if flawed) *marriages*—which mix sacramental mysteries with utter practicalities—are declining with terrible speed, a phenomenon exacerbated by an excessive identification of self and work.

David Foster Wallace's story smokes our minds with the mushrooming loneliness of his atomic protagonist. Schmidt's "self" has been remade in the image of his abstracted and sophistic workplace. Chesterton was fundamentally worried that capitalism's logic would wear away at the deep roots of the family. In "Mister Squishy," we watch not the atoms being smashed, but the progeny of this fission, circling his job in an earthbound orbit, unable to bond, bouncing off the walls of his condo. A conscientious employee, exemplary even. A smashed man, sickly squishy, hard to digest.

12

Portrait of a Paralyzed Priesthood: James Joyce's "The Sisters"

GRAPHIC STORIES, GIVEN by so many victims of Catholic priests and made explicit in (for instance) the Pennsylvania Grand-Jury Report, leave the listener transfixed in terror over how one person could be so broad—*in persona Christi* and unspeakably perverted—at once. Still more startling is the silence that so many victims kept, especially as such quiet moves us to wonder how many more remain stifled by confusion and the maddening pressure to keep up appearances. What stays silenced, what stays suggested or suspected but not known, discolors all the faithful, even those who do not, like the abused, inhabit a place of paralysis.

This sense of paralysis permeates "The Sisters," James Joyce's story of a troubled priest and his troubling relationship with an unnamed narrator. True, his novel *A Portrait of the Artist as a Young Man* culminates in the protagonist Stephen Daedalus's rejection of his Holy Mother in favor of a strict adherence to the priesthood of art ("forging anew in his workshop out of the sluggish matter of the earth a new soaring impalpable imperishable being"). And yet, the Jesuit-educated Joyce remained haunted by the realities of

Catholicity for his entire life. As Father Colum Power notes in *James Joyce's Catholic Categories,* although he formally severed his relationship to the Church, the Irish apostate kept "continuing devotion to the Easter liturgy, to the point of 'secret tears.'" In "The Sisters" he gives us a powerful poetic initiation into the pains that quiet those crippled by priestly abuse.

Paralysis. The word, which "had always sounded strangely in my ears," now "sounded to me like the name of some maleficent and sinful being." Although this first story of *Dubliners* is filled with elusiveness and ellipses, we gather that, for the boy, the word is affiliated with Father Flynn, whose "third stroke" leaves the priest with "no hope." The story starts, then, in an infernal state. When we try to arrive at express and certain answers, we seem to hear the words that hang over Dante's underworld: ABANDON ALL HOPE YOU WHO ENTER HERE.

When the boy descends the stairs for supper, the family friend Old Cotter is sitting fireside, smoking, speaking to his uncle: "No, I wouldn't say he was exactly . . . but there was something queer . . . there was something uncanny about him. I'll tell you my opinion. . . ." Indignant, the boy remains silent but is interiorly infuriated by this "tiresome old fool!" who is, through frustrating indirection and interrupted opinions, casting suspicion on Father Flynn. "I have my own theory about it," Cotter continues. "I think it was one of those . . . peculiar cases. . . . But it's hard to say. . . ." The uncle, less animated in his concern, tells the narrator that his "old friend is gone, you'll be sorry to hear"; still, even here, the enunciation on the considerable difference in their ages, and the idea that the priest was not just a Father but a "friend," advances the sense that their relationship was atypical.

The boy has a hard time absorbing the news, but unsettled by Old Cotter's insinuations, he feels himself "under observation" and strives to continue eating with feigned indifference. The death comes hard on the boy, his uncle suggests to Cotter, because "the youngster and he were great friends." The old Father taught the boy much, and "they say he had a great wish for him." What *is* this wish? We never come to know. Though the story suggests, at various points, that Father Flynn was grooming the boy to follow him into holy orders, perhaps his "great wish" was more nefarious. Cotter's elliptical hints cover the "peculiar case" with darkening fingerprints: might the priest have had a pederastic relationship with his young mentee? As Ali Günes indicates, "even the doubt of such a rumor clearly defiles and defames the image and reliability of the Church and the priest."

Old Cotter won't let up: It is bad for children to be around the likes of Father Flynn "because their minds are so impressionable. When children see things like that, you know, it has an effect. . . ." What precisely the "things like that" could mean remains unnamed, maybe because Cotter, in spite of his outspokenness on the matter, wants to maintain discretion in front of the boy, whose wrath toward the alleger grows.

That night the narrator puzzles with Old Cotter's words, tries "to extract meaning from his unfinished sentences," but he falls asleep before he can make sense of them. In his dreams, the priest, with "the heavy grey face of a paralytic," approaches him, "and I understood that it desired to confess something. I felt my soul receding into some pleasant and vicious region." Here, outside of Cotter's suspiciousness, inside the boy's own soul, our concern increases. What could the priest need to confess to his charge? Why would this lead him into a region both pleasant and vicious—a region defined by connotations of sexual abuse? Our disturbance reaches an unbearable pitch when we find that the purportedly penitent priest "smiled continually" with "lips . . . so moist with spittle." Although the narrator tries to rationalize this bizarre image by remembering that Father died of paralysis, and though he finds that he too is "smiling feebly" as if to "absolve the simoniac of his sin," this does nothing to ameliorate our worry that he has been abused in some way. Instead, he seems to offer evidence, however partial, that the priest was a pederast. Later we learn that when the priest smiled in the boy's presence, he would "let his tongue lie upon his lower lip—a habit which had made me feel uneasy in the beginning of our acquaintance before I knew him well."

With Günes, and wishing otherwise, I too find that this tongued lip "implies sexuality," an implication that gains credence when combined with the spittle-moistened lips of the post-mortem priest of the boy's dreams. Speaking of dreams, when the boy recalls Father Flynn's distended tongue, he is moved to revisit old Cotter's words, is driven to try and "remember what had happened afterwards in the dream. I remembered that I had noticed long velvet curtains and a swinging lamp of antique fashion." Where are we, here? In a bedroom? In the confessional? Once again, our search is cut short, kept in the dark.

When the priest's sisters try to make sense of his death, though they try to press on with the funerary courtesies, they can't help recalling a weird instance wherein the lost Father Flynn was found "sitting up by himself in the dark in his confession-box, wide awake and laughing softly to himself." One of the sisters, Eliza, assures us that his confused (and clearly maddened) state was caused by "the chalice that he broke . . . that was the beginning of it." The chalice, we learn, "contained nothing," which is both reassuring, given that the alternative would mean Christ's Precious Blood spilled on the floor, and curious. For, if the sister is correct in assuming that "it was the boy's fault" that the chalice broke, what exactly could the priest and the boy have been doing to bring about such an accident, that it would be the boy's fault? When "they say" that the narrator is to blame, we can't help but hear yet another iteration of that pattern of priests who try to persuade their victims that *they* are the guilty. The sisters do not wish for their sympathies to be interrupted. At the funerary meal where they "commun[e] with the past" memories of "poor James" their brother, one of the sisters is piqued when the narrator refuses her offer of "a little glass of wine and some cream crackers," a profane sacrament seemingly meant to transubstantiate their disturbed and disturbing brother into a spotless victim. In the last lines of the story, she again tries to absolve Father Flynn: because others found her brother James in a confessional, "laughing-like to himself," when "they saw that that made them think that there was something wrong with him." Notice the way in which she hedges a halo of innocence around her bother: *they think* there is something wrong with him, but, she implies, they exaggerated the case.

Father Colum Power speaks of Father Flynn's "frustrated masculinity" and "unhealthy" religiosity. He roots Flynn's case in the fact that "the Catholic priesthood sometimes bore an authoritarian (as opposed to authoritative) power that is difficult for the contemporary mindset to conceive of; a power and prestige that conjoined the mystical, the social, and the political." Perhaps, he muses, this is why the priest sought absolution for his "simony." Maybe. Maybe it is our unhappy familiarity with too many abusive priests, protected and explained away, that makes it hard to shake Old Cotter's suspicions. But maybe there is more substance in the sense that the broken empty chalice, the loss of the Catholic Church's credibility, is not the *start* of the crisis but the consequence of sins less easy to speak than simony.

We know how often, in cases of clerical abuse, sexual exploitation and monetary exchange have come hand in hand. Are we wrong to shake our heads knowingly when the boy finds himself "annoyed at discovering in myself a sensation of freedom as if I had been freed from something by his death"? Is it only the "old woman's mutterings" that make the boy "pretend to pray" at Father Flynn's funeral? Joyce's story of a paralyzed priest masterfully brushes with all of the signs most of us know from a distance: the elliptical, elusive indirection, the blamed boy. Resorting to a style that is both subdued and cryptic, his portrait of the young man is confused and confusing at once. Old Cotter's allegations are never proven true. All fears of pedophilia may be a misguided projection, prompted by too many portraits of a dubious priesthood smoked and mirrored by a self-interested clericalism. No, such suspicions do not amount to definitive verdicts. Still, in passing through the suspiciousness of Joyce's "The Sisters," we come closer to grasping the sufferings of many of the formerly faithful who, paralyzed by the crisis of sexual abuse, find the chalice of belief half empty.

13

For Whom Chekhov's Bell Tolls

CHEKHOV SANG (LIKE a "little convict") in the church choir that his father conducted. Punctually, the acolyte assisted at the altar, arose early for Matins, and ascended the belfry to toll the bells. But for whom? "And what of it?" he asked, recalling from a distance that pious childhood, "it seems to me rather gloomy. Now I have no religion." Chekhov's agnostic detachment from dogmas is evident in the doctor's prescribed aesthetic: if some artists strive to answer great enquiries and others endeavor to form questions correctly, "only the latter is required of an author."

But his drift from Orthodoxy did not leave the Russian faithless. As he confided to the editor Alexei Pleshcheev, "My holy of holies is the human body, health, intelligence, talent, inspiration, love and the most absolute freedom imaginable." Whereas Dostoevsky portrays the "lover of mankind" as an abstracted humanitarian in dreams who cannot bear particular human beings, Chekov cultivated a distaste for the decadent inaction of those who, "out of boredom, write trivial stories, unnecessary projects, and cheap dissertations." His humanist sympathies drove him to fight a cholera epidemic, organize free clinics, build several schools, and contribute to famine relief. Leonoid Grossman called him "a probing Darwinist with the love of St. Francis of Assisi for every living creature." But the doubting Chekhov also built a bell tower for a village church, and—*Spasibo Gospodi*—the Russian wrought stories in spite of their alleged triviality.

In Chekhov's stories, contends Simon Karlinsky, Christianity and the Church "are totally divorced from the very things they are traditionally supposed to promote in Western Civilization: morality, kindness and ethical treatment of fellow human beings." Yes, but the same tales celebrate the Divine Liturgy with beautiful prose. "The Bishop," for instance, begins during Palm Sunday vigil, as "pussywillows" are passed out in lieu of true palms. "The lights were dim, the wicks were sooty, everything was as if in a mist. In the twilight of the church the crowd heaved like the sea." When the titular character's mother, visiting for the first time in nine years, appears—half-recognized—amidst the pressing crowd, we learn that what first seemed sacred and ethereal is clouded by the pains of illness, for her cantankerous son has the sickness unto death. Lyrical visions, impressionist and lovely, serve as a shroud for his present tense heartlessness.

Later that evening, after attentively reading his "old, long familiar prayers," the bishop recalls his mother's infallible warmth during childhood infirmities, waxing nostalgic until "his memories . . . burned ever brighter, like flames" flicked from votives. A liturgical quality hallows his youth, vesting this time "forever gone" with a garb that is "more festive and rich, than it was in reality." Back then he had followed the procession of a "wonder-working icon . . . hatless, barefoot, with naïve faith, with a naïve smile, infinitely happy." But now he is old, infirm, and incapable of Christ's core commandment. First laughing over his mother's visit, he later wakes for Matins but cannot leave his bed. Something is not right, but he lacks the courage of Tolstoy's Ivan Illych, who could at least muster the modest confession: "Maybe I did not live as I should have."

When at last he meets his mother, she speaks from the heart, daring a confidence: the sight of him handing out palms in church made her weep, "why I don't know. It's God's holy will." Immediately, she blushes with embarrassment, for her son's clerical ministrations have left him cold—like a faint form of God without being. The bishop is startled by her sudden turn; her "timid, deferential expression" leaves him terribly "sad, vexed." We soon find out that he rouses this fear from most of the flock under his watch: whenever he looks at these pathetic provincials, they gape back "small, frightened, guilty." Flirting with the first stirrings of a reckoning, he is "struck by the emptiness, the pettiness of all that people asked about and wept about; he was angered by their backwardness, their timidity; and the mass of all these petty and unnecessary things oppressed him." And then there is his mother: she jokes and chuckles with his fellow priests but turns serious and silent in his presence. On the verge of epiphany, he ducks into the vestry, for the bishop "found peace only when he was in church." As her visit extends, he falls bedbound for months, suffering—supposedly—from gout.

Recovering slightly, he goes to vespers, where he hears the monks sing "harmoniously, inspiredly" of the "Bridegroom who cometh at midnight and about the chamber that is adorned." But the bishop knows not repentance or sorrow for his sins. Rather, the music summons a remembrance of things past, and his celestial daydreams contract, solipsistic: maybe my childhood will be the beatific center of whatever life comes after this; maybe our life on earth will be what we contemplate. For now, his eyes fill with the tears of a man who has achieved all, has faith, and yet lacks "some most important thing" he cannot name.

The missing piece is found when his niece visits his bedside like a beggar, telling of her now deceased father and the dire poverty her family now faces. "Give us a little money," she dares to ask at last, in a "high little voice" that milks many teardrops even from the bishop. His mourning, however, is shorn of meaning, shows not forth the measure of love. Though she needs help *here*, he defers to hereafter, when "the bright resurrection of Christ will come, and then we'll talk . . . I'll help you . . . I will."

Only when the Easter liturgy requires him does the bishop gain "a vigorous, healthy mood." Raising his eyes, he beholds "on both sides a whole sea of lights," hears "the sizzle of candles," and recites the glory of the Son's resurrection. Afterward, on the same Holy Saturday Christ was in the tomb, the anti-Pharisee takes his final rest, unreconciled. I say *anti-* because the Pharisees are "whitewashed tombs, which outwardly appear beautiful, but within they are full of dead men's bones and all uncleanness" (Mt 23:27), whereas the bishop bided time by prettying his insides, but swapped his crosier for a dead man's femur, wielding the bone over his cowering brethren with all the marks of Cain.

Chekhov does not commit the clichéd critique of mindless, deadening liturgy. He does not juxtapose good deeds with dead rites. Rather, while rendering the rituals with mesmerizing prose, he shows how even beauty's summit can become the needle tip of anesthesia—an aesthetic escape for a lukewarm lover of the Lord.

In a letter, Chekhov considers the Bible as bequeathing the best possible morality: "There are neither lower, nor higher, nor secondary moralities, there is one, namely that as was given to us in the time of Jesus Christ, and which now prevents me, you, and Barantsevich from stealing, insulting, lying and so forth." Given that Chekhov lacks faith in the resurrection, we can reasonably read his characterization of Christ as one more "humanization" of the God-man. Pope Benedict XVI captures this revision, trending during Chekhov's time, in his Regensburg Address: "Jesus was said to have put an end to worship in favour of morality. In the end he was presented as the father of a humanitarian moral message." We might suspect that Chekhov, like Harnack, wishes to "bring Christianity back into harmony with modern reason, liberating it, that is to say, from seemingly philosophical and theological elements, such as faith in Christ's divinity and the triune God."

Troubling as Chekhov's reduction of Christ may be, who can find fault in his good deeds. Take his trans-Siberian trip to study the conditions of an island prison colony—a trip that yielded real reforms. We could mistake Chekhov's letter to his brother for a diary entry of Dorothy Day: "We've let millions of people rot in prison for no reason, without thinking, barbarically.... All of us are to blame; yet we don't want to know about it, it's not interesting. The celebrated sixties did nothing for the sick and those in prison, thereby violating the chief commandment of Christian civilization."

Dorothy Day warned against "spend[ing] all our money on buildings," citing Christ's command that we feed the poor. "However," she continued, "there are many kinds of hunger. There is a hunger for bread, and we must give people food. But there is also a hunger for beauty—and there are very few beautiful places that the poor can get into. Here," she said, gesturing to St. Mary's San Francisco Cathedral, "is a place of transcendent beauty, and it is as accessible to the homeless ... as it is to the mayor."

Be wary of an oft-floated false either / or that takes the form of aesthetical / ethical. As Martin Mosebach remarks, "whenever there is a debate about the great Catholic liturgical tradition, it only needs someone to utter the accusation of 'aestheticism,' and it is all over," as the charge is fatal. Chekhov's cantankerous bishop should cull from Christian readers corporeal counterpoints—works of mercy. A tragic muse would have lovers of liturgy shirk the sacred forms to better love mankind. We faithful who feast on Christ's consummate art and who *love him precisely through the chant and through the monstrance, through the chasuble and through the myrrh,* must make certain the chalice of charity spills from the churches, for we are our brothers' keeper or we're Cain, treating Holy Mass as an addict does opium.

14

Flaubert's Fictional Faith

SINCE DOUBT WAS carried into religion through "Christian existentialism," sincere religious experience "has seemed possible only in the tension between doubt and belief, in torturing one's beliefs with one's doubts," relaxing from the torment only to affirm that the human condition and man's belief are both absurd. So suggests Hannah Arendt in her essay "Tradition and the Modern Age." The clearest evidence of her thesis can be found in the fact that Dostoevsky, "perhaps the most experienced psychologist of modern religious belief, portrayed pure faith" in characters such as Alyosha Karamazov, who is "pure in heart because he is simple-minded."

Although Gustave Flaubert professed to be "a mystic at bottom and I believe in nothing," he gave us an unironic portrait of guileless faith that melds the hagiographer's preoccupation with sanctity with the modern fictionist's oblique incorporation of symbols. In so doing, the professed atheist purifies the cynical soul. Félicité, central figure of "A Simple Heart," suffers from the start. Her unforgiving childhood culminates in a deceptive love affair. As servant of Mme. Aubain, she is fiercely devoted to the widow's two children, Paul and Virginie, and she is prodigal in her love for Victor, her neglected nephew. All three children, rotating centers of her affection and selfless acts, disappear, either through death or the distance that comes with worldly success. As Caroline Gordon points out, "Félicité's life follows the same pattern as that of the early Christians. She renounces earthly joys and undergoes many of the same trials that they underwent; she confronts a wild beast when she saves Madame Aubain and the children from an enraged bull" and commits numerous spiritual and corporal acts of mercy; along with "looking after the people who went down with cholera," Félicité comforts the dying "Colmiche, with his cancerous sores," who "bears a marked resemblance to the lepers to whom the early Christians ministered." When he passes, "she had a Mass said for the repose of his soul." Early readers of "A Simple Heart" were certain that Flaubert was satirizing, with a soft scorn, his holy heroine. On the contrary, he wrote, the story of Félicité is "not at all ironic, as you suppose it to be, but on the contrary very serious and very sad. I want to arouse people's pity, to make sensitive souls weep, since I am one myself."

If he succeeds in moistening handkerchiefs, Flaubert does so through subtleties that defy the easy sentimentality of Dickens—no mean feat. As Julian Barnes notes in *Flaubert's Parrot,* "Imagine the technical difficulty of writing a story in which a badly stuffed bird with a ridiculous name ends up standing for the third of the Trinity, and in which the intention is neither satirical, sentimental, or blasphemous."

The story does not easily dodge allegations of blasphemy. After a life overflowing with loss, Félicité receives a parrot. Immediately, she associates the bird with her deceased nephew Victor, "for it came from America"—his destination when he died. "Loulou" too meets the fate of all mortals, but Félicité can preserve him in a manner that would be preposterous and disturbing if applied to now gone children she had loved with abandon: she has him stuffed. The taxidermist, in what could be read as an allusion to the resurrection of the body, presents Loulou more beautified in death than he was in life. The stilled parrot comes "biting a nut which the taxidermist, out of a love of the grandiose, had gilded."

At this point in the story, as her clarity of mind begins to blur, the devout Félicité finds herself "forever gazing at the Holy Ghost, and one day she noticed that it had something of the parrot about it." In a color print depicting Christ's baptism, "with its red wings and its emerald-green body," the Holy Spirit "was the very image of Loulou." Here she seems to reverse a right relationship between image and actuality. The *Holy Spirit* is the image of Loulou, not the other way around. However, seen from the vantage of an innocent soul, such a reversal is not immediately sacrilegious. Take, for instance, William Blake's "The Lamb," wherein the narrator, talking in a childlike manner to the titular creature, says, "He is called by thy name; for he calls himself a Lamb"; here again, it would seem more proper to say that "thou art called by His name," but "meek and mild" as He is, Christ's humility may be better captured in the rendering that gives scandal to an adult too accustomed to hearing songs of experience. Félicité herself, who is in charge of taking her mistresses' daughter to catechism classes, "loved the lambs more tenderly for love of the Lamb of God, and the doves for the sake of the Holy Ghost." Notice the enunciate *direction* of her love. She loves lambs and doves *for the sake of* God; she passes *through* these creatures to the Creator. Félicité buys a print of that image of Christ's baptism that bears an uncanny resemblance to Loulou. Staring now at the print and now at Loulou, she finds "the parrot being sanctified by this connection with the Holy Ghost which acquired new life and meaning in her eyes."

In "The Idol and the Icon," Jean-Luc Marion helpfully juxtaposes two modes of representation and seeing. The idol "fascinates and captivates the gaze precisely because everything in it must expose itself to the gaze, attract, fill, and hold it." The idol, however, is not solely or wholly responsible: the idol "draws the gaze only inasmuch as the gaze has drawn it whole into the gazeable and there expresses and exhausts it." An idolatrous gaze stops at, rests on / in an idol "when it can no longer pass beyond it." A person who has succumbed to idolatrous seeing ceases to transcend, to pass through the visible into the invisible. The icon, on the other hand, "unbalances human sight in order to engulf it in infinite depth." What is essential in the icon "comes to it from elsewhere," to the point that an invisible "strangeness saturates the visibility of the face with meaning."

Flaubert seems to make a faithful reading of his fiction uneasy: has Félicité turned Loulou into an idol, or is the stuffed bird an icon which she passes through in right and just worship? When, after Mme. Aubain dies, Félicité worries that she may lose her lodgings, she fixes an anguished look on the bird "as she appealed to the Holy Ghost, she contracted the idolatrous habit of kneeling in front of the parrot to say her prayers." In this state, light sometimes comes into the room; refracting through the bird's glass eye, it shoots out "luminous rays which sent her into ecstasies." It is clear that she begins by appealing to the Holy Ghost, but Flaubert seems to indicate that she ends in idolatry, prostrate without passing *through* to the unseen Spirit. We also know that throughout her life she found it hard to imagine "what the Holy Ghost looked like, for it was not just a bird but a fire as well, and sometimes a breath." Given this, it would not be unreasonable to presume that she kneels before the seen in order to seize and squeeze a solidified assurance out of the difficult to grasp. Nonetheless, the luminous rays seem, to cite Marion, to "unbalance human sight," to destabilize any sort of simplified refuge in materiality; the glass eyes make luminous a light that takes her as close to the mystical as she comes. (In a letter, Flaubert describes her as "devout but not given to mysticism.")

After Félicité is diagnosed with pneumonia, still living in her increasingly decrepit servant's quarters (in trepidation that she will be removed, she refuses to ask for repairs), the local priest decides to place the Corpus Christi procession altar on Mme. Aubain's property, just outside the simple heart's window. Too weak to make a conventional offering for display on the altar, Félicité offers Loulou. Though the respectable neighbors consider the suggestion "unseemly," the priest "gave his permission, and this made her so happy" that she wills the priest her parrot when she dies. Unknown to the unseeing Félicité, the bird is being eaten by worms. But Flaubert paints her gift as nonetheless beautiful. The altar "was hung with green garlands and adorned with a flounce in English needle-point lace." Beside a little frame containing relics, there are "silver candlesticks and china vases holding sunflowers, lilies, peonies, foxgloves, and bunches of hydrangea. This pyramid of bright colours stretched from the first floor right down to the carpet which was spread out over the pavement." And at last, amidst some rare objects, "Loulou, hidden under roses, showed nothing but his blue poll, which looked like a plaque of lapis lazuli." In "Félicité's Holy Parrot," Myra Jehlen insists that through her decomposing Loulou, Félicité has "reached the outer edge of this material realm, nothing indicates she is going anywhere beyond." Jehlen comes down still harder on the story's subsequent (and final lines). As everyone kneels down before the Blessed Sacrament, a blue cloud of incense wafts into Félicité's room, and "she opened her nostrils wide and breathed it in with a mystical, sensuous fervor. Then she closed her eyes. Her lips smiled. Her heart-beats grew slower and slower, each a little fainter and gentler, like a fountain running dry, an echo fading away. And as she breathed her last, she thought she could see, in the opening heavens, a gigantic parrot hovering above her head."

For Jehlen, there is apparently a strict separation between seen and unseen things; there is no sacramental economy of passing through the visible into the invisible. There are no icons, only idols—material things that suck the soul to themselves and keep them there: "*nothing* of religion occurs" in this final scene, she says, "only things of the earth: incense, a nose, lips, a heart, and, to top it all off, a vision of a real parrot." In "The Catholic Writer Today," Dana Gioia counters the likes of Jehlen, who scoff at bells and incense: "But God gave people ears and noses. Are those organs of perception too humble to bring into church? For very good reason, participating in Mass involves all five senses. We necessarily bring the whole of our hairy and heavy humanity to worship."

The Catholic faith, with its sacramental vision of reality, makes no harsh division between seen and unseen; incense can touch and order the soul. Still, Jehlen presses on. Félicité's final vision of the altar-set parrot "makes Loulou an apotheosis but not an incarnation." He is rather "the final destination of Félicité's love, not a stand-in." How do we know this? Because Flaubert tells us that "she *thought* she saw." He does not indicate that she thought she saw the Holy Spirit in a parrot's form: "the Holy Spirit is nowhere to be seen." Jehlen grants that Félicité does not intend to disregard the Holy Spirit, and thus "there is no blasphemy in her idolatry." Nonetheless, "Loulou neither merges with nor represents the Holy Spirit but preempts it." It is not rash to presume that Flaubert, who "believe[s] in nothing," immerses us into the beauties of Catholic worship and the sublimity of a parrot's coloration in order to replace faith with a kind of idolatrous elevation of beauty in a merely aesthetical (that is to say non-transcendental) sense. But unless Félicité has discarded her earlier associations, we must not stay mired in the final paragraph to grasp her dying relation to the parrot. Remember, the parrot became "sanctified by [its] connection with the Holy Ghost," so that, in Marion's words, the icon's essential meaning is given to it "from elsewhere," saturating the visible with a "strangeness." We would have a much more troubled and troubling case if the protagonist had arbitrarily selected an object of personal preference and purportedly "sacralized" it.

In her reading of the altar scene, Caroline Gordon contends that "the exotic is deliberately stressed throughout this passage," making Loulou appear "not only beautiful but strange." That exoticism was originally affiliated with America, land of the bird's origin and her nephew's destination, but now the bird's exotic character is affiliated with that final foreign frontier of heaven, toward which the exquisite altar aims to elevate us all. The altar, Gordon stresses, is an "excellent preparation for the Resolution," where an "even stranger" thing happens: "the heavens open and the Holy Ghost appears in the form of the parrot she has so loved in life." Is Gordon, a convert to Catholicism, imposing her own wishful thinking in making such a declaration without qualification or contingency?

Jehlen is not wrong to pinpoint the problems produced by Flaubert's inclusion of *thought*. Nor is she wrong to remind us that Félicité sees not the Holy Ghost but the parrot. Flaubert's letter concerning "A Simple Heart" seems to give some credence to Jehlen's doubts: "When she is on her deathbed," he wrote, "she takes the parrot for the Holy Ghost." Immediately after this, he assures us that the tale is "in no way ironic." Geoffrey Wall, attuned to the difficulties at play, suggests that Flaubert is trying to protect his suffering servant, knowing that there is a "delicate tension in the texture of his story. The writing invites us to renounce the agreeable intellectual aggression that we call irony." And yet, he seems to test us, tempt us to our limits. By its very nature, a parrot mimics, imitates. Félicité taught Loulou to say "Hail Mary!" but these words are bereft of the spirit of prayer, which must be moved by the heart and soul and mind.

Is Félicité's final vision also an imitation without substance, a parroted surrogate for what Gordon calls "the kind of vision which comes to the saints"? Remember that when Félicité sees the gigantic parrot hovering over her head, she sees the "opening heavens" above the bird; that is, she does not see *merely* the bird; her gaze does not exhaust itself in the parrot to the point that she cannot pass beyond it—as it would in the case of an idol. Still more, although some readers have concluded that the bird she sees *is* Loulou, Flaubert's withholds any such outright naming. Further, his description of the bird as "gigantic" establishes its distinction from the small stuffed creature; truly, Félicité's affiliation between the Holy Spirit and the parrot could be leading her to conceive of God as an immense bird of otherworldly proportions. In *Christ and Apollo,* William Lynch, SJ, praises images that signify more than themselves "without becoming less actual in so doing." These symbols make the imagination rise to insight while also remaining rooted in the thick and tangible real.

I find myself doubting, finally, that the faith of Félicité, proven throughout "A Simple Heart," is incapable of passing through the density and tang of her fictional vision towards the beatific One. Still, Flaubert has saturated his story with a cautionary ambiguity that leaves us tightrope walking that difficult tension between an Ignatian embrace of imagination (as evinced in Lynch) and a Carmelite's cautionary detachment from "all that can enter through the eye, and to all that can be received through the ear, and can be imagined with the fancy." St. John of the Cross insists that the soul must be "voided" of all such things if she wishes to reach the summits of mystical union. Although Catholicism is intensely sacramental, bidding us to know something of the unseen through the seen, the heights of mysticism demand asceticism. To ascend Mount Carmel, the soul "must be like to a blind man, leaning upon dark faith, taking it for guide and light, and leaning upon none of the things that he understands, experiences, feels and imagines." St. John of the Cross is uncompromising: all of these can cause her to stray: "faith is above all that he understands and experiences and feels and imagines." He does not repudiate the senses as evil, does not dismiss the imagination as intrinsically inclined toward idolatry. There is no harm in breathing in incense with Félicité's "mystical, sensuous fervor." But, the master of the Dark Night teaches, if we always remain circumscribed by the seen and sensed, we will not "attain to that which is greater"—that which is taught totally by faith.

Maybe Flaubert, the mystic who at bottom believes in nothing, was ultimately unable to imagine what faith without sensuousness might "look like." Far different is that other simple-heart, St. Thérèse of Lisieux, who, bereft of tangible gifts which she might place on God's altar, bids us make a sacrificial offering, yes, even of nothingness: "Even when I *have nothing to offer* Him, then I will *give* Him that nothing."

Part III

READING HUMAN NATURE

15

Acolyte of Ambition: Balzac's Lost Illusions *and* Lost Souls

"You CAN LEARN a lot from Mr. B," Bob Dylan wrote of Balzac. "His philosophy is plain and simple, says basically that pure materialism is a recipe for madness. He wears a monk's robe and drinks endless cups of coffee," writing his *Human Comedy* through the silent night. This recorder of modernity is akin to a medieval illuminator whose quills can cull the sublime from the shabby. His *Lost Illusions* should be required reading for every peddler of the pen, and everyone stricken by the climber's desires. For, with homeopathic skill, Balzac cures the soul-sick through artful administrations of what ails us.

Lucien, a self-styled poet and protagonist of *Lost Illusions*, fails to find recognition in provincial Angoulême, where the arts are "roundly deplored." Ready to "avenge the humbleness" of his origins, Lucien leaves home armed with grand visions and—a poetry collection. Maybe Paris, that antithesis of country pettiness, can do justice to the young man's genius.

When, mocked by publishers, his pretentions are proofread into oblivion, he briefly swaps his strivings for friendship with "the Cenacle," a brotherhood of truly talented artists and totally committed philosophers. Led by Daniel d'Arthez, all of them "had that slightly tormented look that a pure life and a fiery mind give to the face, regularizing it and purifying it." This little flowering of resolve blooms fast and dies. Having spent his last monies on firewood, Lucien again borrows from his homespun family. Filching egoism's fluid currency with the confidence of a bank too big to fail, he subjects them to the vicissitudes of "self-made" fate.

Again short on cash soon thereafter, the poet descends into dubious journalism. Lucien's infernal turn coincides with another counterfeit of the good. He cohabitates with a gorgeous actress Coralie whose theater manager purchases canned applause, manufacturing high ratings for her mediocre performances. Balzac's observations on journalism are pessimistic but penetrating; although "news" was in its infancy, he is keen to its fundamental causes and its frightening sovereignty. Claude Vignon, a prolific article-maker himself and colleague of Lucien, anticipates Nietzsche's observation that the newspaper will replace prayer—the ephemeral will eclipse the eternal. The newspaper, surpassing the "role of the priest," can "make its readers believe anything it wants to. Then nothing it dislikes" can possibly be correct, "and it is never wrong." A paper—the people "in folio form"—"will serve up its own father raw, or seasoned only with the salt of its witticisms, rather than fail to entertain or amuse its public." Filled with pithy, painful truths, Vignon's diatribe is that of an addict against his narcotic.

Before long, Lucien is "depraved from the habit of writing both for and against." When different bosses task him with celebrating and decimating the same book, he learns that the newspaper, "like the magic spear of Achilles . . . heals the wounds it inflicts."

Then the Liberal Lucien enters journalism's red-light district, whoring himself to the Royalist papers in anticipation of their likely ascent. Instead, a convoluted tit for tat blackmail awaits. If he does not wish to watch his Coralie paraded through public scorn, he must excoriate a newly-published book by d'Arthez, the soul of the Cenacle. Like a discreet Judas, Lucien pays d'Arthez a nocturnal visit. Penitent before his hallowed friend, Lucien betrays him with a kiss: "Your book is sublime!" he professes, then confesses to having written his damning review..

In one of the most potent reverses in a novel replete with twists and turns, the betrayed d'Arthez helps draft his own death sentence. By perfecting the document that will sink his genius, d'Arthez translates St. Paul's harrowing wisdom into the idiom of editing: "Therefore if thine enemy hunger, feed him; if he thirst, give him drink: in so doing thou shalt heap coals of fire on his head" (Rom 12:20, KJV). D'Arthez then weighs the poet's transgression in the scales of transcendence: "I've always regarded periodic repentance as a great hypocrisy. . . . Repentance becomes just the price you pay for permission to commit your wicket acts. But repentance is a kind of virginity that our soul owes to God: a man who repents twice is a disgusting sycophant. I fear that the only reason you repent is to get your absolution!"

Would that this prophecy remained unfulfilled. For although "from that day on [Lucien] felt devoured by a melancholy that he could not always disguise," he knows no real remorse. Balzac takes pains to make this plain.

Before he is barred from both journalism and socialite stardom, Lucien drives Coralie to an early death. Exhausted, she takes to bed after receiving "legitimate applause, a response that had not been paid for." The spontaneity and sincerity of the crowd's appreciation helps her turn from falsified triumphs. While Coralie lays dying, Balzac hypostasizes the shabby and the sublime. Lucien composes vulgar drinking songs to raise funds for the funeral. The priest proclaims a solemn beatitude that, though meant to bless, comes off as comfortless: "Happy are those who find their Hell here on earth." Sustaining a Catholic coloration shameful to Lucien, Balzac paints the poet's last stance in Paris with an allusion alien to the irreligious striver. After begging alms from Coralie's caretaker, he pines to give the money back, for it "burned in his hand . . . but he was forced to keep it, a final stigmata from Parisian life."

Overcome with illness on his way home, Lucien receives absolution from an unassuming priest who does not know that "for the past eighteen months Lucien had repented so often that his repentance now, violent as it was, had no more value than a well-acted scene—and one that every time had been acted in perfect good faith." The counterpoint to Coralie is clear: whereas the actress, in her death throes, retired from acting, Lucien's living confessions are *semblances*—the accumulated interest of his illusory existence.

The stigmata, nailed into his hands by the city's burning monies, persists even after the prodigal receives a man-made resurrection. Back in Angoulême, he appears at first chastened, relieved to be far from the mutable feast of big city achievements. But his perilous desires are soon petted and purring. At a soirée held in his honor, his haughtiness reaches liturgical proportions. When a lawyer calls him a "man of genius," Lucien "made the kind of gesture you might see in church from a man who finds the censer too close to his nose." Six days after his triumphant return, he yearns for the "wonderful miseries" of Paris. When Angoulême ultimately fails to appreciate him, Lucien serves up a favorite entrée of bohemian "great men": "They're all bourgeois; they can't understand me." Balzac, calling his bluff, discloses his recipe's main ingredient: "he could no longer fool them about his character or his future."

Cornered by his failures and their consequences for his family, he takes refuge in *fate,* that category of inevitability that absolves ethical responsibility: "Many families have a member who is fatal for them, like a kind of illness or infection. That is what I am for you," he writes his sister, promising suicide in recompense.

Ready to off himself, Lucien contemplates ways to die "poetically," eschewing the hideous spectacle of his dead corpse fished from the river. Flowers in his hands, imagining a beautiful death, Lucien is interrupted by a man who seems—"obviously"—to be a priest, but who is actually the serial criminal Vautrin, a central presence in several Balzac novels. With charm and lure that reads as all-too-plausible, the Jesuitical "Father Herrera" tempts Lucien away from the edge by remarking repeatedly upon the young man's beauty and oiling the over-worn engine of ambition.

The scene carries a "supernatural" sense, so says MacKenzie in his translator's introduction. According to the strictures of literary realism, Father Herrera's sudden arrival seriously tests our suspended disbelief. How, then, could we justify this turn? "Is it Providence, working to keep Lucien from his intended suicide, or the opposite, a Satanic kind of intervention?" Herrera, notes MacKenzie (and his extensive notes are extraordinarily helpful), seems more akin to the demonic Mephistopheles of *Faust* than the mundane secularity of the novelistic world.

The decadent writer Barbey d'Aurevilly contended that "Catholicism one day will reclaim Balzac as one of its most devoted and most faithful writers, for in all things he draws the same conclusions a Catholic would draw." But what conclusions can a Catholic extract from a Machiavellian priest who swaps the *analogia entis* for the analogy of a game: when trying to outwit friends at cards, "Do you practice that finest of virtues, openness? . . . You dissimulate, correct? You lie!" Just so, Herrera preaches, in all of life you must perfect your poker face, for "there are no more laws, just customs, and those are only so much playacting—form, always form."

In his preface to the *Comédie humaine,* Balzac wrote that "Christianity, above all, Catholicism" is "a complete system for the repression of the depraved tendencies of man" and "the most powerful element of social order." Herrera's character and counsel are especially heinous because he assumes the "form" of Catholicism while liberating Lucien's depraved tendencies. To paraphrase Aquinas, the greater potentiality a thing has, the more it is disposed for good, the worse it is for that thing to be deprived of good.

Lucien's fall is hard to witness, but a falsified Father is most difficult to find out. For Balzac, the erosion of Catholic order may have been primarily a political tragedy. Nonetheless, if MacKenzie is right that Herrera's presence is mythical-allegorical, are we wrong to come to this chilling conclusion: when religion's restraining power withers, it will be replaced not by an enlightened governance but by wicked ambitions unleashed with a logic that assumes pseudo-sacred authorization?

In the sequel *Lost Souls* (MacKenzie's rendering of *Splendeurs et misères des courtisanes*), he chases the effects of this erosion to their horrific conclusions: Ferrera (whose real name is not Vautrin but Jacques Collin) continues to manipulate Lucien. Living vicariously through the beautiful boy, he plays his marionette to a death that occasions a secular conversion: "Last night, as I sat holding the cold hand of the dead boy, I made a promise to myself to give up the insane battle I'd been waging for twenty years against society. You won't expect me to launch into Capuchin-style pieties, not after what I've already told you about my religious opinions. . . . Well! For these twenty years, I've seen the underside of the world, its cellars, and I've come to see that in the stream of events there's a power that you'll call Providence, and I call chance."

Lucien's death moves the master of the underworld to abandon his post and make himself "the servant of that power that weighs down and crushes us"—helpmate of the police, those "Providences" of Paris. What are we to make of this about face?

Elsewhere, and often, Balzac does not hesitate to tell us what to think. Early in *Lost Illusions*, for instance, after painting a portrait of rurality, he tells us that "the most ridiculous things about us are born out of fine sentiments, by virtues or abilities carried to an extreme. A pride that is never smoothed down by contact with society ends up becoming a rigidity that exercises itself on trivialities." The penchant for moral aphorism is demonstrated in French writers from La Rouchefoucauld ("If we had no faults we should not take so much pleasure in noting those of others") and Pascal ("A trifle consoles us, for a trifle distresses us") to Simone Weil ("Evil when we are in its power is not felt as evil but as a necessity, or even a duty"). One of the delights of reading Balzac is his interplay between intense action and incisive aphorism. But when it comes to his thoughts on Collin-Vautrin-Ferrera, he withholds expressed judgments. Is Peter Brooks right when, in *Balzac's Lives,* he argues that "outlaw and police are just two positions on the social chessboard that can be easily swapped," that these two positions possess an "essential moral equivalence"?

Even if we contend that the police, insofar as they serve law and order, are devoted to a superior end, the authorities' appreciation of Collin's crime-solving swiftness suggests another aphoristic truth: their capacity to contain crime is directly proportionate to their alliance with a criminal. What is unsettling about Collin, Brooks contends, is "that he refuses the distinctions between good and evil altogether. . . . What is truly diabolical [about him] is that he puts in question the very idea of social order," for—like Rousseau—he sees society as a sham social contract wherein law exists to protect the fraudulent. In his preface, Balzac argues the contrary. In spite of the fact that in his novels he has "displayed more of evil than of good," society, "far from depraving him, as Rousseau asserts, improves him, makes him better."

Is Collin, then, "improved" in the end? "Now," he promises, "if you put me into the service of the Law and the police, at the end of the first year you'll be applauding the revelations I'll bring you—I'll be frankly and openly exactly what I should be." Arguing the authenticity of his submission, Collin appeals to the free character of his reversal: "I've given you sufficient proof of my honor," he says to the prosecutor general, "you let me go free and I returned."

This free choice, however, is not sufficient evidence of his lawfulness, as his final soliloquy bespeaks the grave risk of relying on a serial felon. Musing upon the upper crust who have gone unpunished, Collin "allow[s] himself a superb smile.... 'They all believe me, they all act on the revelations I make to them, and they leave me alone and unhindered. I'm going to reign over this whole world, this world that has already been obeying me for twenty-five years.'" Balzac has trained us to abhor the white-collar criminal as epitomized in the banker Nucingen, whose dealings are funded by fake bills and whose obsession with Lucien's lover have hastened the young man's ruin. Nucingen is a "kind of legal Jacques Colin in the world of écus"; a "man steeped in secret infamies, a monster who in the business world has committed such crimes" that every cent of his fortune is "wet with the tears of some family." Balzac dares us not to delight in Collin's plans to punish the fraudulent banker, even if justice is driven by a valet of vengeance.

Henry James called Balzac a "Benedictine of the actual" who "read the universe, as hard and as loud as he could" into whatever his coffee-fueled pen offered up. In *Lost Illusions* and *Lost Souls,* Balzac proves himself an acolyte of ambition, immersing us in addled souls who can't let go until it is too late, subjecting the spirited to catharses and conversion, ridding us of republics writ only in dreams. Practicing his office upon illusive altars, he provides and then clears the incense that enshrines Faustian bargains and purges the reader of Paris spleen.

But Balzac does more than us who homeopathically heal harmful passions. For, even after passing through the thousand pages that comprise these two novels, we have really just covered a corner of the cosmic *Comédie humaine* (which consists of some ninety novels and stories), and a complete reading would see more than the either / or of man in rebellion or death bed faith. As Balzac clarifies in his preface:

> When depicting all society, sketching it in the immensity of its turmoil, it happened—it could not but happen—that the picture displayed more of evil than of good; that some part of the fresco represented a guilty couple; and the critics at once raised a cry of immorality, without pointing out the morality of another position intended to be a perfect contrast. . . . On this point it remains to be said that the most conscientious

> moralists doubt greatly whether society can show as many good actions as bad ones; and in the picture I have painted of it there are more virtuous figures than reprehensible ones. Blameworthy actions, faults and crimes, from the lightest to the most atrocious, always meet with punishment, human or divine, signal or secret.

We can't help but hear Oscar Wilde's romantic rejoinder: "There is no such thing as a moral or an immoral book," he proclaimed in the preface to *The Picture of Dorian Gray,* "Books are well written, or badly written. That is all." The artist, he continues, is absolved of "ethical sympathies," or what he calls "an unpardonable mannerism of style." Wilde would call sin and grace mere colors on the painter's palette: they can each, through contrast or complementarity, contribute to the dramatic action and beauty of a work. "Vice and virtue" are not moral matters, but "to the artist materials for an art."

If, however, they are reduced to "materials," if good and evil lose their metaphysical significance, would they not lose their dramatic weight? In his *Aesthetics,* Dietrich von Hildebrand offers a rejoinder to Wilde: Yes, evil characters can be a "source of great delight," but only indirectly, insofar as they "allow the antithesis between good and evil to shine out even more strongly." A good artist will never let us lose sight of the "horror of the metaphysical ugliness of evil," and will strive to make both the attractiveness and the bankruptcy of that actual evil more intelligible, in fiction, than it would have been if immediately encountered in reality. When it comes to making wickedness intelligible, Balzac is a maestro, but sometimes his depictions of goodness seem less substantial—less metaphysical—and so in the antithesis between good and evil the latter appears the victor.

Not without reason might we wonder whether he unwittingly wrote the *Human Tragedy* rather than the *Human Comedy.* A more obviously comic writer is Jane Austen, in whose novels both the harms and vices and the virtues which alone can overcome them give structure and telos to human lives. As Alasdair MacIntyre argues in *After Virtue*, Austen "writes comedy rather than tragedy for the same reason that Dante did; she is a Christian and she sees the *telos* of human life implicit in its everyday form."

Though Austen may be more expressly ironic and comic, Balzac's comic capacity is discernible—in, for instance, Collin's movement from antisocial criminal to police collaborator. It is also, and especially, evident at the end of *Lost Illusions.* For whereas Lucien's failure to fulfill his self-made forms drives him to a death wish, his provincial friend David (whose regular loans to Lucien threaten the stability of his own family) helps us die to ourselves. David, molded by "the ardent melancholy of a mind capable of embracing the two opposing ends of a horizon," is initially driven by the monomaniacal obsessions of an inventor. When local capitalists trick him of patent rights that could have won him a fortune, he—contra Lucien—tells himself a new story, a tale less glamorous . . . and less melodramatic. He becomes an unknown protagonist of the quiet delights of family life. "I regard the family and not the individual as the true social unit," wrote Balzac at the beginning of his *Comédie.* "In this respect, at the risk of being thought retrograde, I side with Bossuet and Bonald instead of going with modern innovators."

This passage bears a striking resemblance to the final page of *Lost Illusions.* For whereas Lucien remains lost in the trivial pursuits of the individual, David's wife bids him "forever renounce" the fool's gold fate of modern innovators, "those modern day Moses figures obsessed by their burning bush in Horeb." Returned from his manmade mountain, David turns to his land and to his children, not divinized but now more *humane.* The power of that last image, dim and homey though it be, is especially cathartic as an antithesis to Lucien, who is led from the dead end of self-demolition into a false story written by a Father descended from Lucifer.

Man, says MacIntyre, is "essentially a storytelling animal." Without stories that bespeak our true forms, or left with only façades of our final ends, we move, with Lucien, close to the precipice. MacIntyre puts it this way: "When someone complains—as do some of those who attempt or commit suicide—that his or her life is meaningless, he or she is often and perhaps characteristically complaining that the narrative of their life has become unintelligible to them, that it lacks any point, any movement towards a climax or a telos."

Our best human comedies contain antitheses. They let brilliant lies—all too humane—first lead us astray and then leave a bad taste. If they show us man's baseness, they forget not his broadness, his being "a little lower than the angels"

(Heb 2:7, DV). They restore to the plotless a sense of true purpose, and redirect the plotting to a hard-won happiness.

16

Reading the Riddle of Human Nature, from Homer to Dostoevsky

Let strife and rancour
perish from the lives of gods and men,
with anger that envenoms even the wise
and is far sweeter than slow-dripping honey,
clouding the hearts of men like smoke. (18, 105-110)

—Homer's Achilles, the *Iliad*

From the trunk of that tree of vengefulness and hatred, Jewish hatred—
the profoundest and sublimest kind of hatred, capable of creating ideals
and reversing values, the like of which has never existed on earth before—
there grew something equally incomparable, a *new love*, the profoundest
and sublimest kind of love—and from what other trunk could it have grown?

—Nietzsche, *Genealogy of Morals*

Early in Dostoevsky's *The Brothers Karamazov*, a "sentimental society lady whose inclinations were in many respects genuinely good" comes to visit the sapient Father Zossima. Over the course of their conversation, the woman proclaims that she "love[s] mankind so much that—would you believe it?—I sometimes dream of giving up all, all I have, of leaving Lise and going to become a sister of mercy. I close my eyes, I think and dream, and in such moments I feel an invincible strength in myself. No wounds . . . could frighten me. I would bind them and cleanse them with my own hands. I would nurse the suffering."

To shake the society lady from her high self-regard, Father Zossima tells her he "heard the same thing, a long time ago to be sure, from a doctor." The doctor confided in Zossima that, though he "love[s] mankind . . . the more I love mankind in general the less I love people in particular, that is, individually, as separate people." The illustrative anecdote of the doctor's dilemma is very much apropos the sentimental society lady, as her daughter Lise's condition as a paralytic requires much of her attention and, in turn, most of her love. Because Lise, the particular person in the society lady's direct proximity, is in one sense an ideal object of love—she is in need, and she is at hand—we must ask why her mother's impulse leads her instead to dream of mankind.

In *Genealogy of Morals*, Nietzsche contends that "the slave revolt in morality begins when *ressentiment* itself becomes creative and gives birth to values." *Ressentiment* comes when a soul confronts some conflict or failure, some impotence or rivalry, and cannot achieve revenge or recognition: unable or unwilling to take action, such souls are poisoned with small-minded fury that remains entirely pent up inside. As Nietzsche puts it, "The *ressentiment* of natures that are denied the true reaction, that of deeds, and compensate themselves with an imaginary revenge." We can rightly wonder to what extent the society lady's "love of mankind" is an "imaginary revenge" upon the demands that her daughter places upon her, a compensation for her incapacity to undertake great deeds. Zossima's judicious rejoinder resounds loudly in a world wherein claims of "global citizenship" foster an idealism that absolves each "citizen of the world" of any particular, immediate, proximate loves. Rallying cries relegate the crippled Lise to the backstage of that theater of global significance and replace her with the imaginary lepers whom we can kiss in dreams doused with love of mankind. Or maybe, influenced inevitably by those "masters of suspicion" Machiavelli, Marx, Nietzsche, and Freud, we are too quick to demystify, to project dubious motives even where none exist. Maybe our suspiciousness is misplaced. The sentimental society lady's "love of mankind" and the "global citizen's" humanitarian love: are these founded on more than mere *ressentiment*? More pressingly, is *ressentiment* any more than the spoiled fruit of Christian morality?

In his prescient early work *Ressentiment,* Max Scheler contends that Nietzsche "wrongly equated the Christian idea of love with a completely different idea which has quite another historical and psychological origin: *the idea and movement of modern universal love of man,* 'humanitarianism,' "love of man kind," or more plastically, "love toward every member of the human race." Scheler makes a crucial distinction: whereas Christian love demands a definite sacrifice, humanitarian love demands contingent "sacrifice" which is ultimately aimed at enhancing the degree of pleasure experienced in a given society. In *Ressentiment,* Scheler suggests that the humanitarian movement is fundamentally a *ressentiment* phenomenon, as is evident "from the very fact that this socio-historical emotion is by no means based on a spontaneous and original *affirmation of positive values,* but on a *protest, a counter-impulse* (hatred, envy, revenge)." Mankind is more of a "trump card" against a hated thing than an *object* of love: "Above all, this love of mankind is the expression of a repressed rejection, of a counter-impulse against God."

Most of Dostoevsky's novels probe the phenomenon of *ressentiment* with vexing acuity and dramatization, yet perhaps none of his works other than the largely neglected *The Adolescent [A Raw Youth]* so directly explores, in novelistic fashion, the interrelationship of *ressentiment* and humanitarian love. At the onset of part II, Versilov, father of the protagonist, Arkady, brings up the "Geneva ideas" which "underlie today's civilization" and which are founded upon the possibility of "virtue without Christ."

In a somewhat contradictory but frank and perceptive moment, he confesses that humans are "vile" but one can do good on their behalf by "clenching your feelings, holding your nose, and shutting your eyes (this last is necessary). Endure evil from them, not getting angry with them if possible, 'remembering that you, too, are a human being.'" As he clarifies, with startling cynicism, "To love one's neighbor and not despise him is impossible. In my opinion, man is created with a physical inability to love his neighbor. There's some mistake in words here, from the very beginning, and 'love for mankind' should be understood as just for that mankind which you yourself have created in your soul (in other words, you've created your own self and the love for yourself), and which therefore will never exist in reality." Versilov's inability to "break through emotionally to others" even in acts that are objectively moral, grows out of the principle of "doing good without Christ." As Nicholas Rzhevsky notes, "The crucial ideological point is the concept that man 'invents himself to love himself,' for this moral-psychological gesture, Versilov suggests, is what is real while abstractions on the order of 'mankind' never 'really existed.' The argument rests on self-involvement and self-imposed morality in which there are no transcendent objects such as God or merger with 'man-kind,'—the process of love symbolized by Christ—but only the vision of man standing completely alone and shaping himself into a superior being."

On the one hand, Rzhevsky enunciates the "self-imposed" character of this morality, which Pierre Manent, in his *A World Beyond Politics?* traces to Kant: "If for Thomas Aquinas human dignity consists in freely obeying the natural and divine law, for Kant it consists in obeying the law that human beings give to themselves." According to the Christian comprehension of human beings, any dignity that exists comes as given—as a gift—from God, for only God is capable of granting them power to follow their own counsel. For Kant, "the difference is both radical and subtle, to be human *is* a dignity."

Nevertheless, though some of Versilov's sentiments share a certain fraternity with Kant, he cannot embrace life according to nothing more than a Kantian "respect" for human "dignity," for he preserves a pseudo-mystical picture of mankind which, he admits, he would "not be able to live without." During a crucial confession to Arkady, Versilov acknowledges his initial hesitation. Won't a world without God unearth horrors heretofore unknown? Chillingly, as a pensive smile passes over his face, his audacity flashes forth: "I imagine to myself" that after the initial mudslinging and cursing that follow the death of God, "a calm has come, and people are left *alone,* as they wished: the great former idea," their source of nourishment and warmth, has left them, and it seems as though the days of mankind are at their end:

> And people suddenly realized that they remained quite alone, and at once felt a great orphancy. My dear boy, I've never been able to imagine people ungrateful and grown stupid. The orphaned people would at once begin pressing together more closely and lovingly; they would hold hands, understanding that they alone were now everything for each other. The great idea of immortality would disappear and would have to be replaced; and all the great abundance of the former love for the one who was himself immortality, would be turned in all of them to nature, to the world, to people, to every blade of grass. They would love the earth and life irrepressibly and in the measure

> to which they gradually became aware of their transient and finite state, and it would be with a special love now, not as formerly. . . . They would wake up and hasten to kiss each other, hurrying to love, conscious that the days were short, and that that was all they had left. They would work for each other, and each would give all he had to everyone, and would be happy in that alone. Every child would know and feel that each person on earth was like a father and mother to him. 'Tomorrow may be my last day,' each of them would think, looking at the setting sun, 'but all the same, though I die, they will all remain, and their children after them'—and this thought that they would remain, loving and trembling for each other in the same way, would replace the thought of a meeting beyond the grave. Oh, they would hasten to love, in order to extinguish the great sadness in their hearts. They would be proud and brave for themselves, but would become timorous for one another. Each would tremble for the life and happiness of each. They would become tender to each other and would not be ashamed of it, as now, and would caress each other like children. Meeting each other, they would exchange deep and meaningful looks, and there would be love and sadness in their eyes.

Although Versilov's fantastic vision of humanitarian love lacks a step by step process by which adherents could consciously bring it about, although it starts in the *aftermath*, and in spite of the fact that (as he himself grants) this dream will never exist in reality, his scheme is more realistic than the many inextricably utopian formulas propounded in the name of that same love of humanity. Further, the realism of humanism, its achievability, is evident in that it is rooted in a *ressentiment,* "by no means based on a spontaneous and original *affirmation of positive values,* but on a *protest, a counter-impulse* (hatred, envy, revenge)" that is founded upon self-love. Remember that for Versilov, love for mankind is love of a fiction that one fosters in the face of wretched, unlovable, concrete man; "'love for mankind' should be understood as just for that mankind which you yourself have created in your soul (in other words, you've created your own self and the love for yourself), and which therefore will never exist in reality." How are we to hold together Versilov's double vision—of an atheistic world wherein love for mankind reigns, and a love self-founded on the premise that 'love for mankind' will never exist *in reality*? Could it be that what we call "love for mankind" is in actuality—through an almost unconscious circuitry—love for oneself?

To honor this line of inquiry, we should first return to Scheler's early analysis of humanitarianism. August Comte, the leading spokesperson of modern humanitarianism and inventor of the term "altruism," takes offense at Christ's command that one "love God and thy neighbor as thyself." Christianity, he claims, nourishes egotistic impulses in that it commands each individual to care for his *own* salvation. Comte therefore wants to replace this ancient precept by a "new positivistic commandment: 'Love thy neighbor *more* than thyself.'" Scheler is right: Comte "fails to note that it is incomprehensible why our fellow man should have a right to benefaction—since love, for Comte, has value only as a 'cause' for good deeds—for the silliest of reasons: simply because he is the 'other': If I myself am not worthy of love, why should the '*other*' be?" Mincing no words, Scheler roundly critiques Comte's sophistry, for "his tenet is either a hyperbolical pathetic phrase or a nihilistic demand which destroys all vitality and indeed decomposes any structure of being!"

The sensuous, undiscriminating "sympathy for the 'other'—and mainly for his 'suffering'—merely because he is not oneself is a highly leveling and decomposing principle for human life, despite its express purpose of 'strengthening life.'" This decline in the value of life, this "modern humanitarianism" bestows upon love no more than a technical value, as its aim does not stretch beyond 'improvement' of the general welfare. This transvaluation of love, Scheler claims, is truly a slave revolt in morality, "Not a revolt of the slaves, but of the slavish values." That being said, in concrete historical practice, modern humanitarian love and Christian love are now tangled together, a fact that explains Nietzsche's mistake. Many self-proclaimed Christians, for instance, love and think of love like humanitarians.

In "The Empire of Morality," Pierre Manent takes up the task of further distinguishing the different versions of humanitarianism and Christian love of neighbor. Christian love is never aimed at the neighbor in-and-of-herself, but at the *Imago Dei* that is found in every human being. "Nietzsche, though furiously anti-Christian, nonetheless says that to love the neighbor for the love of God is the most refined moral sentiment attained by human beings." Manent helps us distinguish humanitarianism from Christian love in part through a linguistic analysis, for the foundation of humanitarianism is not *caritas* as much as it is *compassion,* or pity, in the modern liberal sense. The capacity for pity is universal because all human beings have a body that is subject to the strong possibility of suffering; human beings are *objects* of suffering. Further, because of the universality of suffering, human beings are also *subjects* of suffering, as Manent notes: "Physical suffering is immediately grasped or imagined. One sympathizes with a toothache, a nervous colic, and two days without eating or drinking more easily than with a moral humiliation, an intellectual preoccupation, or a spiritual anguish. In short, because physical pity is rooted in the senses, we communicate immediately with the other, without the mediation of complex ideas. Pity can be relied on to bind people because it is a sentiment, an affect, or a disposition that does not demand any moral transformation or transcendence of self."

The visible suffering of an "other" says to me, "You too could undergo this," and therefore I make an effort to assuage his suffering. But, in fact, I do not experience this suffering that I perceive so vividly. "I know well that I do not effectively experience it and so I rejoice that I am exempt from it. I experience the pleasure of *not* suffering. Therefore, there is nothing idealistic or utopian in pity as the foundation of social morality."

For Rousseau, if modern mankind is to transcend the isolation and individualism that comprise its ethos and essence, she must cultivate compassion. Once again, we return to the center of this analysis, and at last see how near Versilov's "Geneva ideas," his "virtue without Christ" are to those of Rousseau, that citizen of Geneva: 'love for mankind' should be understood as just for that mankind which you yourself have created in your soul (in other words, you've created your own self and the love for yourself), and which therefore will never exist in reality." What at first seems self-sacrificial is revealed as self-love. As Manent maintains, altruistic pity is morally economical, demanding very little from mankind: "There is nothing in pity that is heroic, since its wellspring is the selfishness of each person. Rousseau was giving us the blueprint that has effectively prevailed in liberal democratic society."

The *other*, whom Comte commanded that we love more than our own selves, is the *pitiable* other, *pitiable* to the extent that she become a self that I have created or abstracted in order to experience the pleasure of pitying. Humanitarian logic is the logic of compassion, and compassion "reduced to itself has two effects. The first, says Manent, is the desire to come to the aid of the suffering and even to risk 'dying for Pristina'; but the second is altogether different, and in the contrary. By turning the attention toward the suffering body, compassion quickens in each of us the desire not to suffer and not to die."

Standing alone at the center of the modern humanitarian empire, compassion offers no satisfactory order, law, or aims. Certainly, in Versilov's rendering, these humanitarians "hasten to love, in order to extinguish the great sadness in their hearts," to, in a slightly different manner than Manent describes, "experience the pleasure of not suffering." Versilov's metamorphosis of love is shocking: *caritas,* that highest of Christian ideals, has morphed into self-interested self-love. All souls, Versilov says, are "left *alone,* as they wished: the great former idea has left them," and all at once the people suddenly feel a "great orphancy," which drives them to begin "pressing together more closely and lovingly." Scheler shows that this "loving" reduction of man to a wholly "*natural being*" is the "*second* step" after the phenomenon of *ressentiment* against "God," against the symbolic concentration of all positive values. "Man is loved because his pain, his ills and sufferings in themselves form a gladly accepted objection against God's 'wise and benevolent rule.'" Scheler notes that wherever he finds evidence of this feeling, he also discerns a secret delight that the divine lordship can be challenged.

Because the roots of humanitarian compassion lie in *ressentiment,* because it is first and foremost a protest against the divine and natural laws, against the mandate that one should love the *Imago Dei* in one's fellow man, it "becomes primarily directed at the *lowest*, the *animal* aspects of human nature, those qualities which "'all' men have in common." We can now configure a common thread of *ressentiment* tying Versilov—who depicts humanitarian "love" as extending to nature ("they would look at nature with new eyes, the eyes with which a lover looks at his beloved")—to Rousseau. For Rousseau, *pity* or *compassion*, unlike the *caritas* of Christianity, is freed from religious doctrines; it cannot lead to separatism. And yet, Manent observes, "the physical pity that Rousseau preaches certainly preserves humanity, since humanity is partly animal, but it tends to weaken the consciousness and sentiment of what is specifically human."

Rousseau's "Geneva ideas" are massively influential, but they by no means contain an exhaustive exemplification of man's attempt to love humankind without Christ. As Max Scheler admits in his later work *The Nature of Sympathy*, "It must be admitted that our treatment [of humanitarianism in *Ressentiment*] goes too far at a number of points." Specifically, he takes issue with his previous attempt to portray a humanism worked up exclusively from *resseniment*-laced rebellion against both patriotism and the Christian command to love one's neighbor as one's self. In *The Nature of Sympathy*, Scheler maintains that the *idea* of humanitarian love has often been "*employed* polemically in this fashion, from motives of ill will," and he further insists that the elevation of love of mankind over patriotism and Christian love of God, the preferential option for the "extremities above what lies nearest the heart, is entirely due to that ill-feeling working itself out." To try and state succinctly Scheler's revised judgment: modern humanitarianism is defined by an "*exaggeration* of the value of benevolence which proceeds from *ressentiment*." The pivotal point of Scheler's reconfiguration is that humanitarian love, what he renames "benevolence," is an inherent possibility in man's intrinsic nature; while it is distinct from Christian *caritas*, and may at times be reactionary, humanitarian love is *positive* in its origin and value. Further, its historical iterations exist beyond Rousseau and his Geneva ideas: "it is to be found in the *humanitas* of earlier antiquity, Stoic and Epicurean schools . . . in the intellectual history of the Chinese, with the spread of Laotse's teaching from South China and its amalgamation with Buddhism; and once again in the modern sentimentally-based democracies of the nineteenth and twentieth centuries."

Just as Scheler reevaluated humanitarian love in order to articulate the senses in which it is not *ressentiment*-ridden, Dostoevsky, too, seems to have broadened his brush in *The Brothers Karamazov*. The nihilistic Versilov can claim that "'love for mankind' should be understood as just for that mankind which you yourself have created in your soul." But exotic extremists such as Versilov are not the only ones who utter humanitarian sentiments. We recall the "sentimental society lady" who, early in *The Brothers Karamazov*, visits Father Zossima, her "inclinations . . . in many respects genuinely good." What are these good inclinations? After all, one could easily read *ressentiment* at the root of her desire to leave Lise and become a sister of mercy, to nurse the suffering and kiss their sores. Aren't these fantasies born of the restrictions which her crippled daughter places on her freedom? For hers is a love that must be borne out in quiet, domestic suffering. Hers is a love that receives no lauds. However, instead of first reading *ressentiment* in her desire, Zossima responds by saying that "it's already a great deal and very well for you that you dream of that in your mind and not of something else. Once in a while, by chance, you may really do some good deed."

Only later does he offer his oft-quoted diagnosis of love in action as "a harsh and fearful thing compared with love in dreams." In the wake of Scheler's reassessment of *ressentiment* and Zossima's judicious, merciful response to the society lady, we can carve out new origins and manifestations of the love of mankind, origins and manifestations not relegated to *ressentiment.* That said, being freed from the law of *ressentiment* is not the same as being freed from the problem of *ressentiment.* For even if, historically, general benevolence can be traced to the Stoic, Cynic, and Epicurian schools, the teachings of Laotse, and even if benevolent love of humanity is an emotion that is intrinsic to man's nature and positive in origin, we live in an ideological age, and "hatred for the divine, hatred for man's spiritual personality and its potential perfection, hatred of one's country and one's neighbor are thus transformed into an ideology," namely, the globalized ideology of global citizenship. While benevolence has not disappeared from the face of the earth, how do we reckon with the likelihood that it will morph into *ressentiment*-ridden humanitarian "love"?

We still find ourselves staring from a precarious pinnacle of thought into the aporia of humanitarian "love" / compassion / pity. How long can we, in good faith, dream Versilov's dream? What sober soul can cleave to the reactionary chatter calling for a return to some Romanticized Christendom? Remember Scheler's insistence that though Nietzsche correctly diagnosed *ressentiment*-ridden benevolence as the major character trait of the modern humanitarian man, he did violence by laying the blame at Christ's beatitudes. Perhaps we can follow Nietzsche's impulse to turn toward the pre-Socratic Greeks, particularly Homer, in an attempt to locate the forces and framework of a world freed from *ressentiment.* In doing so, however, we must remain wary of Nietzsche's own oversimplification of

Greek vitality. Yes, a certain Greek strand countenanced the cruel, chaotic, and irrational world while also (to cite Peter Ahrensdorf) lovingly affirming "the infinite primordial joy of existence." But Greekness was as wily as Odysseus, and not without its own *ressentiments*.

In *Genealogy of Morals*, Nietzsche puts forth his portrait of the "noble" or "Greek" man: "Such a man shakes off with a *single* shrug much vermin that eats deep into others; here alone genuine 'love of one's enemies' is possible—supposing it to be possible at all on earth. How much reverence has a noble man for his enemies!—and such reverence is a bridge to love." Unlike the man of *ressentiment*, who moralizes his weakness into a protective value system and subsequently regards the enemy as "*the evil enemy*," the noble man can endure only that enemy "in whom there is nothing to despise and very much to honor."

Nietzsche situates *ressentiment*, the crowning fruit of Judeo-Christian morality, as opposed to the Greek nobility. He argues that unlike the Christian, who claims to seek not retaliation but "the triumph of *justice*" through the "victory of God, of the *just* God," the Greek relishes and holds in high regard the hope of retribution, the "intoxication of sweet revenge ('sweeter than honey,' Homer called it)." And yet, as Henry Staten makes clear, "nothing could be more indicative of the idealizing falsification of the idea of the 'noble Greek' in which Nietzsche engages, than his attendant quotation of Homer as an antithesis to the dishonest and therefore poisonous vengefulness of the slave mentality." Nietzsche crystallizes his idealization of Homeric

"Greekness" and pessimistic Christianity in the following passage:

> Let me declare expressly that in the days when mankind was not yet ashamed of its cruelty, life on earth was more cheerful than it is now that pessimists exist. The darkening of the sky above mankind has deepened in step with the increase of man's feeling of shame *at man*. . . . On his way to becoming an "angel" . . . man has evolved that queasy stomach and coated tongue through which . . . the joy and innocence of the animal has become repugnant to him. . . . Today, when suffering is always brought forward as the principal argument *against* existence . . . one does well to recall the ages in which the opposite opinion prevailed because men were unwilling to refrain from *making* men suffer and saw it as an enchantment of the first order, a genuine seduction *to* life. . . . It is certain, at any rate, that the *Greeks* still knew of no tastier spice to offer their gods . . . than the pleasures of cruelty.

But does Nietzsche not profoundly misread Homer's presentation of these tastiest spices, of cruelty's "pleasures," this "intoxication of sweet revenge"? For, as Staten illuminates, the very phrase "sweeter than honey," located near the end of *The Iliad* (in book XVIII), is tied not to the satisfaction of unleashed vengefulness, but, rather the dripping poison of a vengeful anger that is never satisfied and ends in Achilles's destruction. Mourning the death of Patroclus at the hands of Hector, Achilles admits that his impotence, his dwelling apart in his tent, is powerful proof that he has been poisoned by *ressentiment:*

> Here I sat/
> my weight a useless burden to the earth,
> and I am one who has no peer in war
> among Achaean captains—though in council
> there are wiser. Ai! Let strife and rancour
> perish from the lives of gods and men,
> with anger that envenoms even the wise
> and is far sweeter than slow-dripping honey,
> clouding the hearts of men like smoke

Achilles, no stranger to anger's obfuscations, prays for the eradication of rancor. He is not shameless, here, championing the wrath that has authored so much ruin. Nietzsche's nostalgic account of ancient heroism falsifies the very heart of Homer's poem, articulated at its genesis: "Anger be now your song, immortal one, / Achilles' anger, doomed and ruinous, that caused the Achaeans loss on bitter loss / and crowded brave souls into the undergloom, / leaving so many dead men—carrion / for dogs and birds." Scheler describes *ressentiment* as a "self-poisoning of the mind which has quite definite consequences. It is a lasting mental attitude, caused by the systematic repression of certain emotions and affects which, as such, are normal components of human nature. Their repression leads to the constant tendency to indulge in certain kinds of value delusions and corresponding value judgments." More than any other emotion, the *ressentiment* phenomenon is connected to hatred, revenge, malice, envy, spite, and the impulse to detract.

The quarrel that commences *The Iliad* is famous. A plague brings many pains to the Acheans. Calchas, the seer, spells out the cause. Chryseis, Agamemnon's war prize, is the child of Chryses, priest of Apollo. Sympathetic to the bereaved father's prayers, Apollo is laying the Achaeans low. Feigning a great soul, Agamemnon swears he will return Chryses. In turn, however, he demands a replacement from among his own men. His mind smoked with fury, he demands Briseis, Achilles's own war-prize. Indeed, Agamemnon faces Achilles forthrightly. He will call for Briseis at the great warrior's hut, "and taker her, / flower of young girls that she is, your prize, / to show you here and now who is the stronger / and make the next man sick at heart—if any / think of claiming equal place with me."

What happens next is of utmost importance for our investigation. Homer tells us that a "pain like grief weighed on the son of Peleus, / and in his shaggy chest this way and that / the passion of his heart ran: should he draw / long-sword from his hip, stand off the rest, and kill / in single combat the great son of Atreus / or hold his rage in check and give it time?" Athena appears, visible to no one but Achilles: "this time, and soon, / he pays for his behaviour with blood," the grey-eyed goddess tells him. "It was to check this killing rage I came / from heaven, if you will listen . . . break off this combat / stay your hand upon the sword hilt. Let him have a lashing / with words, instead: tell him how things will be." Achilles obeys, noting that when immortals speak, man complies, "though his heart burst." Of course, he does conduct a verbal lashing, calling Agamemnon a "sack of wine" with "cur's eyes" and an "antelope heart," and telling the cowardly king that he will suffer remorse for this dishonor. Achilles may vent his spleen, but this verbal valve opening is no real revenge, no catharsis for the rage stirred by his suffering.

In *Genealogy of Morals*, Nietzsche himself observes that "neither for the Christian, who has interpreted a whole mysterious machinery of salvation into suffering, nor for the naïve man of more ancient times, who understood all suffering in relation to the spectator of it or the causer of it, was there any such thing as *senseless* suffering." In order to abolish undetected, unwitnessed suffering, and furthermore to *deny* it, man was compelled to invent gods, which allowed life to "work the trick which it has always known how to work, that of justifying itself, of justifying its 'evil'."

The above instance from *The Iliad* illustrates the insufficiency of Nietzsche's analysis. Athena's appearance and instruction justifies not Achilles's *evil* or his embrace of "life-forces," but his *ressentiment.* She gives his mind-poisoning inaction divine sanction, which in turn represses his rage absolutely, and which gives birth to various "value-delusions." I would like to propose that Achilles (or, from another angle, Homer) invents this visit from Athena, and in so doing we see that *ressentiment*—rather than being the crowning "virtue" of a Christian slave morality, rather than being heretofore unknown before modern humanitarian love—transforms slavishness into virtuous submission in the Western world's oldest poem. But *The Iliad* does not glorify Achilles's resentful wrath. Rather, as Staten postulates, "we recognize in Homer's story of Achilles both levels of the economics of ressentiment described by Nietzsche, the empirical level at which Achilles suffers an actual injury for which he demands compensation and, behind this, the transcendental level at which the injury of time—Achilles' death sentence, sealed at birth, is ultimately the cause of his resentfulness." As accurate as Staten's reading is, we need to reiterate the importance of Athena's sanctioning. From the vantage point of our *allegation* against the Achilles-Athena alliance, her command runs circles around Nietzsche's idealizations. Achilles wished to take vengeance. Instead, mandated by a goddess to pathetic inaction, his soul is poisoned by ruinous wrath. The Christian God bids us to "turn the other cheek." Of course he does, Nietzsche scoffs. Whoever invented him was incapable of having his vengeance, and so he clothed his own impotence with divine sanction. But Athena's prevention of vengeance precedes Christ's appearance by hundreds and hundreds of years.

The affinity between *The Iliad* and the Gospels as texts tied to *ressentiment* does not end here; it is precisely the further affinities that will allow us to war with Nietzsche's allegations. We must return to Nietzsche's contention concerning the roots of *ressentiment:* "From the trunk of that tree of vengefulness and hatred, Jewish hatred—the profoundest and sublimest kind of hatred, capable of creating ideals and reversing values, the like of which has never existed on earth before—there grew something equally incomparable, a *new love*, the profoundest and sublimest kind of love—and from what other trunk could it have grown? . . . This Jesus of Nazareth, as the living Gospel of Love, this "Savior" who brought bliss and victory to the poor, the sick, the sinners—did he not represent seduction in its most sinister and most irresistible form?"

If this be so, if Christ's love comes not as the antithesis of, but as the crown of "Jewish" hatred, then it simultaneously serves as the crown of Greek hatred. For, as Simone Weil explains in her essay "The Iliad, Or the Poem of Force":

> But the purest triumph of love, the crowning grace of war, is the friendship that floods the hearts of mortal enemies. Before it a murdered son or a murdered friend no longer cries out for vengeance. Before it—even more miraculous—the distance between benefactor and suppliant, between victor and vanquished, shrinks to nothing: *But when thirst and hunger had been appeased,/ The Dardanian Priam fell to admiring Achilles./ How tall he was, and handsome; he had the face of a god; And in his turn Dardanian Priam was admired by/ Achilles,/ Who watched his handsome face and listened to his words. And when they were satisfied with contemplation of each other...*"

How can we fail to find here the same spiritual force that allowed the "Greeks, generally speaking, to avoid self-deception"? The fruits of such frankness were great: "they discovered how to achieve in all their acts the greatest lucidity, purity, and simplicity," fruits of a spiritual force that, for Weil, is "transmitted from *The Iliad* to the Gospels by way of the tragic poets." Whether there is textual or anthropological evidence for this spiritual transference is, for this present examination, inconsequential. It is enough that forgiveness and love of enemy emerge as more than reactions of slaves—as so much more than the twisted sublimation of *ressentiment.*

In "Priam and Achilles Break Bread," Rachel Bespaloff remarks on the majestic moment when Priam visits Achilles to reclaim his son's dead body. Priam exhorts Achilles to remember his own father "and take pity on me. I am far more pitiable than he, for I have endured what no other mortal on earth has, to put to my mouth the hand of a man who has killed my sons." Bespaloff asserts that this speech lacks all vehemence, that this absurd errand he shoulders has nothing base about it, as it is "equal to the love that sustains him." Suddenly we see Achilles emerging as his own victim, at least as much as Priam's sons were. Achilles the conqueror is "struck dumb; he seems to come to himself and be cured of his frenzy." "Hatred is disconcerted and relents. The two adversaries can exchange looks without seeing each other as targets, as objects which there is merit in destroying." Achilles invites Priam to "come now, sit upon a seat, and let sorrows rest in our minds, in spite of our pain. Chill grief is profitless." Although he is remorseless, Achilles is, in Bespaloff's words, "overwhelmed by compassion," to the point that he comforts and praises Priam. After Hector's body is anointed with oil, Achilles weeps, then breaks bread with Priam. Afterward, as though the bread were almost a type of the Eucharist, we behold what Bespaloff calls a "premise of truth, where *forgetfulness of an offense* in the contemplation of the eternal is made possible (pardon for an offense being unknown to the ancient world)." Bespaloff posits Priam as the poem's dominant character, the poet's delegate, the one who "typifies the watcher of tragedy, the man who sees it all, more completely and more truly than Zeus on Mount Ida because he is also a sufferer in the drama he is witnessing. Thanks to him, the prestige of weakness triumphs momentarily over the prestige of force. When he admires the enemy who is crushing him and justifies the stranger whose presence is the ruin of his city, the old man gives absolution to life in its totality."

The Iliad, then, is as much the poem of Priam's *forgetfulness of offense,* his absolution, as it is of Achilles's rancor, regardless of the disproportion in lines devoted to each of them respectively, for, as Scheler notes, in terms of authentic "Christian" love, what matters is not a maximum amount humanitarian welfare, but "a *maximum of love* among men." And Priam's presence before Achilles, though it be no container of pardon or forgiveness per se, certainly incarnates central characteristics of Christian love. For what could be more miraculous—albeit more subject to Nietzsche's critique—than Luke 6:27–29: "Love your enemies, do good to them that hate you. Bless them that curse you, and pray for them that calumniate you." Scheler is adamantly against Nietzsche on this point, for this precept of "love your enemies" demands more than the mere passivity "which is only 'justified' by the inability to seek revenge. . . . Nor do they seek to shame the enemy in secret vengefulness, or indicate a hidden self-torment which satisfies itself through paradoxical behavior. These precepts demand extreme activity against the natural instincts which push us in the opposite direction."

Remember Versilov, the post-Christian humanitarian, armed with his admission that humans are "vile."

Dostoevsky's novelistic creature exemplifies hidden self-torment and the secret vengefulness when he indicates that one can do good on others' behalves only by "clenching your feelings, holding your nose, and shutting your eyes (this last is necessary). Endure evil from them, not getting angry with them if possible, 'remembering that you, too, are a human being.'" For Weil and Bespaloff, Priam, the pre-Christian Greek, incarnates something like love even to the man who murdered his son. Entering the enemy's tent, Priam exemplifies the sort of strenuous reformation of the natural instincts which Christ demands. When the prestige of weakness triumphs momentarily over the prestige of force, he defeats both *ressentiment* and rage.

Let me be clear: Priam's heroic presence in the tent of Achilles is not synonymous with Christian love, which remakes and transfigures us through sanctifying grace. However, as the lives of the saints and Priam's treatment of Achilles make clear, there is something heroic about *caritas* and its pagan precedents, a substantive force which humanitarian compassion cannot replace. Christ does not forbid his followers from having enemies; he does not command that the distinctions of "friend" and "enemy" disappear from the face of the earth. But he does demand a level of heroism that we can justly call excellence. Not the heroism of Achilles, or Agamemnon, but the heroism of Priam. The Trojan father does not revere the "other" merely because he is the "other," for Achilles is not a blank-signifying "other" but the man who killed his son. There is no trace of humanitarian "benevolence" in Priam's deep affinity with his enemy. There is "nothing [in benevolence] that is heroic since its wellspring is the selfishness of each person," and, furthermore, because the pity humanitarianism demands is too general. Such sentimentality cannot muster the moral strength which is necessary if we are to forget our enemies' wrongdoings or grant them real forgiveness.

Not the authentic and positive capacity for *humanitas* but the *ideology* of the "new humanitarian empire" is the Achilles's heel of our age, driven, like his festering rage, by the phenomenon of *ressentiment.* As Pierre Manent warns, it is a question of *moral* weakness. Put simply, "in humanitarian action, *one does not know what one is doing.*" This is so in spite of the fact that nothing is clearer and more defined than the purpose of humanitarian action, built as it is on humanitarian compassion, that plastic simulacrum of Christian love: "to save lives, to end violence . . ." But in the name of humanitarian intervention, in the name of reducing human suffering through compassionate missions, "anyone is authorized to do anything whatsoever." To be even more blunt, "the humanitarian demand is a real demand, but one should not ignore that, left to its logic alone, it means the war of all against all," the condition of the state of nature. For in the state of nature, "everyone is authorized to judge and to punish violations of the law of nature, and that leads to the war of all against all." And when natural benevolence begins to wane, what humanitarian aid can replace it?

This harsh truth of humanitarianism now established, it may not seem so ironic, so idiotic, so Quixotic, to look to *The Iliad* in order to learn how to revere "the other," and "the enemy" in the time that remains—in this span that precedes that true and only paradise, where mankind will learn war no more. We, inhabitants of that most subtle humanitarian empire, can hold ourselves above *The Iliad's* impact, like those dreamers who "considered that force, thanks to progress, would soon be a thing of the past," or we can join those others "whose powers of recognition are more acute and who perceive force, today as yesterday, at the very center of human history," for whom "the *Iliad* is the purest and the loveliest of mirrors." For if Heraclitus is in part right that "war is the father of all and king of all, who manifests some as gods and some as men, who makes some slaves and some freemen," it is equally true that "Love is the father of all and king of all, who manifests God as man, who sifts rancor's slaves from the freemen."

And yet, as Pierre Manent argues with great acuity and persuasive acumen in his *Metamorphoses of the City*, "the ending of the *Iliad* is extraordinarily powerful emotionally, but it also has a complex and precise design. One must not lose sight of this complexity and precision by giving way to emotion, by giving the last two books, particularly the last, a sentimental interpretation." If, therefore, we are to turn again to the *Iliad*, to learn again from it, we must resist all sentimental lenses. Priam's visit to Achilles, Achilles's willingness to let Priam return his son's corpse to Troy for proper burial rites, these events, Manent contends, "have nothing to do with the hitherto irreconcilable enemies discovering their common humanity in a flow of emotion that envelops the reader or hearer." Although Achilles has taken Priam under his protection, the Achean's anger could be rekindled by the slightest offense; he himself says as much. Achilles *is* altered in that "he is able to keep his wrath at bay and be motivated by something else," that something being neither "compassion or humanity . . . even if keeping his wrath under control allows for deeds and actions that among us would reveal compassion and humanity." What has changed, then? Manent points to Achilles's increased awareness of his own mortality, and by extension the mortality of all men. After all, Achilles at first failed to recognize Hector's mortality. He dragged his corpse around the city, senselessly "killing" him again and again. He rejects the reality of his enemy's death. As Manent concludes, "It is only when one recognizes the honor due to all corpses, including those of the enemies," that one has completed "his education in humanity."

Manent's words are meant as cautionary. He wishes us to be more restrained in our reading of *The Iliad* than was Simone Weil, for whom the *Iliad* demonstrates that "the purest triumph of love" when, as "the crowning grace of war . . . friendship . . . floods the hearts of mortal enemies." Still, perceptive as Manent's analysis is, effective as it is in counterpoint to Simone Weil's idealization of an enemy's *humanity,* we have reason to pause before any impulse to return to the primordial shores of Western Civilization in our search for our *humanitas* that is not riddled with *ressentiment.* It is easier for an Achilles to act without rage than it is for a modern to reclaiming "noble Greekness" without bringing his humanitarian *ressentiment* with him.

Our chastening comes via Versilov, when, in *The Adolescent [A Raw Youth]*, he recounts before Arcady a strange dream:

In Dresden, in the gallery, there's a painting by Claude Lorrain—*Acis and Galatea* according to the catalog, but I've always called it *The Golden Age,* I don't know why myself. I had seen it before, and then, some three days earlier, I had noticed it once again in passing. I saw this painting in my dream, but not as a painting, but as if it were something happening. However, I don't know precisely what I dreamed; it was exactly as in the painting—a corner of the Greek archipelago, and time, too, seemed to have shifted back three thousand years; gentle blue waves, islands, and rocks, a flowering coast, a magic panorama in the distance, the inviting, setting sun—words can't express it. Here European mankind remembered its cradle, and the thought of it seemed to fill my soul with a kindred love. This was the earthly paradise of mankind: the gods came down from heaven and were united with people.... Oh, beautiful people lived here! They woke up and fell asleep, happy and innocent; the meadows and groves were filled with their songs and merry shouts; a great surplus of untouched forces went into love and simple-hearted joy. The sun poured down warmth and light on them, rejoicing over its beautiful children.... A wonderful reverie, a lofty delusion of mankind! The golden age—the most incredible dream of all that have ever been, but for which people have given all their lives and their strength, for which prophets have died and been slain, without which the people do not want to live and cannot even die. And it was as if I lived through this whole feeling in my

> dream; the cliffs and the sea and the slanting rays of the setting sun—it was as if I could still see it all when I woke up and opened my eyes, literally wet with tears. I remember that I was glad. A feeling of happiness unknown to me before went through my heart, even to the point of pain; this was an all-human love."

This tantalizing dream recurs in "At Tikhon's," a suppressed chapter of Dostoevsky's later novel *Demons*, the nihilistic Stavrogin confesses to the bishop Tikhon that he raped his landlady Matryosha's daughter, and that near the end of the rape, "a most strange thing happened, something I shall never forget, something that quite amazed me: the little girl flung her arms round my neck and all of a sudden began to kiss me frenziedly" with a face filled with rapture. After several delirious nights, during which the girl repeats the phrase, "I killed God," she encounters Stavrogin again and "suddenly she raised her tiny fist and began shaking it at me from where she stood."

This act of despair first seems to sadden Stavrogin, but then he finds himself cheerful, and not depressed, at which point he "formulated for the first time in my life what appeared to be the rule of my life, that I neither know nor feel good nor evil and that I have not only lost any sense of it, but that there is neither good nor evil (which pleased me) and that it is just prejudice: that I can be free from any prejudice, but that once I attain that degree of freedom I am done for."

During the same confession, Stavrogin waxes wistful about none other than Claude Lorrain's "Acis and Galatea," the same painting that spurs Versilov's utopian dream of purely humanitarian love. Stavrogin's words match Versilov's with a startling exaction. At the end of his exposition on the humanitarian "Golden Age," however, Stavrogin recounts the fact that this dream morphed into a vision of "Matryosha [the girl he raped], wasted and with feverish eyes, exactly the same as when she had stood on my threshold and, shaking her head, had raised her tiny little fist at me."

After Stavrogin raped Matryosha, and after she cried out "I killed God" several nights in a row, Matryosha committed suicide. This act of despair first seems to effect Stavrogin, but then he finds himself cheerful, and not depressed, at which point, as noted earlier, he can be rid of all prejudice, can shed the categories of good and evil even though, once he is completely freed, he will fall into despair.

Dostoevsky dramatizes something far more profound than a mere moralistic warning. In putting the same "Golden Age" dream of a utopian "love of mankind" in the mouths of both Stavrogin and Versilov, he confirms Max Scheler's revised contention that "love of mankind" can be born of both a *positive* intrinsic human impulse and a sick *ressentiment.* Stavrogin's "Acis and Galatea" seems a clear cover for his own depraved deed. Versilov, though susceptible to nihilism, is no Stavrogin. His son Arkady sees an authentic love in him. And yet, as George A. Panichas argues in *Burden of Vision*, "inherent in Versilov's vision of a 'humanistic utopia' is a profound sorrow. . . . It is the humanistic ideologue who is speaking here of his Idea, of the thought without which he could not have lived, as he confesses. Dostoevsky's insight into the illusion of humanism is piercing and prophetic. Can there be love without God?" Versilov desperately desires to answer this question with a *yes*, but ultimately he cannot: "at the very heart of Versilov's vision of felicity one finds the spiritual emptiness that no humanist ideologue can permanently dispel; Versilov's greatest virtue is an uncorrupted sincerity, the secularist's limitive counterpart to grace."

Stavrogin's story contains uncanny similarities to Nietzsche's "The Madman" parable, even as it does not perfectly match it. After he rapes the girl, she most disturbingly cries out, "I killed God" repeatedly. She seems to take upon herself the experiences of guilt and shame, consequences of a sense of good and evil, that Stavrogin lacks. In Nietzsche's parable, the madman runs into the marketplace seeking God, only to be mocked and laughed at, for "God is dead! God will stay dead!" (*Gay Science* 95-96). God has bled to death under man's knives, and there is no consolation for the "murderers of all murderers" (96). The men of the parable ask themselves, "Must we not ourselves become gods just to seem worthy of it? There has never been a greater deed; and whoever is born after us will, because of this act, belong to a higher history than all previous history" (96).

Although it is the girl, and not Stavrogin, who cries, "I killed God," Stavrogin's response to the deed echoes the men of the marketplace. He says that, *for the first time in his life,* after he rapes the girl, he formulated the fact that "I neither know nor feel good nor evil and that I have not only lost any sense of it, but that there is neither good nor evil (which pleased me) and that it is just prejudice," and that, having attained that degree of freedom, he is done for.

Manent warns that the problem of humanitarian love is a problem of *moral* weakness: "in humanitarian action," which is founded upon benevolence and modern compassion, "*one does not know what one is doing.*" This is so in spite of the fact that nothing is clearer and more defined than the purpose of humanitarian action, built as it is on humanitarian compassion, that doppelgänger of Christian love: "to save lives, to end violence . . ." But in the name of humanitarian intervention, in the name of reducing human suffering through compassionate missions, "anyone is authorized to do anything whatsoever." This description eerily describes Stavrogin's position beyond good and evil.

In "A Memoir of Mary Anne," Flannery O'Connor writes that "in the absence of faith now, we govern by tenderness. It is a tenderness which, long since cut off from the person of Christ, is wrapped in theory. When tenderness is detached from the source of tenderness, its logical outcome is terror. It ends in forced labor camps and the fumes of the gas chamber." We can say the same of any humanitarian love in dreams. However *positive* its origins, when such a love latches onto a humanitarian ideology cut off from the source of tenderness, its logical outcome is the destruction and depravation of human *being* in the name of the globalized pseudo-conscience that is humanitarian compassion.

Part IV

READING CATHOLIC FICTIONS

17

The Problem of Pity: Misguided Mercy & Dante's Infernal Purgation

I, one man alone,
Prepared myself to face the double war
Of the journey and the pity.

—Dante, *Inferno,* Canto II

It is a pity that compassion has conquered our public conversations, our churches, and our hearts. (In this chapter, I will at times use the words "compassion," "pity," and "mercy," even as I make necessary distinctions along the way.) Occasions for pity proliferate to the point that many of us experience what the protagonist of David Lodge's novel *Therapy* calls "compassion fatigue," which is "the idea that we get so much human suffering thrust in our faces everyday from the media that we've become sort of numbed, we've used up all our reserves of pity, anger, outrage, and can only think of the pain in our own knee." Alongside "compassion fatigue," others are plagued by misconstrued mercy, misplaced pity, and an abundance of attendant errors; those who advocate misguided compassion often dignify their bad counsel by calling it "pastoral."

The problem of pity, already addressed at length in the prior chapter, brings to the fore our need to discriminate between poisonous pity and virtuous pity. Poisonous pity strives to persuade us that the emotional response that others elicit ought to be the lodestar of our ethical lives. Virtuous pity, or what Thomas Aquinas calls *misericordia*, is married to justice, regulated by reason, and driven by doctrine. Dante teaches us this necessary discrimination dramatically. In order to be cured of our pitiful plague of compassion, we must pass through *The Inferno,* putting ourselves under the tutelage of Virgil and Dante, and, more to the point, we must learn to measure our mercy against the just mercy of God.

In Canto V of *The Inferno,* in the circle of the carnal, Dante meets the famed Paolo and Francesca; in consequence of their illicit affair, these lovers glide through hell's whirl like grotesque mating doves. Seeing Dante, Francesca immediately recognizes his pity—and she pounces on it, telling her own "piteous tale." Anticipating his question as to how they ended up in the inferno, she three times proclaims that *love* led them there. Having read the rhyme of Lancelot, she and Paolo, "alone with innocence and dim time," lost custody of their eyes until they could hardly read further, and "one soft passage overthrew" their caution and their hearts. As she tells this tale, "out of pity," she says, even though it will make her weep, Paolo stands by her side, himself crying "so piteously," Dante writes, that "I felt my senses reel / and faint away with anguish." He swoons, falling as a corpse might to hell's floor.

As he begins his descent into the inferno, Dante prepares himself "to face the double war / of the journey and pity." In other words, taking up the metaphor of war Dante himself gives us, pity is, in a certain sense, *the enemy.* As such, it would seem that our aim must be to conquer or banish it. However, as we will see, it is possible to win this war by pressing pity into the service of the highest faculties God has given us. But before we take a look at the way pity plays out in *The Inferno,* it will be necessary to parse out several of its types, its perils, and its conditional goodness.

Let's return for a moment to *A World Beyond Politics?*, in which Manent takes up the task of distinguishing between the different versions of humanism and humanitarianism, in large part to demonstrate their indebtedness to—and incompatibility with—Christian love of neighbor. Manent unveils the paucity and fragility of modern humanism's moral foundations. For Jean-Jacques Rousseau, one of the fathers of this humanism, pity is a moral sentiment that is able to unify human beings in a world witnessing the death of the common good. This bears repeating, as the lack of clarity in this regard is a cause of countless errors: Christian love is never aimed at the neighbor in and of himself, but at the *imago Dei* that is found in every human being. Humanitarian pity, on the contrary, is tethered solely to our all-too-human selves, and is morally economical: whereas the cardinal and theological virtues demand significant moral and spiritual ardor, humanitarianism's low-bar compassion fits perfectly with modern liberalism's reductive, earthbound explanation of human nature.

There is a catch, though, that casts us back to the nature of pity, and which prevents us from dismissing all forms of it as disordered. Jesus himself is regularly "filled with pity." We read that, as he walked through cities and villages, casting out demons and healing the sick, "seeing the multitudes, he had compassion on them: because they were distressed, and lying like sheep that have no shepherd" (Mt 9:36). Later in Matthew's Gospel, we read of two blind men who cry out to Jesus for mercy and that, "having compassion on them, [Jesus] touched their eyes. And immediately they saw, and followed him" (20:34). Or consider the following moving passage from the Gospel of Luke:

> And when he came nigh to the gate of the city, behold a dead man was carried out, the only son of his mother; and she was a widow: and a great multitude of the city was with her. Whom when the Lord had seen, being moved with mercy towards her, he said to her: Weep not. And he came near and touched the bier. And they that carried it, stood still. And he said: Young man, I say to thee, arise. And he that was dead, sat up, and began to speak. And he gave him to his mother. (7:12–15)

Pity precedes each of the aforementioned healings, which demonstrates that there are certain good acts that cannot come to be without pity. In the *Inferno* itself, Dante's first word is "miserere": "Have pity on me, whatever thing you are, whether shade or living man," Dante cries out at the sight of Virgil (I.65–66). Explaining "why I came to you and what I heard when first I pitied you," the author of the

Aeneid recounts that Mary herself instructed him to work toward Dante's salvation with "high counsel, pity, and with whatever need be for his good" (II.50–67). "Blessed be that Lady of infinite pity," Dante exclaims as Canto II comes to a close; he recognizes that without her pity, he would yet be lost in the wood.

In his *Summa Theologiae* (II-II, q.30), Thomas Aquinas asks how taking pity could be a defect in the person who pities, given that God himself pities. We cannot recognize dependence and respond righty to disfigurement without pity—at the bare minimum—or something that is both similar to it and yet surpasses it. It would seem, though, that this something is *misericordia.* Aquinas probes the problem of *misericordia*, which can be translated as "pity," but which we ought to leave in Latin to avoid the connotative meaning of pity as pure sentiment, unguided by reason—as sentimentality, a sign of moral failure. Most literally, *misericordia* means *miserum cor,* or pitying heart. *Misericordia*, Aquinas teaches (citing St. Augustine), is a heartfelt grief or sorrow over another's distress, "impelling us to succor him if we can."

In order to establish the *motives* of pity, Aquinas turns to Aristotle, who in his *Rhetoric* defines pity as "sorrow for a visible evil, whether corruptive or distressing." Such evils, he writes, provoke pity even more if they are contrary to deliberate choice, "when it is the result of an accident, as when something turns out ill, whereas we hoped well of it." Finally, Aquinas argues, "we pity most the distress of one who suffers undeservedly." Pity rightly practiced hinges on this word *undeservedly.* Aquinas explains that it is of the nature of a fault to be voluntary, and insofar as it is voluntary, it "deserves punishment rather than mercy." However, because a fault "may be, in a way, a punishment, through having something connected with it that is against the sinner's will," it may call for *misericordia*, for pity.

Although pity can be felt or demonstrated wrongly, then, it would be wrong and deeply damaging for us to banish it from our hearts and minds. Both Aquinas and Aristotle note that a virtuous person looks upon his friend as another self. This means he counts his friend's grief as his own. But Aquinas also notes, as Rousseau did later, that a person can feel pity for those who are not his friends, especially when he realizes that what has happened to them may happen to himself. The old and the wise, he says, know well that they may fall upon evil times. On account of this, "feeble and timorous persons, are more inclined to pity."

Others are naturally unlikely to know pity, especially "those who deem themselves happy, and so far powerful as to think themselves in no danger of suffering any hurt." The proud are inclined to think that those who suffer have merited it; thinking the suffering wicked, they refrain from pity. The angry also are bereft of pity, for, as we read in Proverbs 27:4, "anger hath no mercy, nor fury when it breaketh forth."

How, then, can we learn to pity rightly? First, we must learn the parameters of pity rightly understood. In the *Summa,* Aquinas considers the objection that pity cannot be a virtue. As Aristotle teaches, he notes, virtue is above all else a choice, "the desire of what has been already counseled." But pity seems to hinder counsel. In addition, mercy seems to belong to the appetitive power; as a feeling, it cannot be an intellectual virtue, and because God is not its object, it cannot be a theological virtue. Finally, because it does not belong to justice, and is not about passions, pity cannot be a moral virtue.

Aquinas admits that distress over another's distress may be a mere movement of the sensitive appetite. But we must not on these grounds discard it, as "in another way, it may denote a movement of the intellective appetite, inasmuch as one person's evil is displeasing to another. This movement may be ruled in accordance with reason, and in accordance with this movement regulated by reason, the movement of the lower appetite may be regulated." Augustine, too, knew that this was true, for in *The City of God*, he argues that "this movement of the mind obeys the reason, when mercy is vouchsafed in such a way that justice is safeguarded"—for instance, when we give to the needy or forgive the repentant. *Pity,* then, *misericordia*, is a virtue insofar as it is practiced justly, which is to say, according to reason.

Crucially, Augustine notes that we can show pity through an act of forgiveness, but such could only meet the demands of justice if the object of our pity were repentant. It is here that we encounter one of the major flaws in Dante's misguided pity for Paolo and Francesca. As I demonstrated earlier, Francesca exploits Dante's error. Seeing that, though Italian, he has an Irishman's bleeding heart, that he assumes that these two lovers have been "brought to this sorry pass" through "sweetest thoughts" and "green and young desire," none of which he condemns, she thrusts upon him what we have come, in common parlance, to call a "sob story." Francesca's tone is self-pitying, and like Dante, Paolo is melted "to tears of pity and of pain." Crucially, whereas at the start of his journey Dante called out for *miserere*, here the Italian reads "*lagrimar mi fanno tristo e pio.*" Thus does Dante, the author of *The Divine Comedy*, distinguish between right and wrong understandings of pity by employing different words to signify each.

Francesca places a large portion of the blame for her current state on the author of the Arthurian legend.

> For when we read
> how her fond smile was kissed by such a lover,
> he who is one with me alive and dead
> breathed on my lips the tremor of his kiss.
> That book, and he who wrote it, was a pander.
> That day we read no further. (V.130–135)

The author of Lancelot and Guinevere's affair, in this case Gallehault, was, as the very spelling of his name suggests, a *galeotto*, the Italian word for pimp. Francesca's allegation betrays her unrepentance, and Dante's dizzied response to her demonstrates his incapacity to discern the proper object and parameters of pity.

Is this not the case in so many of the contemporary conversations of our time? For many, pity is and should be indiscriminately expressed toward the other, whether that person has cancer or is a slothful student, whether he inhabits a district with heavy lead levels in the water or is actively engaged in a homosexual relationship that is purportedly unjustly condemned by the dominant culture. In an age of diminishing demands and disappearing duties, it makes sense that pity would ascend to the throne of liberal individualist morality.

Like Dante, many practice pity as they do precisely because, in Manent's words, "[it] does not demand any moral transformation or transcendence of self." (I should note that some who are inclined to anger and pride may find themselves nodding, but only because they have made their deficit of pity something to extol.) Dante's transformation comes first through the instruction that Virgil provides, which tempers the poet's pain and helps him to see the parts within the whole. When the "sighs and cries and wails coiled and recoiled" overwhelmed Dante, and he was tempted to feel bad, Virgil "put forth his hand . . . with a gentle and encouraging smile."

Dante's pity is also purified through his encounters with the souls in purgatory, who, though in a state of punishment, are entirely at peace with it. They have come to recognize that pity must not contradict the dictates of justice. As he moves from the *Inferno* to the *Paradiso*, Dante comes to see various punishments as merited; he sees that although the effects of sin may cause us sorrow, we ought not to pity the sinner to the point that we try to rearrange the architecture of hell—or, I might add, to abolish hell entirely, putting in its place a pitiful cosmos of our own making.

In mentioning justice, I cannot help but anticipate the objection that God's highest attribute is *misericordia*, "just mercy," or "just pity," and not justice per se. This would be welcome news to those who mistake a morally impoverished, misdirected pity for the *misericordia* of God. But, with Aquinas, we should take seriously the objection that can be formulated as follows: Since, in God, mercy takes precedence over all other virtues, so, in our practice, pity must take precedence in our own moral economies; while sin *x* might "in justice" merit punishment *y*, we ought "in mercy" to respond in a forgiving manner.

Aquinas would respond to this by acknowledging that one virtue *can* take precedence over another: first, in itself, and second, in comparison to its subject. He grants that, considered in itself, *misericordia* does take precedence over other virtues, as "it belongs to mercy to be bountiful to others, and, what is more, to succor others in their wants, which pertains chiefly to one who stands above. Hence mercy is accounted as being proper to God: and therein his omnipotence is declared to be chiefly manifested."

However, with regard to its subject, *misericordia* is *not* the crowning virtue, unless its subject is greater than all others. For as man has God above him, charity, which unites him to God, is superior to *misericordia*, by which he "supplies the defects of his neighbor." With regard to his neighbor, though, mercy is the greatest, "even as it is higher and better to supply the defect of another, insofar as the latter is deficient."

He who promulgates the supremacy of compassion is right, then, in the sense that pity is the greatest virtue we can exercise toward our neighbors. He regularly errs, however, in his practice of this compassion. When contemporary churchmen call for radical ruptures with any number of perpetual Church teachings, they often appeal to the supremacy of pity, which is the sentiment so often affiliated with appeals that we be "pastoral." Appeals to pity that enunciate the affective elements often aim not merely to change feelings, but to alter truth.

In the seventh circle of hell, which is inhabited by the violent against nature, Dante must again reckon with the problem of pity, must discriminate between pity as mere affect and pity as directed, in justice, by the intellect. For here Dante meets a band of famous Florentine sodomites. His affectivity is not yet fully educated, even if he has made some gains since Paulo and Francesco. Still, the poet's interactions with the homosexuals are remarkable in that, as Robert Hollander notes, "Virgil, who so often warns Dante when the latter begins to admire or become sympathetic (or overly concerned with the damned), here is urgent in his approbation of these three sinners."

"These are souls to whom respect is due," Virgil says. "Do as they ask."

Subsequently, we receive an extended description of the third round of the seventh circle. Darting flames hem the narrow passage through which Dante and Virgil walk. Forming themselves into a wheel, the sodomites begin "their ancient wail / over again." Iacopo speaks on behalf of all, perhaps courting Dante's pity by openly hoping that their scorched appearance and the misery of their place will not bring them into contempt. In response to Iacopo, Dante desires to embrace them:

> I would have thrown myself to the plain below
> Had I been sheltered from the falling fire;
> And I think my Teacher would have let me go.
>
> But seeing I should be burned and cooked, my fear

Overcame the first impulse of my heart
To leap down and embrace them then and there.
(XVI.45–51)

Dante scholar Joseph Pequigney says, "Dante the pilgrim's reaction is rather one of sympathy than the usual and anticipated antipathy, and one that dramatizes Dante the author's outlook, which is, for the time and place, remarkably benevolent." Hollander concurs, arguing that "the fact that here, as in *Purgatorio* 26, he chooses to put homosexuals in a good light when there was no apparent compelling reason for him to do so surely should cause us to ask further questions about Dante's views concerning homosexuality."

We are right to read in these passages Dante's immortalization of pity for the sodomites. That being said, both Hollander and Pequigney fail to acknowledge a trinity of truths hidden in plain sight. Indeed, both their readings are forced to mute several elements of the text.

First, although Dante experiences a pronounced affective pity for them, this pity comes in the context of the canto's overwhelmingly political preoccupation. These Florentines are not merely sodomites but members of the "good Guelphs," the lost cause, who could have saved Florence from the awful aftermath of the battle of Montaperti (1260).

Second, although Dante's disposition toward the sodomites may be strikingly compassionate given the norms of medieval culture regarding homosexuality—in Dante's day, penalties for sodomy could include confiscation of property and even capital punishment—we know clearly that

Dante's own education into virtue, Dante's pilgrim conversion, is far from complete. Given this, we cannot regard his pity as evidence of the poet's "progressive views" concerning homosexuality.

Finally, and perhaps the most poignant point for our purposes, the sodomites are yet—for all the sentiment that Dante might feel toward them—in hell. As I noted earlier, for Aristotle, those who are beset with anger and pride are often unable to pity. I should also note that those who detach pity from justice and make it their lodestar are particularly liable to pride, even as, because pity comes with such tenderness, it can be difficult to diagnose the arrogance with which it is often affiliated.

Pitiful arrogance has moved many to make claims that would rearrange the architecture of the afterlife. For this, too, Dante provides a corrective. For whatever the poet's feelings toward the damned may have been, he knew that *misericordia* is married to justice, regulated by reason, and structured by doctrine, a truth that plays out in that his own pilgrimage takes place within the norms that take form through the Word of God. Pity souls he might, but this does not blur his vision: although he deems its inscription "harsh," Dante can still read—and teach us to read rightly—the sign affixed to the gate of hell:

> SACRED JUSTICE MOVED MY ARCHITECT
> I WAS RAISED HERE BY DIVINE
> OMNIPOTENCE
> PRIMORDIAL LOVE AND ULTIMATE
> INTELLECT

18

What Waugh Saw in America: An Anglo-American Romance

Dilatasti cor meum

—Psalm 119:32

AT FIRST SIGHT, Evelyn Waugh envisioned America as Aimée Thanatogenos, anti-heroine of his Hollywood novel *The Loved One.* She is a naïve young beauty whose mind is decorated with "sparse furniture," who is "dressed and scented in obedience to the advertisements; brain and body scarcely distinguishable from the standard product." A year later, in 1948, Waugh crossed the Atlantic again. Though he remained vexed by the States' forbidding foreignness, on second glance his ironic distance was lessened, leaving Evelyn with a lover's blindness. Her birthmarks, he found, were not all blights that demand excision. Discovering her Catholic side, the smitten Waugh took the country as his loved one.

Waugh could be a mean man when he wanted to. Even when he didn't ("but I do the very thing I hate" (Rom 7:15)), the author of *Vile Bodies* ("who shall change our vile body?"

(Phil 3:21, KJV)) had a proclivity toward cruelty. His friend Nancy Mitford famously asked him how he could reconcile "being so horrible with being a Christian. He replied rather sadly that were he not a Christian he would be even more horrible . . . and anyway would have committed suicide years ago," she recollected. Waugh bore an especial antipathy to Americans ("the bloody Yanks"), whom he considered barbaric, bereft of tradition—the apogee of vulgarity.

And so it was with considerable trepidation that his agent, A. D. Peters, pondered the Anglo author's travels to Hollywood, where in early 1947 Waugh was set to negotiate the film rights for *Brideshead Revisited.* Peters, trying to level the ground for his client's coming, sent a censorious missive from New York: "I must tell you that you have the reputation here—both at M.G.M. of being a difficult, tetchy, irritating and rude customer. I hope you will surprise and confound them all. . . . They are children; and they should receive the tolerance and understanding that you show to children." But, as Waugh's biographer Selina Hastings retorts, "tolerance and understanding were rarely conspicuous in Evelyn's attitude toward children."

The trip was a recipe for tragedy. Waugh's first New York impressions included the "great booby boxes" (illustrious American skyscrapers), which he found "absolutely negligible in everything except bulk. . . . They bear the same sort of relation to architecture as distempering a ceiling does to painting." Like some twentieth-century Dante lost in the high rise booby traps, Waugh described his taxicab travels as infernal—"sitting through all eternity in a traffic block"—though who among us hasn't found gridlock hellish?

In Beverly Hills, the art of compromise was doubly doomed. American film executives possessed a stunted grasp of the book's Catholic undercurrent. Still further, as Waugh complained without naming *Brideshead*, "A script was recently condemned as likely to undermine the Christian conception of marriage. The story was of an unhappy married man and woman who wished to divorce their respective partners and remarry one another." As the trip's purported purpose disappeared from MGM's spotlights, the foreigner assumed a journalist's mantle. His article "Why Hollywood is a Term of Disparagement" (*Daily Telegraph and Morning Post*, 1947), disparages the film industry's capitulation to the "great fallacy of the Century of the Common Man . . . that a thing can have no value for anyone which is not valued by all." Whereas not so long ago a book which sold a mere five thousand copies could shape a generation, "a film must please everyone." And at a price that is not worth paying. Waugh saw an intrinsic inhumanity in the film star's life, which, he quips, "is as brief as a prize fighter." The technicians are too enterprising, threatening to make pyrotechnics, rather than the art of acting, the center of the film. And then there are the farcical commonplaces that govern the industry. A script writer, wishing to hang a map on his wall, requested a hammer and nails. A unionist arrived and indicated that the carpenters would strike if he hung the thing himself. These sorts of impositions, Waugh concluded, keep the cost of moviemaking exorbitant: "The capitalist at the head of the company is concerned solely with profits; the proletariat allow profits only to those who directly work for their pleasure; in this miniature class-war the artist vanishes." In the final lines of the article, he insists that the absurdities under which Hollywood works are insuperable and fears that artists will "be seduced there to their own extinction."

Meanwhile, down the road at an absurd "necropolis of the age of pharaohs" called Forest Lawn Memorial Park, Waugh the endangered artist was gathering the stuff of his next novel—*The Loved One: An Anglo-American Romance.* Eighty miles of pipe kept the lawns golf course-grade, and the place's solemn funerary purpose was nowhere betrayed, not until Evelyn entered the "Slumber Rooms" and found there, sometimes on couches, embalmed bodies looking "dandified," effusing an air of "happy childhood at play." Countless concealed radios crooned the "Hindu Lovesong." Caged birds accompanied these soothing melodies with their ample twittering.

The ideal, Waugh wrote in his article "Half in Love with Easeful Death: An Examination of Californian Burial Customs" (*Tablet,* 1947) was to "shade off, so finely that it becomes imperceptible, the moment of transition" traditionally called *d-e-a-t-h.* Dr. Eaton, mastermind behind the avante-garde burial home, encouraged all to "be happy because they for whom you mourn are happy—far happier than ever before." His optimistic necropolis had "consciously turned its back on the 'old customs of death,' the grim traditional alternatives of Heaven and Hell. . . . Dr. Eaton is the first man to offer eternal salvation at an inclusive charge as part of his undertaking services." Waugh, having witnessed rearranged corpses "fresh from the final beauty parlor," was left wanting the traditional attire of a naked soul sitting at the judgment seat, bodies surrounded by "marble worms writhing in the marble adipocere," threatening to eat what flesh remains. Eaton's achievement was meant to mask from a highly civilized people the cautionary realism of Christianity: hell awaits the wicked. Instead, all buried here passed from the indestructible steel shelves that kept their remains to the "endless infancy" of an insured, purchased paradise.

These strange burial customs were reincarnated in *The Loved One,* Waugh's grotesque sendup of the New World's artificial mastery of death. "It is not possible to be funny about corpses for 25,000 words," his agent cautioned. Waugh answered by prefacing the book with a conspicuous warning. The novel is only a "little nightmare" that bears no resemblance to the "vast variety of life in America."

In the opening pages, however, we find English countrymen "exiled in the barbarous regions of the world." After dotting the landscape with huts and setting a scene familiar to so many novels of Graham Greene, Waugh reveals that this barbarous region is Hollywood. Though put off by the primitive manners, the English are acclimating to the "generous" Americans, who "don't expect you to listen." The secret of social casualness is born of a simple fact: "Nothing they say is designed to be heard."

The novel's hero, Denis Barlow, is the shame of his fellow expats; having failed in the film industry, he has taken up work at the Happier Hunting Ground. His boss Mr. Schultz tries to capitalize on the fact that folks talk to their pets "like they was children." The Brit promises doggy daddies an anniversary remembrance card "without further charge": "*Your little Arthur is thinking of you in heaven today and wagging his tail,*" it reads. The "Grade A service" includes, at the moment of committal, "a white dove, symbolizing the deceased's soul, liberated over the crematorium" of the dead. The entrepreneurial Happier Hunting Ground was forged "in emulation of its great neighbor"—Whispering Glades. The latter, developed by The Dreamer, promises all bereaved "a New Earth sacred to HAPPINESS." Here the master mortician, Mr. Joyboy, assures that "leave-taking" meets the purchaser's preference, though his fondness for the mortuary hostess has him applying the product labeled "Radiant Childhood Smile" to all the corpses without discrimination. (Incidentally, Denis Barlow finds this smile "entirely horrible . . . a painted and smirking obscene travesty.") Here a deceased woman is not merely embalmed. She reclines on a chaise-longue holding a telephone, "as though dressed for an evening party."

Denis finds himself beholden to Whispering Glades when his compatriot Sir Francis commits suicide and requires safe passage to a happier place. He is greeted by the mortuary hostess, Aimée Thanatogenos, who plies her beautician's trade for benefit of the beatified cadavers. Ms. Beloved Bringer of Death bears that American lack of manners that made Waugh squeamish. When Barlow solicits her services, she tries to triumph over him with the therapeutic: you must not shrink in anxious rejection of death, but rather "discuss it openly and frankly," thereby removing "morbid reflexions." The answer, she insists, is "to bring your dark fears into the light of the common day of the common man."

He eventually concludes that he has seen her before. She is one with all of her sisters of the reception desk and airliners. She is "the standard product" who would "croon the same words to him in moments of endearment and express the same views and preferences in moments of social discourse. She was convenient." But Barlow, spawn of a more ancient civilization, requires mystery and manners: "He did not covet the spoils of this rich continent, the sprawling limbs of the swimming pool, the wide-open painted eyes and mouths under the arc-lamps." Just when he consigns this "sole Eve in a bustling hygienic Eden" to cartoonish shallowness and tragic American innocence, an epiphany enraptures him: she is all he has sought during his solitary era of exile.

At Whispering Glades, you can buy tickets to W. B. Yeats's ethereal Lake Isle of Innisfree; the poetic place has been pinned down, built to buoy up weary travelers. When Barlow goes out to the isle seeking the muse, he meets Aimée again instead. Soon thereafter he confesses his poet's soul to her and, all romantic, she too becomes besotted. Denis stoops low to exploit her American naivety of literature and history. She thinks he's composed the Keats he quotes ("I have been half in love with easeful death"). Plagiarizing poetry becomes a boon for Barlow, though Ms. Thanatogenos nearly catches him when, stealing Shakespeare, he compares thee to a summer's day.

Finding him unsettlingly "Un-American," the self-described "progressive" writes to a newspaper columnist named Guru Brahmin (who is comprised of exactly two men and a secretary) soliciting advice. How could she marry a man who shows irreverence toward the excellences of Whispering Glades, which she thinks "an epitome of all that is finest in the American Way of Life"? Still more, the English poets he cites are too despondent or ceremonious for this Californian courtship. Citing their melancholic verse, he can't compete with the movies and the crooners. And then, finally, Denis is not gainfully employed. Doesn't he realize that "an American man would despise himself for living on his wife?"

No, he says, "the older civilizations" have no such prejudices. Desperate for cash, the man remakes himself in an all-American fashion, taking correspondence courses to become a "non-sectarian clergyman." But when the lovesick Aimée discovers his "unethical" piracy of British Verse, she heeds the Guru's surefire advice and kills herself at Whispering Glades. With borrowed vulgarity, Barlow sees through his new business of "non-sectarian services expeditiously conducted at competitive prices." Before he can cinch his first client, though, a fellow Brit finagles him into sparing the Old Country further embarrassment. And so it goes that the Englishman takes his leave, his ticket fully funded by the expatriate Cricket Club. The romantic lie of the Anglo-American match cannot withstand the novelistic truth: Waugh severs the macabre alliance, consigning The Dreamers to the columbarium of history.

Whether motivated by masochism, by a whim of magnanimity, or monies affixed to a *Life* magazine article on Catholicism in the States, Waugh returned to America in

1948 (November to December) and again in 1949 (February to March). Additionally, Fr. Francis X Talbot, the Jesuit president of Loyola University of Maryland, had proposed that Waugh deliver a circuitous series of lectures, which came to be called "Three Vital Writers: Chesterton, Knox, and Greene." During these second sightseeings, he met Dorothy Day, whom he described as "an autocratic ascetic saint who wants us all to be poor." He gave Day and her *Catholic Worker* fellow travelers lunch in an Italian restaurant. Although she did not approve of the cocktails he disseminated at considerable expense, they conversed for many hours. (Waugh would later visit the *Catholic Worker* contributor and National Book Award-winning writer J. F. Powers in St. Paul, MN. Powers, impoverished both voluntarily and on account of his own improvidence, did his part to dispel the Stateside rumors that cartooned Waugh into more of a character than he already was: "Saw Waugh . . . all a lie about liveried servants. Carried out his dishes himself," Powers reported.)

During the same reluctantly-taken travels, Waugh stopped at Gethsemane Abbey in Kentucky. Thomas Merton was indebted to his literary better, who provided extensive edits to the "long winded" *Seven Storey Mountain,* so that the book came out in England one third shorter and with Waugh's recommended title, *Elected Silences.* The younger Merton repaid his debts in part through spiritual friendship, advising Evelyn to "say the Rosary every day. If you don't like it, so much the better." The monk meant the beads to assist with Waugh's anxiety over imperfect contrition, which to Merton's mind was a man "with intellectual gifts" arguing himself "into a quandary that doesn't exist." In his review of the book he helped rewrite, the Englishman showed greater benignity toward the U.S. scene: "Americans . . . are learning to draw away from what is distracting in their own civilization while remaining in their own borders."

Elected Affinities, with its "fresh, simple, colloquial" ethos, came as a revelatory shock for "non-Catholic Americans," who were altogether unaware of "warmth silently generated in these furnaces of devotion." Waugh goes further, anticipating that the USA will soon be the scene of a flourishing monastic revival. Championing the Benedictine option long before the Benedict option became *chic,* Waugh proclaimed the modern world increasingly uninhabitable, putting us back in the age of Boniface, Gregory, Augustine: "As in the Dark Ages the cloister offers the sanest and most civilized way of life."

Back in the Shire, Waugh complained that he'd "seen enough of USA to last me fifty years," this even as *Life* published his article "The American Epoch in the Catholic Church" (1949), which betrays a conditional surrender to the peculiar prospect that Providence may be "schooling and strengthening" the people of the New World "for the historic destiny long borne by Europe."

Waugh starts out with a regular scholastic *disputatio* of objections. It would seem that the hallmarks of the American character are "unsympathetic to the habits of the Church": compulsive revolt against traditional authority; obsession with mere activity; the blind embrace of novelties; the strangeness of Latin on democratic lips; "their dislike of dogmas that divide good citizens and their love of the generalities which unite them."

The objections continue. America, child of the West, is marked by "late-eighteenth century 'enlightenment' and the liberalism of her founders has persisted through all the changes of her history and penetrated into every part of her life." Thus, many American prelates preach representative majority government as "of divine institution." The transatlantic traveler seizes upon a ship metaphor to elucidate the essential dogma of the country: separation of Church and State. Government is the captain of a liner, who has received the capacity to command from his passengers. Though the public rooms may be rented out for motley religious assemblies, blasphemy is permitted only in the privacy of the bars. This, according to Waugh, was the ideal which the "doctrinaire liberals" of America's founders conceived: very little government is to be tolerated, and the private sphere has a vast and inviolable circumference. In many enlightenment experiments, the State ("whether conceived of as the will of the majority or the power of a clique") has commandeered more of that supposedly sacrosanct privacy. As a result, the "discrepancies between the secular and the religious philosophies" have become more prominent, "for many things are convenient to the ruler which are not healthy for the soul." In America, in spite of her idiosyncrasies, this damnable decay has been delayed.

It would seem, finally, that America's anti-Catholicity would stunt the New World from being a nursery for Popery. Waugh is careful to enunciate the strength of these prejudices: "It was the Quebec Act tolerating Popery in Canada, quite as much as the Stamp act and the Tea Duties, which rendered George III intolerable to the colonists." And yet we must not mistake the strength of a stabilized minority religion, as is the Catholic faith in the United States. We must not cling to the rosy lie that "from the age of Constantine to that of Luther there was a single, consistently triumphant, universally respected authority." No, the Church, even when she faced fewer or weaker enemies outside her walls, "has always been at grips with enemies inside." In spite of its depth of tradition, and the Church's profound and prolonged influence in Europe, there "conversions barely keep pace with apostasies" whereas in America the Catholic Church is "subject to both the advantages and disadvantages of an underprivileged position."

It may be true that, generally speaking, American Catholics wax latitudinarian when it comes to doctrinal matters, and that they shirk the ascetic life. But Waugh distances himself from generalities of this sort, framing them as limited caricatures of the sort he employed to damn the New World from a distance. After all, Catholicism is not entirely alien to the American spirit. Take New Orleans. Yes, witchcraft is to be found there, syncretized with the creed and the rosary. But on an Ash Wednesday there Waugh witnessed "one of the most moving sights of my tour." Filthy streets confessed the excesses of carnival. Still, across the street, a Jesuit church was "teeming with life all day long; a continuous, dense crowd of all colours and conditions moving up the altar rails and returning with their foreheads signed with ash" and admonished with a "Dust thou art." In the "desert of modern euphemisms," where falsifying niceties such as "under-privileged" and "emotionally disturbed" threaten to conceal what Flannery O'Connor called our "essential disfigurement," here, in Catholic New Orleans, all day long souls were told of their poverty in the plain and lovingly painful style of the Church.

Waugh tempers his celebration, reminding us that New Orleans has never known persecution, which is never healthy; it can even be enervating if toleration is carried over too long a time. In Maryland, on the contrary, though Catholics practiced in temporary peace, they met maltreatment. The old Catholic families of Baltimore "have much in common with the old Catholic families of Lancashire," Waugh remarks. The countryside around Leonardstown, too, is haunted by the tradition of Jesuit missionaries, slipping in disguise from family to family, celebrating Mass in the hidden parts of plantations.

Persecution came to black Catholics not from Protestants but from "fellow-members in the Household of the Faith," who possessed a supernatural knowledge of their faith that surpassed that of their clergy. Although Waugh is attuned to the efforts of white Catholics to make amends for these scandals of the distant past, he elevates the "thousands of coloured Catholics who so accurately traced their Master's roads amidst insults and injury."

The goods of Catholic colleges have also emerged at least in part from uneasy relations between Church and State. Though poor, American Catholics have "covered their land with schools," incited by the conviction that in a non-Catholic land only a whole education can incubate the Faith. True, Catholic colleges cannot compete with

Harvard or Oxford when it comes to specialized scholarship and preparation in the physical sciences. But Waugh channels Tocqueville, considering it a "very great thing that young men who are going out to be dentists or salesmen should have grounding in formal logic and Christian ethics," that they could "prove syllogistically that the natural rights exist" and "give the fundamental reason why usury is wrong." Or that they might know "the difference between soul and mind" and be able to "give and explain a definition of Sacrifice."

Waugh chooses these questions at random from a Jesuit college exam, and cites them as the reason why Catholics could keep pace when the discussion moved into general concerns, whereas, when he witnessed their secular peers, "one got the impression that outside their particular subjects everything was shapeless and meaningless." Not to mention, and not unimportantly, Notre Dame's "holy places are crowded before a football match."

But Holy Mother Church, Waugh concludes, does not exist to produce philosophers. (Nor writers. "The Church and the world need monks and nuns [such as were then flourishing in Trappist Abbeys and Carmelite cloisters] more than they need writers. The Church can get along very well without them.") She exists to produce saints, and, "what is plain to the observer is that throughout the nation the altar rails are everywhere crowded." From just such popular devotion do the Faith's finest flowers crop.

In "Americanism," that amalgamation of all that Americans call "the good life," it is Christianity, and "preeminently Catholicism" that plays the redeeming part. Waugh assures his readers that the "Americanism" produced and parodied by the fears of Europeans is a fiction. "There is a purely American 'way of life' led by every good American Christian that is point-for-point opposed to the publicized" hyperboles pumped out by Hollywood and popularized the world over. Still, Catholics are tempted to capitulate; everywhere the Americanism of antiauthoritarian latitudinarianism and vulgar materialism beckon. More so than their fellow Protestant citizens, they feel pressured to prove themselves faithful to the "way," to fit in. J. F. Powers, Waugh noted, was keen to this tension: his Irish priests are "faithful and chaste and, in youth at any rate, industrious, but many live out their lives in a painful state of transition; they have lost their ancestral simplicity."

Waugh's great expectations were tempered most by the threatening "neutrality" of the State: "neutral—a euphemism for 'unchristian.'" Mercantile forces seek to replace the Christ child with Santa Claus and his reindeer. The visitor from abroad witnessed, in early Lent, the Easter Bunny's arrival at a train station, police posse and brass band in tow: "pagan commerce is seeking to adopt and desecrate the feasts of the Church," and if the matter lands in the hands of public authority, we know which side the neutral State will likely favor. Given the liberal regime's incompetence in religious matters, and given the huge differences that divide the various religions practiced by U.S. citizens, "the neutral, secular State can only function justly by keeping itself within strict limits." It was not for him, a foreigner, to predict how long the U.S. government will withhold from perilous encroachment. Nonetheless, Waugh seemed to see that encroachment hovering in the distance, however far. He seemed to see the barbarians descending from the hills of Hollywood, howling the end of the "American Epoch in the Catholic Church." But Waugh the foreigner has fallen for his forbidden loved one, and he will not bespeak her unbeautiful birthmarks in public.

When the mercurial man undertook a final sailing to the U.S. in 1950, he rode the coattails of his *Life* diagnoses. Waugh was welcomed, in the words of Pam Berry, "in a quaint Catholic light" which showed him to be "a noble gentle person who is capable, oh, yes, from time to time of naughty spitefulness, but who is on the whole a saintly, good person, healed and beatified by the Church." Oddly enough, Waugh's last foray into foreign America was occasioned in part by the publication of his novel *Helena,* a novelistic treatment of the ever-controversial Constantine's saintly mother.

But Waugh was no saint. The tormented artist was quite cognizant of his hot temper, and knew that his miniscule benevolence could be poured out, lukewarm, into fragile little teacups. "How to reconcile this indifference to human beings with the obligation of Charity," he confided in a friend. "That is my problem." As George Weigel has noted, in his later years, the novelist undertook a purgative "spiritual quest for compassion and contrition. As for many of us, the contrition likely came easier than the compassion."

Selena Hastings says that as a corrective to his misanthropy, the Catholic writer "channeled a substantial portion of his income to Catholic charities." In the case of *The Loved One*, all translation royalties were bequeathed to the primate of the country concerned. His agent wrote to relate various archbishops' gratitude and directives, indicating the various orphanages, etc. that would receive Waugh's alms. Almsgiving covers a multitude of sins, but this kind of charity can be easily caricatured: the cantankerous man continues to crank but holds out his liberality as a kind of red herring. *The Loved One* did not need to be translated into "American" English. Therefore no charities in the States received royalties. But Waugh, infatuated by the good things of his stateside fling, gave American Catholics something perhaps greater: he showed his dilated heart by bestowing upon them the flirtatious impermanence of an epoch.

19

The Sound and the Fury, Symbolizing Something: Walker Percy and Jacques Maritain on the Paradoxical Miracle at the Limits of Language

For my son, *Søren*

In his happy little tome *Hermeneutics as Politics* (recommended breakfast reading, preferably prior to coffee), Stanley Rosen demonstrates that those who are obsessed with language in our time tend to come to the conviction that there is no deep, meaningful relationship between signs and the things they signify. In the wake of this fracture, a cynical conclusion reigns: there is, finally, nothing but interpretation: "there is nothing 'out there' but ghosts of uninteresting truths; truth is superstition." In his essay "Sign and Symbol," Jacques Maritain insists that we revisit and reinhabit the Scholastic solution to the problem of language: correct, he says, there exists no literal link between sign and signifier. And yet, there is a "certain presence—presence of knowability—of the signified in the sign; the former is there *in alio esse,* in another mode of existence."

Signs, while used by humans, play a great part in the psychic life of animals. Just this morning my son *Søren said, unprompted, "Dad, parrots can talk like us."*

"But do they understand the words they use?"

"Yeah, they do. I saw a parrot that knew what it was saying. Every time the phone rang, it said, 'Pick up the phone, pick up the phone.'"

For animals, as for humans, signs *do something,* and yet for us the sign is also "the keystone of intellectual life." In order to trace how this key to the intellect is turned, we must sort out the distinct meaning of a sign. "An animal employs signs without perceiving the relationship of meaning," Maritain explains. "To perceive the relationship of meaning is to have an *idea*—a spiritual sign."

Maritain contends that the marvel of perceived meaning is most remarkably evident in the awakening intelligence of blind deaf-mutes, "imprisoned souls." The philosopher-novelist Walker Percy, who persistently probed the troubled relationship between language, meaning, and being, also pauses before the blind deaf-mute's consciousness of *meaning.* Percy considers such extreme cases singularly important in the study of signs and symbols. Helen Keller's teacher could help her to interpret the word as a *signal* that "*did* something," but what she "could not make [Helen] understand was that the word *water* was not a command to *do* something with water, but *meant*, denoted water." Once, by a mysterious flash of insight, Keller understood that this "is" water, "what she had to know immediately was *what everything else was!*" Consciousness, moving from sign to symbolized meaning, requires that everything *be* something, but finds paradoxically that the "one thing in the world which by its very nature is not susceptible of a stable symbolic transformation is *myself*."

An approach informed by both Maritain and Percy's philosophies of language, sign, and symbol will guide us as we engage with Percy's novel *The Moviegoer*, in which the protagonist Binx Bolling voices creative intuitions regarding the "miserable, anxious awareness" paid for the gift of language, and comes to find in his mentally disabled but linguistically luminous brother Lonnie an almost holy truth about our use of symbols. Those whose sufferings limit their use of language can reveal how miraculous our capacity for meaning-making really is. Taking this paradoxical miracle as his premise, Percy helps us to fall in love with language, to see that love is impossible outside of human symbolization, outside of *homo symbolificus*—man the symbol-monger.

Peter Augustine Lawler notes that Percy "agrees with Aristotle and Saint Thomas that discovering the truth and communicating it to others may be the greatest of the human pleasures," even as "man experiences himself as an alien because he cannot, through language or thought, formulate or locate his own place in a cosmos that is otherwise dyadic." *Dyadic* is a jargonish word used by Percy's semiotic mentor Charles S. Pierce to mean "composed of stimulus-response sequences." Percy, with Pierce, distinguishes *dyadic* (response-stimulus) from *triadic* behavior in order to differentiate various human uses of language. Whereas in dyadic language the self is submerged in the sequence of stimulus-response, in *triadic* behavior the self stands *apart* from stimulus-response sequences and uses symbols to navigate through them.

In order to distinguish between dyadic sign use and triadic symbol use, Percy establishes the two categorizations of *environment* and *world.* It is possible (if reductive) to think of the human person as an organism that maintains homeostasis in an open system in spite of all changes in an environment. The organism responds to those segments of its environment to which its genetic code has been predisposed to through evolution. In such a case, segments of the environment without biological significance are ignored. Learning, in an environment, consists of modifying certain neurons in the organism's central nervous system in such a way that it will "respond to certain signals in an environment by a behavior oriented toward other segments of the environment." An environment allows for only dyadic relations.

The triadic moment occurs when organism B understands sign A as *meaning* something, as more than a signal to flee or approach. While a signal is *received* like any other stimuli in an environment, a symbol or a "sign requires a sign-giver." When the sign and symbol user crosses the triadic threshold, she has, in addition to her environment, a *world.* As I noted earlier, Percy is particularly interested in the crossing as it happens in blind-deaf-mutes because it contains great mystery and meaning. In *The Message in the Bottle*, he muses that "three short paragraphs in Helen Keller's *The Story of My Life* veiled a mystery, a profound secret, and . . . if one could fathom it, one could also understand a great deal of what it meant to be *Homo loquens,*

Homo symbolificus, man the speaking animal, man the symbol-monger."

Helen had always responded to stimuli like any good animal. If she wanted cake, she spelled it in the hands of her teacher Miss Sullivan. But one day on a walk, a threshold was crossed:

> We walked down the path to the well-house, attracted by the fragrance of the honeysuckle with which it was covered. Someone was drawing water and my teacher placed my hand under the spout. As the cool stream gushed over one hand, she spelled into the other the word *water*, first slowly then rapidly. I stood still, my whole attention fixed upon the motion of her fingers. Suddenly I felt a misty consciousness as of something forgotten—a thrill of returning thought; and somehow the mystery of language was revealed to me. I knew then that "w-a-t-e-r" meant the wonderful cool something that was flowing over my hand. The living word awakened my soul, gave it light, hope, joy, set it free! There were barriers still, it is true, but barriers that could in time be swept away.
>
> I left the well-house eager to learn. Everything had a name, and each name gave birth to a new thought. As we returned to the house every object which I touched seemed to quiver with life. That was because I saw everything with the strange, new sight that had come to me. On entering the door I remembered the doll I had broken. . . . I felt my way to the hearth and picked up the pieces. I tried vainly to put them

> together. Then my eyes filled with tears; for I realized what I had done, and for the first time I felt repentance and sorrow. I learned a great many new words that day.

Maritain maintains that, in the blind-deaf-mute experience, in order for one to *know* the relationship of signification which will usher them into a world of meaning, "some external help is indispensable. . . . The miracle of awakening to the life of thought will come to pass precisely when—thanks to the patiently repeated attempts of the teacher who refuses a desire and suggests a sign, an *artificial, conventional* sign, intended to obtain the satisfaction of the refused desire—the child suddenly will *discover* by some sort of sudden eruption of the idea, the signification of this conventional sign . . . and from that moment on progress proceeds with astonishing rapidity."

Keller's experience intersects with the scholastic insistence (which in a sense is both pre- and post-modern) that there is a "certain presence—presence of knowability—of the signified in the sign; the former is there *in alio esse,* in another mode of existence."

For Ferdinand de Saussure, the sign is "a union of signifier (the sound-image of a word) and signified (the concept of an object, action, quality)." Percy calls the relation between the sign (signifier) and referent (signified) "a particularly mysterious property." This mystery is located in the "troublesome copula 'is,' when Helen said that the perceived liquid 'is' water (the word)." According to Jacques Derrida's deconstructionist linguistics, "the referent of a signifier is merely another signifier." Derrida is in this way an echo of the ancient rhetorician Gorgias, who argued "that by which we reveal is logos [words], but logos is not substances and existing things.

Therefore, we do not reveal existing things to our neighbors, but logos, which is something other than substances." Michel Foucault, laboring in this non-vineyard of deconstruction, argues that what is needed is to think *difference*, discontinuity, "to dissociate the reassuring form of the identical" because "we are difference." But, cautions Rosen, this rejection of the metaphysics of presence, of, we can add, the medieval theory of *in alio esse*, places us as players in a nihilistic world of absence. "If the world is a text written by *difference*," he writes, "it is a tale by an idiot, a nonsubjective subjectivity or idiot savant, hence a tale full of sound and fury, signifying nothing." Percy grants deconstructionist postmoderns of Derrida's ilk a nod, and then he shakes his head, no: The word "water" is not *water*, but then again it *is*.

Percy's first published novel, *The Moviegoer*, dramatizes the problem: are we mere organisms in environments, responsive to arbitrary signals, or humans in world using signs and symbols in order to transcend ourselves? Binx, a film-ingesting stock market agent and the novel's narrator, is home visiting his mother and family. It is Sunday. As such, he happens to attend Mass with them. Although the family falls into a great commotion trying to get to Mass, the moment the rite begins they become, in a sense, the pre-symbolizing "imprisoned souls" described by Maritain, deaf and mute to the meaning around them: "it is as if it

[Mass] were over before it began—each has lapsed into his own blank-eyed vacancy."

In this context we witness a purely dyadic response when "the bell rings for communion," that is, when the bell signifies that the bread and wine are now Body and Blood. Roy, Binx's stepfather, responds to the bell as though it were what Percy calls a "signal." For a dog, the word "ball" is merely a "signal"; hearing its master shout "ball," the animal responds as it does to so many other stimuli from his environment. "Ball," says the master, and the dog goes to look for it.

Roy behaves a bit like a Pavlovian dog. The bell rings, signifying that the Eucharist, source and summit of grace, *is*. And yet when the bell rings, "Roy gets heavily to his feet and pilots Lonnie [Binx's handicapped half-brother] to the end of the rail," where he is to receive the sacramental Host. All Binx sees of Lonnie is "a weaving tuft of red hair." We know that Lonnie, in the presence of the Eucharist, begins to tremble, because "when the priest comes to him, Roy holds a hand against Lonnie's face to steady him. He does this in a frowning perfunctory way, eyes light as an eagle's."

We, with Binx, are spectators seeing only a shade of what is happening at the communion rail. Roy is dutiful but disengaged, while Lonnie, shaking, seems to wax mystical in the presence of the Eucharist. Does Roy move beyond stimulus-response into a moment wherein he understands that Lonnie, or Communion, simply *is*? The metaphor "eyes light as an eagle's" offers both clarification and confusion. Are Roy's eyes glazed-over-light or sharpened-light, like an eagle's? Either way, Percy estranges the experience of the Eucharist by juxtaposing the signal-response to the bell with the real presence of the Eucharist, which, more than a signal or symbol, is a sacrament.

In "Sign and Symbol," Maritain describes a sacrament as "something external and sensory which signifies an effect of interior sanctification to be produced." In the Catholic tradition, sacraments are sacraments "in a super-eminent manner: they effect that which they signify (if the subject does not put obstacles in their way by his contrary disposition)." Friedrich Theodor Vischer, seeking proof for his hypothesis, read in the sacrament of the Eucharist a central instance of the identity between the sign and the signified. Against this imposition of theory, Maritain insists that "the sacred words, 'This is my body' in no way assert an identity; they operate (as an instrumental cause) a change (transubstantiation). Far from resting upon an identity between the sign and the signified, the sacrament of the Eucharist adds to the relationship of sign to signified that of cause to effect and implies the intervention of the First Cause producing the most radical change of which we can conceive, a change which affects being in so far as it is being."

We will soon see that this change *in being* of which Lonnie partakes is paralleled, *in alio esse*, in his language. "Lonnie's monotonous speech gives him an advantage," Binx says, "the same advantage foreigners have: his words are not worn out. It is like a code tapped through a wall. Sometimes he asks me straight out: do you love me? And it is possible to tap back: yes, I love you." Heidegger overstates the case when he says that "language is the house of being." Being exists beyond language. Nonetheless, language can be further from, or closer to, the being it bespeaks. Lonnie's language, more than most, builds a hospitable home for being.

After Mass, Binx tells Lonnie, "I don't think you should fast. . . . You've had pneumonia twice in the past year. It would not be good for you." Lonnie says he is fasting "to conquer a habitual disposition." He uses the peculiar idiom of the catechism in ordinary speech. Once, Binx relates, "he told me I needn't worry about some piece of foolishness he heard me tell Linda, since it was not a malicious lie but rather a 'jocose lie.'" With his particular language, Lonnie can, like a poet, recover mystery, can, in a sense, "wrench signifier out of context and exhibit it in all its queerness and splendor."

Before we can speak of this recovery of signifier and signified, we must trace the devolution signs undergo. Percy argues that at first the "signifier serves as the discovery vehicle through which the signified is known," as in the case of Helen Keller "discovering water through *water.*" Afterward, the signifier is transformed by the signified. The signifier *water* becomes informed by the utterly loose-substance-spray of chill when a shower is first turned on, by the heavy, down-ward tending rush of water going down the throat. Finally, there is "a hardening and closure of the signifier, so that in the end the signified becomes encased in a simulacrum like a mummy in a mummy case."

For instance:

First Tourist: What is that?

Second Tourist: Oh that, that's only Niagara Falls.

In such an instance, Percy observes, "a devaluation has occurred," as the thing itself—in this case, water—has, "disappeared into the sarcophagus of its sign." The unique looseness and soft-hardness flow or spray of water is "assigned to its class of signs, a second-class mummy in the basement collection of mummy cases."

Nietzsche posits roughly the same semiotic process in "On Truth and Lying in a Non-Moral Sense," although his primary aim is to critique scientific abstraction. Humans, he says, first generalize sense perceptions, transforming these sensations into concepts, cool concepts that convince their makers they can master the world. "Something becomes possible," he writes, "in the realm of these schemata which could never be achieved in the realm of those sensuous first impressions, namely the construction of a pyramidal order based on castes and degrees, the creation of a new world of laws, privileges, subordinations . . . something regulatory and imperative." Nietzsche cherishes the transformation of sense-perceptions into metaphor, because, he contends, every metaphor is individual and unique and therefore beyond classification, beyond scientific good and evil. Scientists construct a great edifice of concepts, an edifice that resembles in its rigid regularity the "Roman *columbarium*." While Nietzsche pinpoints science as the primary cause of this devaluation, Percy sees this sad process performed by and participated in by humans broadly speaking.

Nietzsche (in prescribed solutions) and Percy (in practice) both posit poetry as the source by which the world undergoes a rebirth that ransoms it from its tragic, conceptual coma. For Nietzsche, concept-making is part and parcel with the human will to truth. Man forces and forges truth into words through sheer force of will, striving to make himself more powerful than he actually is. For Percy, man, who has devalued language through symbolization now dead, is more reminiscent of the "Last Man" we meet in *Thus Spoke Zarathustra*. Because the symbols "love," "creation," "star," and "happiness" have been devalued through deadening use, the Last Man lives as though the deep things these words signify simply do not exist.

Percy contends that the "semioticist most acutely aware of this devolution of the sign and its renewal through the defamiliarization of art is the Russian formalist Victor Schklovsky." For Schklovsky, as perception becomes habitual, it also becomes automatic, unconscious. Were someone to compare the sensation of speaking in a foreign tongue, for instance, for the very first time, he would fast find the chasm that divides the lively freshness of his initial discovery from the automatic, half-articulated compromise of his current condition. Through this "algebraic" method of thinking, the poetic approach is replaced by a dull, prosaic one: "Objects are grasped spatially, in the blink of an eye. We do not see them, we merely recognize them by their primary characteristics. The object passes before us, as if it were prepackaged."

Percy gives us a glimpse of this "prepackaging" of objects in Binx's mother. Binx tries to "shake her loose from her elected career of the commonplace" by asking her whether his deceased father was a good husband. "Was he!" she says. "And what hands! If anyone ever had the hands of a surgeon, he did." Binx takes this in: "My mother's recollection of my father is storied and of a piece. It is not him she remembers but an old emblem of him."

For a moment, because of Binx's prodding, she is shaken from her automatic answer and she recalls a time when her husband would not eat: "It was like he thought eating was not—*important* enough. You see, with your father, everything, every second had to be—" She breaks off, and upon prompting, responds, "I don't know. Something." Binx again asks what was wrong with him, but she only replies, "He was overwrought," she says in "her regular mama-bee drone and again my father disappears into the old emblem." Most of the time, his mother knows not her husband but sarcophagusic signifiers pointing not to him but to, in Binx's words, "an old emblem." Again, for Percy and Nietzsche, as for Shklovsky, art is a prime device through which the object, hidden behind the emblem, disappeared into its sarcophagus, can be recovered.

As Shklovsky says, poetry restores sensation to our half-conscious, compromised perceptions: art "makes a stone feel stony," it leads us to knowledge of a given thing by means of extended perception—through sustained, wide-eyed, sensuous sight instead of automatic, abstracted "recognition."

Derrida ends with the devolution of the signifier that can do nothing but point us to another signifier. Shklovsky and Percy grant this devolution but something like the virtue of hope obtains in their souls: they believe in the resurrection of signification, that what the sarcophagus once contained *in alio esse* will be raised from its deadness.

In *The Moviegoer*, Percy leads us to knowledge of the Eucharist through the organ of sight instead of recognition. He estranges the Eucharist through art in the scene of Lonnie's shaking tuft of red hair and Roy's accompanying eagle eyes. Literally, in *The Moviegoer*, Lonnie leads us to knowledge of a thing, but not quite through the organ of sight as opposed to recognition. He *estranges* objects by using the "peculiar idiom of the catechism in ordinary speech." Shklovsky writes of the artist who, rather than *naming* things, describes them as if seeing them for the first time. Lonnie, like Hellen Keller, *sees and names* things in such a way that they are seen as if for the first time, and it is in this Edenic moment that we stand in a sense as if beside Adam as he named animals. Lonnie, like Adam, names things in order to know them, to inhabit the world with the irradiating meaning of being. Of course, Lonnie is speaking of quite the animal—sin, and (again) he does not get at it by means of a metaphorical snake. Listen as he further interacts with Binx over the question of conquering a "habitual disposition":

> "What disposition is that?" [Binx]
> "A disposition to envy."
> "Envy who?"
> "Duval."
> "Duval is dead."
> "Yes. But envy is not merely sorrow at another's good fortune: it is also joy at another's misfortune."

Binx suggests that Lonnie is not hurting the dead man Duval with his envy, but Lonnie says, "It is hurting me. You know what capital sin does to the life of the soul."

"Yes. Still and all I would not fast. Instead I would concentrate on the Eucharist. It seems a more positive thing to do."

"This is true . . . but Eucharist is a sacrament of the living," Lonnie says somewhat mysteriously, implying that, *symbolically*, he is deadened due to envy. Lonnie, for all of his very real limitations, invites us into a richer world, one wherein a hierarchy of vices ("capital sins") can become "habitual dispositions," and thus must be habitually conquered through penance, charity, and grace. Here, in this world, we leave behind the old "environment" which would make "instincts" of our "sins" and we walk through a cosmos in which all things are oriented to our final end—salvation.

Of course, in a certain sense humans and animals both exist in environments: both use and respond to signs. In addition, both humans and animals die. But, just as only humans know the *meaning* of signs, only humans know the natural fact that death is certain. For Percy, Lawler gleans, "that miserable, anxious awareness is the price to be paid for the gift of language, for thinking about the mystery of human existence."

Through his singular relationship to language, to the symbol, to the possibility therefore of symbolic death (death *in alio esse*), Lonnie reveals an awareness that is anxious and a lexicon with which he can ransom that mystery, and can therefore find redemption of everyday sins from the environment in which they have been held captive as simple stimulus-response actions beyond human symbolization and therefore beyond human freedom. In Keller's account, immediately after she experienced language as a symbol, she experienced sorrow over shattering the doll: "My eyes filled with tears; for I realized what I had done, and for the first time I felt repentance and sorrow." Lonnie's relationship to the language of the catechism remains *living*, and therefore he is able to "discover" sin, to *name* sin in even subtle situations.

"When I name an unknown thing or hear the name from you, a remarkable thing happens," Percy notes. "In some sense or other, the thing is said to 'be' its symbol. The semanticists are right: this round thing is certainly not the word *ball*." But until it becomes, at least in some sense, the word *ball* in our consciousness, the ball will remain unknown to us. Percy, like Maritain, points to the Scholastics, whose theory of symbolic meaning he sees as far more adequate. He too points to the great Scholastic commentator John of St. Thomas, who observed that "symbols come to contain within themselves the thing symbolized *in alio esse*, in another mode of existence."

When a man names a thing, says "this is water and is cool," an unprecedented thing happens. Here man goes beyond merely interacting with things: "He stands apart from two things and says that one 'is' the other. The two things which he pairs or identifies are the *word* he speaks or hears and the *thing* he sees before him." Until this point, until man utters *A is B*, "he will never know A or B; he will only respond to them." In a Percyan key, man is more foolish than a bee, but the bee cannot tell the truth; it can merely respond, react, to its environment. Unless Lonnie articulates his "habitual disposition to envy," until he articulates envy as "not merely sorrow at another's good fortune" but also "joy at another's misfortune," he would not *know* envy, and would only respond (with joy) at the stimuli (another's misfortune) of his environment.

Soon the conversation between Lonnie and Binx breaks off, and the two part. After Binx kisses his half-brother goodbye, however, the latter calls him back. But, Binx notes, "he doesn't really have anything to say." At least, he does not have anything to signal:

> "Wait." [Lonnie says.]
> "What?"
> He searches the swamp, smiling.
> "Do you think that Eucharist—"
> "Yes?"
> He forgets and is obliged to say straight out: "I am still offering my communion for you."
> "I know you are."
> "Wait."
> "What?"
> "Do you love me?"
> "Yes."
> "How much?"
> "Quite a bit."
> "I love you too."

Here Percy parallels a scene in John's Gospel. Binx and Lonnie have just finished Communion; Jesus and his disciples have just eaten breakfast:

> When they had finished breakfast, Jesus said to Simon Peter, "Simon, son of John, do you love me more than these?" He said to him, "Yes, Lord, you know that I love you." He said to him, "Feed my lambs." A second time he said to him, "Simon, son of John, do you love me?" He said to him, "Yes, Lord; you know that I love you." He said to him, "Tend my sheep." He said to him the third time, "Simon, son of John, do you love me?" Peter was grieved because he said to him a third time, "Do you love me?" And he said to him, "Lord, you know everything; you know that I love you." Jesus said to him, "Feed my sheep." (Jn 21:15–17)

Again, there is something fresh and full about Lonnie's way of being in the world. As Binx noted earlier, Lonnie's words are "not worn out. It is like a code tapped through a wall. Sometimes he asks me straight out: do you love me? and it is possible to tap back: yes, I love you."

In a sense, Lonnie is a sign pointing us to Jesus. Percy posits a sign as "something that directs our attention to something else," and this directing of our attention is "brought about by past association." In another sense, Lonnie is a symbol, a symbol that "does not direct our attention to something else, as a sign does. It does not direct at all. It 'means' something else. It somehow comes to contain within itself the thing it means." Having just received the Eucharist, Lonnie could be read as a symbol, containing in himself the thing he means—Christ. Maritain reminds us that "the sacramental sign is no longer merely a *practical sign*, it then becomes an *instrumental cause* of which the very

Cause of being makes use to produce grace in the soul." Having received the sacrament, Lonnie becomes a symbol.

At the end of his essay "Sign and Symbol" Maritain argues that "nothing is clearer than the importance of the sign in social life," because the sign "invests human affairs with *meaning* (signification) and fills them with something more than they physically are, makes out of men and their gestures a mirror, a sign, a symbol through which passes *another thing*, and to this extent gives social life an intellectual and indeed a poetical *quality*." In *The Moviegoer*, Lonnie may be a "Helen Keller" helping us to discover signification and therefore sin.

He may also be a sign mirroring Christ for Binx. Dwelling on the wonder of signification, Maritain argues that it is in a sense of little importance that a sign's significance be forgotten over time, or is morphed, or is indistinct. What is essential is that there be sign and signification: "Not knowing precisely what a given sign signifies, I am free to have it signify *everything* for me. In a sense, poetical joy and affective exaltation will then only be more vast and more indeterminate." And yet, on the edges of this *everything* dwells the great *nothing* spoken of by Shakespeare's Macbeth, for whom all of life, *everything*, is "a tale / Told by an idiot, full of sound and fury, / Signifying nothing." Amidst the sound and fury of *The Moviegoer*, Lonnie may signify many things, but there is one thing he symbolizes more than any other.

Wrestling with three incarnations of the literary term "Christ-figure," Robert Detweiler "speaks of the *sign*, where the character is but Christ in disguise, of the *mythological archetype*, where the character and Christ are seen as representing the same recurring life-pattern, of the *symbol* in which a character's redemptive role in a story is indicated through some overt parallels to the Biblical Christ." Lonnie is a symbolic sign. At the novel's end, Lonnie dies of hepatitis. The day before he is gone, Binx visits him to find that "he had conquered a habitual disposition"—his envy. Just before dying, he became a living man. The day his breath finally expires, Lonnie's half brothers and sisters are left outside in the car all morning while his mother stays at her dying son's bedside. Binx, until this point an observer and interpreter, comes urgently out of the hospital room: "I have to find the children," he says hastily. Binx comforts the children with kisses. If Lonnie symbolizes Christ *in alio esse*, Binx becomes Lonnie in another mode of existence, becomes, thereby, an unexpected vessel of faith, hope, and love:

"Binx," one of Lonnie's brothers asks, "when our Lord raises him up on the last day, will Lonnie still be in a wheelchair or will he be like us?" Binx says, "He'll be like you." To which young Donice replies, "You mean he'll be able to ski?"

> The children cock their heads and listen like old men.
> "Yes."
> "Hurray" cry the twins.

When Binx offers to take the children to the Audubon park, they scream *Yes!* and say, "Binx, we love you too!"

You can see just how tricky it is to parse out the fissures and sinews that exist between signs and signifiers, symbols and sacraments. The mysterious character of these relations coax us into intensive investigations of reality. And this is the point: to extract something of the supersaturated meaning that marks our lives, we must assume the posture Flannery O'Connor described as being "hotly in pursuit of the real." Piecing together the work of Percy and Maritain, and trying to put things as succinctly as possible, Lonnie is a sign *symbolizing* Christ. In him we find a "certain presence—presence of knowability—" which we find more fully in the unbloody sacrifice of the Eucharist and in the sufficient sacrifice of his life. Christ is in Lonnie *in alio esse.*

Lonnie is both sign and symbol in the story, but his meaning bleeds beyond both in that he receives the Eucharist. Lonnie offers up the sacrament, which effects a *change in being* for Binx. In the final scene, where Binx interacts with the children, we see more than a mere change in behavior. We see an indisputable change in Binx's being. We see him respond to Christ's command (one which Lonnie *presences* to him anew): "feed my lambs" and "tend my sheep." Of course the shift is not and should not be *storied.* We see him, even after his contact with what Lonnie and what the children signify, even after the remarkably childlike interaction with the children, move into a movie-like image of his beloved Kate in his mind, and he remains again abstracted "until my brothers and sisters call out behind me."

Percy begins *The Moviegoer* with a quote from Kierkegaard's *The Sickness Unto Death:* "The specific character of despair is precisely this: it is unaware of being despair." As we now know, Percy contends that consciousness—from *con-scio*, "I know with"—comes about through language. For he calls consciousness an "act of attention to something under the auspices of its sign . . . an act which is social in origin." One who lives in despair without knowing he is in despair is like the deaf mute whose life is dictated solely by signals. To use Kierkegaard's metaphor of the self, such a soul lives *only in the basement* for his entire life. The basement is the *aesthetic* way of life in which one is in despair so as not to be conscious of having a self. He who inhabits the basement lives in obedience to desires alone, and never reaches the ethical first floor—from which he might arrange his life in accordance with the required. The debased basement life is twice removed from Kierkegaard's religious second floor, what he calls the ideality of actuality, where all things are made new. Binx, whose tenancy in the basement has gone on too long, is nearly subsumed under a flood of pleasant fictions and their fabricated promises. He first lives for the fiction of the movies, but *The Moviegoer* reveals that the harmful fantasies which distract us are not limited to the second-rate blockbusters by which too many of us measure our lives.

Rather, as Simone Weil shows us in her essay "Morality and Literature," "the substance of our life is almost exclusively composed of fiction. We fictionalize our future, and, unless we are heroically devoted to truth, we fictionalize our past, refashioning it to our taste. We do not study other people; we invent what they are thinking, saying, and doing." Reality may provide us with raw material, but we tend to refashion it until all values are reversed. Explicating Weil's essay, John M. Dunaway notes that "a law of human psychology perpetuates this tendency until we are confronted with a violent shock of reality—such as contact with a saint or with affliction or crime. The only other thing that can overcome the force of fiction in our lives is the work of great literary genius," poetical passages filled with the density of the real. Such *poesis* ransoms the significance of symbols, which give to us *worlds* which, existing within good and evil, grant us the possibility of *conversion*—conversion at the level of language, yes, and yet also at the level of the soul. Remember Maritain's insistence that in order for one to *know* the relationship of signification of which they are to make use, "some external help is indispensible." In *The Moviegoer*, Binx's aesthetical, basement existence is interrupted by contact with the saintly Lonnie and, in an entirely connected sense, children.

For us, this "external help" comes from Percy's poetry, which makes us *feel* the stoniness of our hardened hearts by giving us God *in alio esse.* Who among us is not lost in those Pharisaical fictions which Christ called "unseen graves over which people unknowingly walk"? When we are half-asleep in cemeteries of buried significance, hemmed in by our secret sins (signs that signify nothing), great poems can prepare spaces in our language which do not yet exist, opening our very beings to the gravity-suspending, despair-defying, language-illumining action of grace.

20

"Stay in Your Lane or You'll Get into 'The Trouble'": J. F. Powers and the First Commandment of Fiction

"WHAT INSULTS MY soul," Zadie Smith confesses in *The New York Review of Books*, "is the idea—popular in the culture just now . . . that we can and should write only about people who are fundamentally 'like' us: racially, sexually, genetically, nationally, politically, personally."

The First Commandment of Fiction has mutated from "*write what you know*" to "*stay in your lane.*" This narrowing stricture, perhaps meant to prevent accidents and keep us safe within ourselves, is at odds with the essence of good fiction, which, Smith says, has always "suspected that there is far more to people than what they choose to make manifest," and which unflinchingly probed the "profound mystery of consciousness" in a manner that stimulated deep and humanizing curiosity concerning "others."

In his short story "The Trouble," the (Caucasian) Catholic writer J. F. Powers weaves between black and white lanes. Imagining the reader into some of the singularities that have marked African American Catholicity, he thereby makes tangible the universality of the faith, even though, as a fictionist, he also makes manifest that which divides. In doing so he tries to eschew cheap platitudes of "unity" in order dignify the sufferings of his fellow travelers. At times he comes close to one of the casualties of fiction's false consciousness—caricatures. Still, Powers does not chalk race as the final demarcation. Rather, the chiaroscuro story strives to remind all comers of what Flannery O'Connor calls our "essential disfigurement."

"The Trouble" takes us into an urban "race riot." The young narrator, a black Catholic, moves from window-watching observer to soul-sickened sufferer of the riot's casualty. His Mama, caught up in the mobs as she came home from work, is carried inside their apartment. One of her bones "had poked through the flesh . . . all bloody like a sharp stick, and something terrible was wrong with her chest." Earlier, the young man's Old Grandma kept shooing the kids away from the window where they longed to "see some whites get killed for a change." That morning all of them, even those "too young to know what the hell," witnessed a limping black man get bricked in the head until "it got all red and he was dead."

Now, as his grandmother mutters her French prayers (*Mére du Christ, priez pour nous, Secours des chrétiens, priez . . .*), the wound gets intimate: the violence threatens to bear him away. When they bring Mama in, a bespectacled black man cites a poem by the Catholic convert and former Marxist Claude McKay. "If we must die let it not be like hogs hunted and penned in an inglorious spot," he cries, rallying his race to organize and fight the thing to a finish.

If the kingdom of heaven suffers violence, its kernels feed the narrator's soul, sprouting when he's so sick he can't eat. While he's caught up in McKay's call to "meet the common foe," as Mama lays dying, he seizes a sight they've all been waiting for—"a white man that was fixing himself to get nice and killed." The young man, running with a bugle, is chased by "about a million coloreds." But as the pale enemy comes closer and "the worse it got for him," the more the narrator pulses with prayers for the "fool white man with the bugle to get away." Watching it all, Old Grandma saves the chased bugler. When she sneaks him into their apartment, this pricks the narrator to get "hold of a funny idea." "I told myself the trouble is that somebody gets cheated or insulted or killed and everybody else tries to make it come out even by cheating and insulting and killing the cheaters and the insulters and killers. Only they never do. I did not think they ever would."

Powers immediately pinches us with a problem, prevents the story from becoming a paltry parable. The white man, who says he hates to "give us any trouble," feigns innocence. He'd just been passing by, he says, when "a hundred nig—when he was attacked." His cut-short racist rant is only part of the trouble. The "victim's" story whitewashes what actually happened. As the narrator noted earlier, the bugler was one of "three dozen whites" who were "chasing two coloreds" down the alleyway. Everybody saw this because Old Grandma had just crossed that way, ducking into the store and returning "with something in a brown bag."

The white man, worthy of unsought prayers, hangs around the apartment with utter awkwardness, his shame on silent display. He looks fundamentally funny to the narrator, who tells us that the only whites who came to see them were "the man for the rent" and Fr. Egan, their priest. As Powers's fellow traveler Evelyn Waugh saw, in America, black Catholics faced "sharper tests" than their white co-religionists, for the source of their persecution was not Protestant prejudice but "fellow-members in the Household of the Faith." In "The American Epoch in the Catholic Church," Waugh lauds the African American Faithful who possessed a supernatural knowledge of their faith that surpassed that of their hypocritical clergy. Waugh is attuned to the reparation by which some have tried to amend these scandals. Still, "honour must never be neglected to those thousands of coloured Catholics who so accurately traced their Master's roads amidst insults and injury." Waugh observes that a particularly noteworthy contingent of black Catholicity took shape in New Orleans. Powers too points to this relative anomaly to the American scene: "Our family wouldn't be [Catholic]," the narrator remarks, "if Old Grandma and Mama didn't come from New Orleans, where Catholics are thicker than flies or Baptists."

Powers paints chiaroscuro throughout "The Trouble." Wounded Mama is "all bandaged up in white." Grandma opens the brown bag when the pale priest comes to administer Last Rights: inside the brown bag hides not the salve of alcohol (as foreshadowing seemed to hint), but "two white candles." The priest plucks cotton out a little black bag and, dabbing it in the oil of unction, anoints bandaged

Mama with the sign of the cross. The new pastor has come to replace a priest who only lasted a week before "poor health" took him elsewhere. Daddy reveals that he "was transferred to a church in a white neighborhood because he couldn't stand to save black souls." Brushing the story with still more shades, the priest who prays over Mama is named Father Crowe—a painful allusion to the Jim Crow laws that enforced racial segregation. Powers paints in black and white in spite of—or because of—the fact that the white man with the bugle is "Catholic too." *Are the anti-fiction foes of Zadie Smith right?* he seems to ask. Can we only know "people who are fundamentally like us"—race, in this case, being more fundamental than Catholicity?

On the surface, the story comes to a close without achieving commonality across characters. Daddy threatens to murder the white man if his wife dies, even though all present profess the bugler's "innocence." "Just because you're white, yeah," he menacingly says. The white man, in turn, clings to the Catholic card, begging the cleric to accompany him through the anticipated mob outside. "You won't be the first one to hide behind a Roman collar," Fr. Crowe says.

It is Grandma's Catholic faith that colors the story with governing images capable of reigning above the chiaroscuro of racial tensions, even if it doesn't dispel them or offer easy answers. It is not just that her influence is felt in the narrator's epiphanic "funny idea" concerning cyclical violence. Just before Mama dies, Old Grandma "took down the picture of the Sacred Heart all bleeding" and set it beside the departing soul, where, candles make the "Sacred Heart, punctured by the wreath of thorns, look bloodier than ever."

Christ's heart bleeds for Mama's, bleeds a bright and unifying red.

Although his interior agonies remain hermetically sealed, Daddy's final gesture mimics his son's earlier reach for forgiveness. His wife, having just barely received extreme unction, dies. He shuffles "draggily" over to the departing white man and says, "in the stillest kind of whisper, 'I wouldn't touch you.'" Waugh may be right (in his review of *The Prince of Darkness*) to be wary of the ending of Powers' "Lions, Harts, Leaping Does," as it is true that his "gentle account of the death of the old friar" is tinged with the "sentimental." But the end of "The Trouble" escapes this allegation. The narrator falls breathless, overcome by too many intersecting sufferings, this in spite of his Daddy's hinted forgiveness and his mother's reception of the sacraments.

And yet "The Trouble" only narrowly dodges another sort of sentimentality—the recreation of "others" in a manner that too easily pleases. As John V. Hagopian remarks, in this story, both whites and blacks come close to "conveniently" fitting the "stereotypes of the liberal mind," which would ideologically romanticize the object of its sympathy and struggle to render well the consciousness of the characters.

Consider *Terrorist,* a late novel wherein John Updike fails badly because from the very beginning, what Hagopian calls "the liberal mind," asserts itself awkwardly, committing an offence against the art of fiction. For fiction excels at the imitation of characters' interiority, and to succeed, it must manifest the character's, not the author's, consciousness. Powers flirts with failure, but, as Sister Bernetta

Quinn asserts, the author's thirst for justice is tempered by a "symbolically significant structure and by a rather subtle imagery" that reconciles the "outer and inner worlds" at stake in the story.

Catholicity passes through the particular into the universal. As Waugh wrote, regardless of the palpable differences that mark the world's manifold cultures (he cites a Eucharistic procession in Spain, wherein firecrackers exploded under the feet of the clergy), "any altar boy" could tell you that "the 'incantations' of the Mass are identical whether in Guadalupe or Gethsemane, Ky," regardless of plain differences. Powers's Catholic faith proclaims this. But the fictionist in him permeates otherness, sinks into the necessary particularities that complicate our unities—the indignities that we cannot perfectly share. There, from within the story, with all the agonies only art can give us, he crafts the wounds that mar the body of Christ without bugling out a propagandistic moral. J. F. Powers's civil disobediences evince his unwillingness to cow to convention. In fiction, too, the Irishman refuses to stay in his lane, and it gets him into the kind of trouble without which it is difficult to live wholly.

21

Caroline Gordon Lost and Found: The Malefactors

The reputation of Caroline Gordon concerning her contribution to the Catholic literary tradition has suffered repeated mortifications, so much so that one cannot help wondering whether they may be merited. When her importance is recalled at all, Gordon is reckoned as the wife of Allen Tate and the indispensable editor and mentor of many. Without her rallying praise and exacting advice, Walker Percy may never have gotten out from under his burned early novel *The Charterhouse*, and *The Moviegoer* may have remained an existentialist *essai* (which in the original French signifies a *try* or *attempt* as opposed to a finished thing) rather than a National Book Award recipient.

When Robert Giroux wavered over *Wise Blood*, Robert Fitzgerald asked Gordon to apply her sharpened sensibilities to the manuscript, which O'Connor came to call "Opus Nauseous No.1." Gordon immediately recognized that "this girl is a real novelist" and wrote to the young talent a long letter filled with earnest appreciations ("There are so few Catholics who seem possessed of a literary conscience") and painstaking criticisms ("I don't think that your title is prepared for enough") that gave the novel a needed transfusion. O'Connor was not oblivious to the "great pains" which her elder took; she remained overwhelmed by Gordon's "very generous" criticism and her "highly energetic and violently enthusiastic" acumen, even as her adept mentor made her "feel like [an] illiterate grandmother."

In spite of this awesome arc of influence, Gordon's own fiction has remained, in the main, untouched. A number of her novels, long out of print, have been lost to prospective generations of readers. Of late, Gordon has been "found" again. In the last few years, we have seen the publication of *The Letters of Flannery O'Connor and Caroline Gordon,* edited by Christine Flanagan. In *Good Things Out of Nazareth* (whose title is taken from Gordon's own description of the Southern Catholic literary movement), Gordon plays a major part. And, finally, Cluny Media, as part of its sustained putsch to bring many "Catholic novels" back into print, just republished two of Gordon's important works: *How to Read a Novel* and *The Malefactors.* Given this surge of recognition, it is perhaps not peculiar that Cluny is also bringing *The Strange Children* back into print in the summer of 2020.

Gordon wrote two novels in the years immediately following her conversion to the Catholic faith. *The Strange Children,* published the same year as *Wise Blood* (1952), was nominated for the National Book Award alongside works by J. D. Salinger and Truman Capote. *The Malefactors,* which followed four years later and came out as a Cluny Classic in 2019, is a novel of the "Lost Generation." In the story, Tom and Vera Claiborne inhabit a farm at Blencker's Bridge, headquarters of a lively influx of family and friends and literati. When they turn away from painting and poetry, these bohemians make life "a party every day," which is to say that things turn south. As her misanthropic husband takes a mistress, Vera roots herself in bulls—not the brutal beauties of Hemingway's matadors, but rather raising prize bulls and serving as "president of the Red Poll Breeder's Association of the Atlantic Seaboard States." After an attempted suicide, Vera brings her bull to a Catholic Worker farm, where, pathetically late, Tom comes to confront himself in front of her.

The odds of this "strange book" (to cite the original jacket cover) were undermined before it reached readers' hands. Gordon had originally dedicated the work to Dorothy Day, who is fictionally refracted in the character Catherine Pollard. Day was astonished to find herself rendered, in Paul Elie's words, "as a holy seductress with a blasphemous past"—including participation in a Black Mass. Although Gordon considered the book as "a tribute, an act of devotion," Day wrote "forceful letters" demanding that the "To Dorothy Day," as well as her character's dabbling in Satanism, be exorcised.

As Bainard Cheney notes, "The decision, just before publication, to eliminate the dedication, gave the publisher cold feet, and the novel was shelved rather than promoted: perhaps a considerable reason for its small sale." Fifteen years after its initial appearance, Cheney tried to champion the novel back into print. He cited *Collier's Encyclopedia* entry for 1956, which registered *The Malefactors* as "probably the finest novel of the year—in certain respects if not in all."

He summoned the strength of Arthur Mizener's *New York Times* review, which insisted that "her books have grown more skillful with time" even as "not many people seem to notice. The decades go on tossing up their temporary immortals . . . and Miss Gordon goes unnoticed." Cheney's collection of celebrations bids us to tease out causes for the constancy of this oversight, an unmerited mortification. Regularly, Gordon's reviewers insist that this novel is a rare feat, and regularly these cries are trampled underfoot. Surely Gordon's book suffers not merely from—to cite Hamlet—"the slings and error of outrageous fortune."

Although *The Malefactors* is more than the "spiritual hangover of the Lost Generation" (as *Time* magazine called it), the novel cannot entirely dodge one critic's charge: "tedious." And so, before accentuating its excellences, I must try to enumerate the elements that magnify the tedium.

First, the past exerts a persistent influence on the present-tense action. As Gordon explained to a friend, three dead men (the poet Horne Watts, as well as the fathers of Tom and Vera) "unfold chronologically, counterclockwise to the main action." Intentional as the intervening flashbacks may be, at times they stretch on for pages *between* dialogic exchanges happening in the *now*. Not infrequently, the reader is rudely awakened from mesmerizing, ghosting portraits of torturous and torturing father figures by a character's response to a question we forgot had been asked, or by the "reappearance" of another character outside Tom's consciousness who, in our past-bound reverie, we forgot was in the room.

Second, the novel introduces us to too many characters too quickly. By beginning with a *féte* at Blencker's Bridge, Gordon provides the material occasion for the massive cast that we meet in the first thirty pages, but she overwhelms us with convoluted townie and familial relations and expatriate associations. Just when we have found some steady ground, following a single conversation that has been continuous for a decent duration, she asks us to juggle a new troupe. This weakness disappears as the novel moves to part II. Further, on a second reading, this flaw is far less distracting, and perhaps a partial explanation for being pulled in so many directions, through so many subplots, is that we are following these (spiritual) drifters of the "Lost Generation," but a saturation of diverging directions enervates the action nonetheless.

And finally, Gordon's attempt to write saints—her efforts to transpose Peter Maurin and Dorothy Day into compelling figures charged with captivating sanctity—makes for some of the weakest characterizations in the book. "She certainly had a hard time making those CW [Catholic Worker] people believable," O'Connor admitted. As Paul Elie observes, O'Connor would never write a novel like *The Malefactors*, "in which good and thoughtful people discuss the quandaries of religious faith in an earnest and intelligent way. Good people, she believed, are especially hard to write about." Here, O'Connor concurs with Simone Weil, who insists that "imaginary evil is romantic and varied; real evil is gloomy, monotonous, barren, boring. Imaginary good is boring; real good is always new, marvelous, intoxicating." While Weil's appraisal is too categorical, we know how hard it is to make goodness compelling in fiction. From Dickens and Dostoevsky to David Foster Wallace, capacious writers have mastered troubled souls and only with marked problems crafted holy souls.

When Gordon's agent approached O'Connor requesting a kind of *quid pro quo* in exchange for the elder's public praise of *Wise Blood* and *A Good Man is Hard to Find,* the "real novelist" with a "literary conscience" ducked, indicating that "it would be impertinent for me to comment on the book, simply because I have too much to learn from it." Nonetheless, O'Connor did write a review. She grounds her analysis in an interpretation Louise Cowan advances in "Nature and Grace in Caroline Gordon": "Though the surface of her novels . . . moves toward destruction and despair, the current in their depths moves in a strongly different direction." O'Connor stares at the superficial glare that threatens to blind readers to its subterranean and sometimes super-subtle merits.

Although *The Malefactors* is "profoundly Catholic," it remains "doubtful if it will receive the attention it deserves from the Catholic reader, who is liable to be shocked by the kind of life portrayed in it, or from the reader whose interests are purely secular, for he will regard its outcome as unsound and incredible." The "outcome" she mentions is the conversion of Tom Claiborne, his strained but not entirely uncanny turning toward the Catholic faith. This most difficult aspect of the novel is its most complete achievement. O'Connor goes so far as to say that here we have "undoubtedly the most serious and successful fictional treatment of conversion by an American writer to date."

In *How to Read a Novel,* Gordon cites Aristotle, contending that all great narrative art falls into two parts: complication and resolution. In a masterpiece, she says, "the Resolution is always embedded in the Complication from the very start." *The Malefactors* is not a masterpiece, but Gordon does set up the complication—and its prospective resolutions—immediately and masterfully.

Waking late, Tom rises on the day of the *fête* to find Vera leading her prize bull. At once we behold one of the novel's controlling symbols (the Red Poll) and we grasp their marital *de facto* separation, as he wearyingly resists each of her requests with the same palpable indifference. He wishes to avoid a visit to his sick aunt's room, though when he reluctantly goes, he finds Catherine Pollard performing a corporeal work of mercy.

"Hell of a way to entertain a guest," he says, feeling badly for Cat. But he finds her *facing* instead of hiding from human fragility, which gives him a healthy shock. He wants someone else to pick up Vera's cousin Cynthia from the train station, but when he grudgingly fulfills his wife's request, things quickly become complicated.

Tom and Cynthia's interactions are charged with indirect but evident erotic tension. Although Tom remembers Cynthia as "savorless broth," upon seeing her he has to restrain himself from giving her "Southern kisses," and he speaks awkwardly of his age ("I'm getting to be an old man"), as though to simultaneously acknowledge and diminish the force of his attraction. We learn that on his wedding day, the drunken Claiborne fell down near Cynthia, who pulled from her bridesmaid bodice one of her poems and begged the famous poet for his opinion. Too drunk to think, he declined. On the ride home, Cynthia speaks glibly of her strained marriage, and Tom wonders if this Dantean Francesca has already found her Paulo: he does not admit that already he has half-submitted his application for this adulterous role.

Tom is a difficult man to love, a fact which elevates Vera in the reader's troubled heart; still, although it is hard to witness his habitual solipsism, Gordon renders his own agonies with soft touches that solicit concern for his soul rather than condemnation. His mentor Horne Watts committed suicide: when drunk enough, the poet (modelled after Hart Crane) spoke of himself as a "holocaust," arguing that the artist must sacrifice even love to offer himself on the Muse's altar. But Watts's artistry, so promising at first, had dried into a single paltry lyric composed over a run of years, and he leapt from a ship crossing the Atlantic; "it was the sea that got him in the end, and sharks, not flames, that picked his bones." This abdication into the abyss oppresses Tom throughout the novel, pulling at him sometimes to follow the man to whom he remained in debt. His imagination reels with hyperbolic visions of others close to the edge. Seeing Cynthia sitting on a bench, he wonders whether it was "the shadow of a tree trunk or the wavering walls of a chasm? It crept on across the grass and she set her cup down and leaned farther backward, her hands clasped in her lap. . . . Did she know that her bench stood on the lip of a chasm?"

Besides these nervous delusions, Tom never had a proper raising: his father was a gambler who frequented whorehouses: "He could not ever remember looking his father in the face without feeling the necessity to look away. . . . It was not because his father had looked unkind or arrogant that he had found it necessary to avert his gaze from his face, but because he looked unhappy," and, for children, "unhappiness is the cardinal sin."

Tom's early successes with poetry won him laurels and editorships, but he cannot conscientiously ride on the coattails of these youthful victories. In shame, he has "fallen into the habit of deceiving Vera." Her happiness, he knows, depends on his. She "could not give herself over wholly to rustic delights unless she was convinced he was enjoying himself too." And so he chooses the ruse of writer in his garret, frustrated by the "demands" she places upon him, as if wishing she were as apathetic to his threatening malaise as he is toward his fellow man. Although he has written only a handful of pages of middling poetry in many years, each day he asserts that "I've got some things to do," and, shutting himself into his office, he locks the door. The lock is a safeguard against shame; once, a servant entered the room to find the poet asleep on the sofa instead of communing at the altar of the Muse.

It comes as no surprise when Cynthia, houseguest at Blencker's Bridge, appears in Tom's office "in a white dress," bearing a manila folder filled with poetry. At this very moment, Claiborne looks out the window to find his wife watching cows with "Tom Abel," the dairyman. Already Tom has seen in his wife's affiliation with other men his own failings: "Was it because he was the kind of man he was that his wife had to have a fellow like Max around?"

Max, a painter and friend of Watts, is a homosexual and therefore poses no triangular threat to his relationship with Vera. His response to her consultations with Tom Abel, however, is more alarming: "For him her actions had been so long divorced from reality that they had lost all significance." Cognizant of the dried-up irrigation ditch that separates him from his wife, Tom turns toward Cynthia and confesses, "I haven't been able to write anything for a long time." She preys upon this declaration of poetic impotence, indicating how eager she is to have him admire her poems and then trading his confession for a volatile confidence. Although Tom knew that Vera's father committed suicide (for it was his wife who found her progenitor dead at his easel), and gossip had suggested that her old man was homosexual (providing a plausible reason for her close kinship with Max), Cynthia tells him more: in his last days, Vera's father painted grotesque pictures of himself, pictures that his daughter had purportedly burned but which are almost certainly instead locked up in the attic—in the Claiborne attic just above them.

Tom and Cynthia ascend into the attic, and just before they open the aluminum container concealing the controversial paintings, Cynthia starts pressing closer to him, whispering his name. He raises his head to find his wife as witness to their proximate infidelities. Vera swears that there are no paintings of her father's. They are "*Mine!*" she declares, averting "her eyes from his while she contrived the first lie she had ever told him." It is obvious that Cynthia was keen to Vera's secret. It is obvious that Vera's first falsehood is in part a consequence of Cynthia's cruelty and of her husband's own flirtations with misspent intimacies.

The affair between Tom and Cynthia accelerates, as they consummate their predictable passions in a cave to which he retires "when things get too much for him." She takes up an apartment in New York City, and he assumes an editorial position at *Parade*, a newly-launched literary magazine. As Anne M. Boyle writes in *Strange and Lurid Bloom: A Study of the Fiction of Caroline Gordon*, the author "turns her attention to the salvation of the frustrated, intellectual, emasculated man" who needs to recover his manhood. Tom's adultery is a cheap assertion of virility, whereas his assumption of an editorial position requires daily work. Soon thereafter it "occurred to him that he had spent half his life avoiding offices. He wondered whether it had not been a mistake." The discipline that his duties demand reorient his restless soul and, unexpectedly, he experiences "stirrings of his imagination" for the first time in years. Gordon's treatment of Tom's spiritual ascent is marked by novelistic action that obtains on multiple levels. Awful as his treatment of Vera is, he does not suffer the downward spiral of a primary color morality tale. His reliance on his wife's wealth, his simultaneous retreat into and alienation from the land had increased his sloth. Wrong as he is to run off with Cynthia, Tom nonetheless gains dignity from the work he does now out of necessity.

The last third of the novel is leavened with these sorts of ironies and reversals. Instead of ending up in a bohemian hovel, Tom's absent friends offer him (and perhaps implicitly Cynthia) their ornate apartments, a habitation so gaudy that a drunken guest once admits, "*You*—in this apartment! Several people told me about it, but I had to see it to believe it." The inebriated Molly does more than mock the dissonance between Tom's literary pretentions and this exorbitant locale. Pulling her into a dark room, he finds he prefers the lightlessness, which as though conceals "from the world at large . . . some poverty." Gordon's articulation of the paradox is perfect: the ornamentation and lavishness of his borrowed apartment, when revealed, expose Tom's deepest impoverishment. He has gained the whole world in exchange for a starving soul. "Oh, you have a ten-dollar word for everything!" Molly chides, "But you don't fool anybody but yourself. . . . I don't think you're really bright at all. If you had been, you wouldn't have fallen for that little bitch." Molly's condemnatory words are cooked by the same alcohol that Tom has been using for years to cool his own banal selfishness. When she relays Vera's indication that she never wants to see him again, it is clear that he is piqued by the pain of such extensive severance; the wife he took for granted, and took advantage of, is no longer the tree of stability around which their home has been built.

Tom retreats into that familiar, shallow solipsism, peddles the platitude that "people our age often discover that their first marriages were a mistake," but his protest is no match for Cynthia's sunken countenance, which he is forced to confront once Molly and the party guests exit. "There was an expression on her face that he had never seen before," he muses, "as if somebody you had never seen or heard of were suddenly standing at the window of a house you had supposed unoccupied."

Gordon takes us into yet another room of meaning, down another one of these crooked corridors with which their borrowed home is pregnant. Beyond the pleasantries of poetry, beyond the pressings of the flesh, he does not know Cynthia at all, does not realize that she is using him for his reputation and influence, as a temporary residence from which to launch her writing career. Or rather, he *did* not admit this. Now, to Cynthia, he says, "You're on the way up [into the lair of the glittering literati]. It's easy to see that. I've got a notion that I may be on the way out." Once he has helped her get published (and he has), and once the hardships of their unrespectable cohabitation strain her success (and tonight's party, punctuated with the punch-drunk Molly, has, oh it has), she will find new quarters, new literary lovers. But before she leaves, Cynthia relates that their mutual friend and psychiatrist has diagnosed him with—. Although she cannot finish her phrase, she need not, for we can do the diagnosing ourselves, a judgment that brings no real pleasure in life: Narcissism. *Narcissist*, a label she lobs at him when he denies his love of Vera with the devastating admission that "I'm not in love with any woman," the indirect confession that he cares only for himself. (And, as he is drunk with a good dose of self-hatred, this dynamic solicits a wince.) His rejection of the pat diagnosis is followed by a fierce desire to be covered in darkness.

Into this courted lightlessness comes an intrusion into his consciousness—foreign words whose source momentarily eludes him: *While all things were in quiet silence and night was in the midst of her course.* The words are from the Word, from Wisdom (chapter 18). In the biblical book, this scene of night silence is succeeded by the following: "Thy almighty word leapt down from heaven from thy royal throne as a fierce conqueror into the midst of the land of destruction." These words wrestle with his wasteland soul until, though still harsh, he has heart enough to profess his awfulness, and Vera's goodness. "You and Vera are very different," he says. "She's got her faults, but she is a woman . . ." The scene's pitch could break glass, and at last Tom's most obfuscating window, dirtied by impossible smudges, shatters. Although he is unable to tell Cynthia what she is, if she is "not a woman," when his Francesca asks him what *he* is ("And you? What are *you*?"), he can finally look inside and find the right words: "A son of a bitch. That's what I am. A son of a bitch." And with that he leaves the room.

The scene is like a bottle of spoiled champagne, brought out for the party guests but imploded instead, staining the lovers' appearances. There is something in it of a Greek tragedy, of the "reversal" Aristotle describes in his *Poetics.* In *How to Read a Novel*, Gordon explains that the reversal is caused not by a change in the heart or mind of a given character (although such changes may follow), "but by an incident: something which, happening suddenly, crystalizes the action and hurries it toward Resolution." Although "there is nothing illogical about it" (and there is nothing illogical in this reversal of *The Malefactors*), "it has in it all the elements of surprise which make a plot . . . work." Molly's disapproval was not entirely unexpected; she had recently refused to invite Cynthia and Tom to a house party. She surprises us, however, by her frothing forthrightness. Tom's confession seemed permanently deferred; we should not have been surprised had he withheld it even until the curtains closed on the novel's last page. However, we have been waiting, *hoping* that he could name his sin.

Given his habituation into self-centeredness, *The Malefactors* would be severely wounded had Tom hit the bulls-eye with his first self-condemnation. Denigrating himself in front of his temporary muse is a major gain, but his name calling remains vague—does not reach the precision that real conversion requires. Given his condition, it is no wonder that the deeper healing begins at least initially with tender regard for his hurt self. Tom visits his cousin-psychologist George Crenfew, who, seeing that the sun is falling too strong on Claiborne's face, "went over to the window and adjusted the blind so that the sunlight did not fall so strongly on [his] face. Claiborne felt that he had never before received such exquisitely thoughtful attention. Tears came into his eyes." Gordon gives us George's action in such a way that its goodness radiates with beauty: a small good thing that helps the stubborn bull surrender.

Tom tells his cousin of a troubling dream, which, superficially, would be deeply unsatisfying if the novel ended here, or if too much hinged on their analysis of his haunted passage through a dreamscape cave, where a father throws his own head over a cliff before directing his son away from the abyss, threatening to throw the son's head over also. Gordon's depiction of the descent into the cave is improved in that it bears echoes of Aeneas's descent (in Virgil's *The Aeneid*) into the underworld in search of his father Anchises. George argues that it is the mythologists and poets, more than reductive psychologists, who gives us images to live by.

The cousins spend much of the "session" not engaging in saving psychology so much as reminiscing about Claiborne's actual father. For George, when they were boys, the elder Claiborne "taught me about the heroes"; he wasn't wholly a failure and negation, as he was for Tom. Tom himself brings an ironic tease: "Pretty run-of-the-mine, I imagine? Lack of a father pattern, don't they call it?" he asks, and his question pierces our sense that this *is* cliché. But, having acknowledged that, the novel presses on, invites us to consider that it is common because it is deep, it is familiar because it is of utmost import: Sophocles's Oedipus could solve the Sphynx's riddle with his "mother-wit," but Tom, George suggests, needs an "Old man." George can play the part, if imperfectly. He plays it by offering a paternal interpretation of his cousin's dream. Crenfew wonders whether the dreamscape father, in threatening to toss the son's head into the abyss, was warning his charge that he was "*too* bright" for his own good. Claiborne again tries to take refuge in his own lights. "Can't be too bright these days," he quips, and in quick succession calls his wife a fool, for he has learned that after an attempted suicide she has moved to one of Catherine Pollard's farms: "My wife's a *fool,*" he accuses. "You know what she's doing now, George? Tending pigs." George's response roots the Cartesian poet in reality: "Well somebody's got to tend 'em—till they make a plastic pig." And besides, the novel seems to suggest, the pigs are a sort of surrogate for the prodigal Tom.

When Tom arrives at the outskirts of "Mary Farm," the gas station attendant tells him of a woman who recently pulled up in a truck, jumped out, "and they let the end gate down and she took aholt of the bull's halter and her and him walked up that path as cool as a cucumber. You don't see a sight like that every day." You don't, but Tom did—only he failed to marvel.

Near the end, then Gordon reintroduces one of the novel's controlling symbols, the bull. On the literal level, we find that Vera has given her "prize bull" to the Catholic Worker farm. But, as Cheney explains, "he also signifies the brass bull, in which St. Eustice and his family were burned to death." In one of the novel's many side plots, Catherine Pollard has commissioned Max to paint a mural for the chapel of St. Eustace, which is connected to the Mott Street house of hospitality. During the *féte,* which fell on the saint's feast day, Max had displayed a painting of his called "The Vision of St. Eustace," which depicts "a Roman general who was converted when the stag he was hunting turned at bay and he saw Christ hanging on the cross between its horns." George's wife, Marcia Crenfew, upon seeing the painting, had asked, "Can't the cross be a phallic symbol?" at which point Tom, irreligious though he was, lost control and shouted *No!*

No, the novel says. Just say no to ideological symbolism. No, the bull is also not a heavy-handed symbol of Tom's tamed virility. The animal, which the novel breeds us to read as affiliated with martyrdom, moves from the source of Vera's pride to alms for the poor. Still, Gordon's controlling symbol isn't over-easy. Its senses are many. In

"Companions in the Blood," Vivienne Koch contends that the novel's opening part in honor of Vera's Red Poll obtains an "atmosphere of sweating humans and hygienic animals" that "slowly builds to a sinister portentousness reminiscent of the cattle show in *Madame Bovary*"; talk of bulls leads to an extended conversation on "artificial insemination" which crescendos into a huckster's foolproof breeding methods, all of which are rejected by some Pennsylvania Dutch Dunkards as "a sin against creation and against God"; the latter, Koch argues, is "a parable on the animal level for the larger motive of *The Malefactors*": to determine the ways in which man can be fruitful and multiply, and what obstructs this capaciousness.

As we, with Tom, follow Vera and her bull to "Mary Farm," we may as well be with Mary Flannery O'Connor as with Dorothy Day; the place is ridden with freaks and outcasts, displaced persons and misfits: "One of them," like O'Connor's good country person, Joy Hulga, "had a wooden leg." Claiborne, moved by these misfits' willingness to feed him, gives away his cigarettes. Tom finds Vera tending not the Red Poll but a mentally ill Joseph Tardieu and a "maimed child" who makes a "discordant cry." Vera greets him with a nay: "I'm not going to get a divorce," she says. As the spouses converse, the child begins to "utter his strangled cry." Gordon lets Tom be Tom. He moves from the precipice of sorrow to resentful paranoia: Vera has decided not to get a divorce, he concludes, because she is going to adopt the child, and "the authorities don't like broken homes, as we laughingly call them." Irate insults escape his loosened tongue. She could marry again, in a few months, he mocks.

She should just get a divorce. Vera gives him silence, does not ask for anything. Her quiet humility overwhelms him, humiliates and harrows him. "I did not know what it would be like to have her look at me and ask nothing," he muses, and, still hurting, continues to hurt her.

His parting words are refined instruments of torture: "Spend the rest of your life working in an orphan asylum," he says, "or an insane asylum, if that suits you better. . . . Have a religious conversion!" A sound "as discordant as the cries that came from the child's mutilated throat" escapes her. "I think maybe I have had it!" she shouts back. The double entendre is just right: yes, yes, she has had it with Tom's antics, and, yes, yes, she has had that conversion. It is only left for him to follow. In the words of the novel's epigraph, taken from Maritain, "it is for Adam to interpret the voices that Eve hears."

As Tom huffs off, he runs into a priest who is also a recovering alcoholic. Father suggests that Tom stay on the farm, let things cool a bit and lend the workers a hand. But Tom won't have it; in a final, barely-controlled assertion of his arrogance, he refuses to stay in the "men's dormitory," which, the priest tells him, is "the old chicken house." Out of the chicken house and onto Mott Street, Claiborne searches out Catherine Pollard and finds her in St. Eustace chapel. Pollard, it turns out, has been praying for him since "soon after George called," as Crenfew told Catherine that Tom had gone to see Vera.

"I wish I could have seen you before you went," she tells him. "I would have reminded you that a wife is subject to her husband as the Church is subject to Christ." When

Tom objects that neither he nor Vera is Catholic, Catherine corrects him: "Surely you know that Vera is in the Church. She was baptized when she was a child."

No, he says, no, he did not know that. "I didn't know anything." Tom turns to kiss her cheek, a reversal of the libidinal kisses he wished to plant on Cynthia when he first picked her up at the train station. Comedy and Christian chastity kiss: Catherine turns her head so that his mouth "fell warm on her mouth." The kiss of peace sealed, he hastens to Mary Farm, where "he could sleep in the hay if there was no bed. He could be sitting there on the bench with the other bums when she came down in the morning." The allusion to Christ's parable of the prodigal is plain. Amazingly, it works on the reader both literally and allusively—efficaciously, on both levels—because Gordon has established the agrarian backdrop from page one. Also, here, in these final lines, is a brushstroke of Bethlehem. He could, like Christ, be born in the hay. He could, we know, be born again into a second sight, if he is already willing to see himself a bum—what O'Connor would call a "figure for our essential displacement" who attains depth because, like so many of her misfits, Tom's story is one of the action of grace upon a character "not very willing to support it."

In his *Commonweal* review of *The Malefactors,* Father John W. Simmons considers conversion as "a special invasion of grace into a particular life. If the artist, in his effort to summon the mystery, gives a maximum plausibility to the motives and conditions leading up to conversion he risks an attenuation of the essentially free character of Grace." But this is only part of the difficulty: "If he gives a maximum permissiveness to Grace he risks making his character seem the puppet of Grace. In this case it is the art which seems implausible, for God becomes an almost literal *deus ex machina.*" Father Simmons finds in Gordon "a novelist who had not only avoided with her usual consistency the *clichés* of her craft but had come closer" than any other Catholic writer to "encompassing the elusive miracle" of rendering conversion in an artistically arresting way without cheapening either nature or grace.

"It seems to me that all good stories are about conversion," O'Connor wrote to her friend Betty Hester. Remember that O'Connor also hesitated to criticize *The Malefactors* "because I have too much to learn from it." Writers and readers working in the vineyard of the Word can learn a great deal about the workings of nature and grace and the artistic imitation thereof from a careful passage through Gordon's novel—especially its final turnings.

In *Art and Scholasticism*, Jacques Maritain posits what is necessary for the emergence of great artists and the perfection of all artistic aims. Among other things, he cites the "absolutely indispensable maintenance of a sufficiently high level of culture in the average of artists and artisans." It would be absurd, he says, to ask every one of these artists to be an "original genius." The greatest writers often rely on lesser ones to reach the heights of their improvements. "All artists borrow," says Etienne Gilson. What distinguishes talent from genius is not what they borrow but "the way in which they borrow. Because talent dovetails, adjusts, organizes and composes, it sews the things it borrows onto the work it produces." Genius, on the other hand, "takes them up to make them its own"; genius smelts them into metal which is cast into a new mold. The genius, we might say, sees what others have achieved and, while not denigrating it, says, with the genuine artist's admixture of magnanimity and humility that often appears to be arrogance, "I could do better." But the genius may only know what needs improving by first encountering works well-made, good works that, in different hands, could have been great ones.

Gordon may not have been a writer of genius, but she was a Catholic novelist of considerable talent. She appears on the scene, just now, like a "Lost Generation" matador with an impressive *muleta*—that stick-hung cloth bullfighters bring out for the last third of the match. Her red cloth is rich with the threads of so many masters: Faulkner and Flaubert, Joyce and Henry James. She amazes us, though, not by dodging bulls' horns (although we know she can do this too), but by corralling the lost animal into the stable, and by tucking the found creature to sleep under the glimmering *muleta*, lowing under the weight of grace.

22

Mistakes Were Made in A Canticle for Leibowitz

WALTER M. MILLER'S *A Canticle for Leibowitz* chants a litany of misdirection that resonates powerfully in our "post-truth" age. Miller, who helped bomb Monte Casino Abbey before becoming a Catholic convert, starts the novel in a comedic key—a fusion of funny and cynical ironies.

Saint Leibowitz Abbey persists in the quiet work of preservation against a violent backdrop of deliberate forgetting (called, euphemistically, "The Simplification"). A desert-dwelling novice uncovers a fallout shelter and mistakes a nuclear blueprint for a holy relic. For fifteen years he illumines the blueprint, inking out a gilded and glorious artifact. Aloof to this and other documents' true purpose, he and his brethren unwittingly contribute to still more nuclear warfare. Through ages alternately dark and enlightened, *Canticle* makes plain our painful capacity for untruth. And yet, even when mass-deception reaches a radioactive level and the monks wane helplessness against their leaders' lies, the novel fosters a meager but substantive resistance, reminding us that institutionalized obfuscation must not eliminate our vital war against self-deception.

When our leaders lie, we, too, can become acclimated to the tallest of tales: that our acts are not "facts" but Rorschach blotches interpretable into oblivion. Miller loosens this "post-truth" preoccupation from our present era, plunking down the same problem in a far out future. In politics, the novel grimaces, truth is always scarce, *in saeculo saeculorum, Amen.* Still, Miller registers the increase in occasions for scandal and distrust that attend promises of transparency. The more we hope in the prospect of responsive rule, the more embittered we can become. When rituals of transparency become platforms for a far more sophisticated dishonesty, cynical faithlessness spreads freely until we find the phenomenon Patrick Deneen pinpoints in *Why Liberalism Failed*: "Overwhelming majorities regard their governments as distant and unresponsive."

As Romano Guardini puts it, "there is a growing sense of there being no one at all who acts, only a dumb, intangible, invisible, indefinable something which derides questioning," a phenomenon he finds captured by Kafka's grim novels. In *Canticle,* this sense waxes during the section of *Canticle* whose tone, technologies, and regimes are closest to our own. With nuclear war nigh, a Defense Minister participates in that symbol of accountability known as the press conference. When a lady journalist requests his comment on a scientist's report concerning high radiation counts, the Minister swerves: "I have not read that statement," he says. Asked whether the scientist in question is competent, the Minister weaves: "He has never been employed by my department." When she presses him for a more "responsive" answer, he insists that his reply was "quite responsive. Since he has never been employed by my department, I have no way of knowing his competence or responsibility. I am not a scientist." The Minister's attitude of distrust is contagious. We have no way of knowing his competence or responsibility. He distances himself from the scientist and from science itself, reducing "truth" to something (someone) that needs to be vetted and supervised before it can be properly publicized.

We know why he is loath to assent. Reticence eliminates commitment and thus—superficially—removes culpability. "To communicate a fact seemed always to lend it fuller existence." This line comes from thc mind of the monk Brother Joshua, who has just discovered scandalous radiation levels. He hesitates before telling his abbot, wary of lending facts existence. Upon hearing these levels, Abbot Zerchi assures his trusted monk that if there were a war going on, they would know. But then he reels, realizing the groundless desperation in his implicit trust. "The government *must* know," he muses. "And yet we hear nothing. We are being protected from hysteria. . . . What is the fundamental irritant, the essence of the tension? . . . Ask a dozen experts, get a dozen answers." The pains of post-truth persist, surviving several apocalyptic scenarios, shaking an Abbot on the verge of another.

As nuclear warfare continues to wreck the globe, the lady reporter again asks answers of the Defense Minister, noting that he "appears rather calm, in the face of the facts." Two international laws have been violated. Warlike acts have been committed. The Defense Minister epitomizes a deflection that has fatigued so many of us: "Madam, as you very well know, we do not have a *War* Ministry here; we have a *Defense* Ministry. And as far as I know, only *one* violation of international law has occurred. Would you mind acquainting me with the other?" As the tedious exchange of officious obfuscations continues, the reporter risks an outright confrontation. The Minister seems to "attempt to shift the responsibility for a full denial from your own—" But she is cut short by his own accusations. *She* is taking a tone. She lacks propriety. The press conference peters out pathetically.

Watching it all on a TV screen, Abbot Zerchi seems to read Guardini: "When this happens, when to the question 'Who did this?' neither 'I' nor 'we'" answers, "the exercise of power has apparently become a natural force." The outcome is obvious. "Are we doomed to do it again and again and again?" he wonders, recalling the falls of formerly great empires. Miller's answer is an unnerving *yes*, for the escalation continues unabated, decimating the earth and but for burdened survivors ruined by radiation. "Lucifer," code name for the bomb, blackens the horizons. The Abbey, in cooperation with orders from New Rome, moves the Benedict option into space, where they will establish a "daughter house" of monks.

Meanwhile, the monastery of St. Leibowitz opens its ancient quarters to the wounded, working out a tense agreement with "Mercy Camp" doctors who, by law, must read "hopeless cases" their right to state-sponsored euthanasia. The Abbot debates Dr. Cors, a Mercy Camp worker who puts the facts to sleep with a too-tender pity. Cors embodies Flannery O'Connor's contention that tenderness without Christ turns into terror: "It ends in forced labor camps and the fumes of the gas chamber." And, we might add, Mercy Camps. At the entrance to these zones of false solace, the Abbot orders his monks to paint a truer sign: "ABANDON ALL HOPE YOU WHO ENTER HERE." With this allusion to the words that hang over Dante's *Inferno,* the Abbot gives the facts of euthanasia their right name.

The Abbot strikes Cors in the face when the doctor wrestles a radioactive baby from his arms. Miller makes the prospect of a radioactive child unnervingly painful. The baby cries without ceasing. The Abbot's fist, though, tells the whole truth, even if later he must confess his own sinfulness. Confession, in *Canticle,* is the enduring correction to self-deception.

Lucifer falls again.

Knocked out in the ruins, grasping for consciousness, Abbot Zerchi's doom seems complete. In the dark, alone, he wrestles with Doctor Cors, still trying to persuade the absent medic that his constructed morality lacks metaphysical veracity. Can't you see, he says to no one, the paradoxical logic of "society and Caesar"? The children of this world work hard to "minimize suffering and to maximize security," only to pervert these ends and arrive at their opposite: "maximum suffering and minimum security." None of this can be denied. But the Abbot must persuade the hardest opponent: *me.*

In her essay "Truth and Politics," Hannah Arendt argues that "current moral prejudice tends to be rather harsh in respect to cold-blooded lying, whereas the often highly developed art of self-deception is usually regarded with great tolerance and permissiveness." She reminds us that in Dostoevsky's *Brothers Karamazov*, when the perpetual fibber Fyodor asks Father Zosima what he must do to gain salvation, the latter prescribes one thing: "Above all, never lie to yourself!"

"The trouble with the world is *me*," Abbot Zerchi confesses, "with a little help from the father of lies." His admission does not absolve the untold number of Caesar's untruths; it does not discount the gravity and reality of these masked. *Canticle* is not a tract counseling quietism. Rather, it is a sober actualization of the Jewish hermit's dictum: "The children of this world are consistent too." Externally defeated by this terrible consistency, the Abbot is crushed under a deeper responsibility he had previously only glimpsed. Tempted to imitate the fabricators who rule, we too wish to "blame anything, blame God even, but oh don't blame *me*."

As the novelist Charles Baxter contends, there is such a thing as the "poetry of a mistake." The Defense Minister peers out from behind the passive voice. "Mistakes were made," he mutters. But when a character confesses with colloquial frankness, then "the action retains its meaning, its sordid origin, its obscenity, and its poetry." Especially read against the Defense Minister's misdirection, Abbot Zerchi's own admissions are truly cathartic. Still, we cannot help wince at the meagerness of his conversion, wondering what it amounts to when amidst the ruins of reality. What healing would come if even one of our rulers would not exit the press conference when invited to chant that hymn of Christian remedy: the trouble with the world is *me*.

23

Christopher Beha's Capacity for God: Sophie Wilder *Revisited*

In his new novel *The Index of Self-Destructive Acts*, Christopher Beha, editor for *Harper's*, makes grace a noisome concern, not least through the controlling metaphor and self-proclaimed prophet Herman Nash, whose apocalyptic preaching from a New York city fountain alters a veteran's life: the latter abdicates the stability of his family's ill-gotten wealth, almsgiving his millions to heed Christ's call: look at the "fowls of the air," who "sow not, neither do they reap, nor gather into barns; yet your heavenly Father feedeth them." Nash announces an end that is nigh, assures a definitive date, and ultimately mysteriously disappears. But before he abandons his fountain perch, Nash gathers crowds, numbers which multiply almost miraculously as clips of him preaching are passed around the internet, some treating "the thing with irony, or as a kind of performance," while others are won over by the man's apparently arresting presence. Unfortunately, this authenticity is hard to believe. Neither Nash nor Eddie are Beha's best creations. While we receive some telling details that draw us into the preacher's presence ("with white hair that shot from his head in electrified waves and the wild gray beard of a prophet of old"), most of these moments lack the level of immediacy called for by both the man's charism and his persistence through the novel. Admirable as Beha's foregrounding of the "ultimate concern" is, in his new novel Beha is better at humanely portraying the tittering, vain, self-imploding "New York set" than those overcome and altered by the Otherness of God. Even if *Index* does not render grace with the same immediacy and capacious persuasiveness as *What Happened to Sophie Wilder*, given the importance of his new novel for both the form itself and for writers of faith, now is a good time to revisit Beha's first novel.

Beha's promise comes in part from deep artistic debts. Unlike many writers of contemporary fiction, he is openly apprenticed (and wonderfully indebted) to great novelists such as Henry James. (The characters of *Wilder* purportedly live in a house once inhabited by James himself, though one doubter proclaims that "probably it's bullshit.") Like Flannery O'Connor, who read James "from a sense of High Duty," Beha is both beholden to the large-canvas achievements of past literary masters and committed to present-tense idioms and present-day conflicts. *Arts & Entertainments,* for instance, chases our obsession with celebrity culture. Beha's corpus also bears the marks of the French novelist Balzac, whom Henry James called all writers to learn from if the novel is to regain "its wasted heritage." Beha's three novels, like the interwoven tales of *La Comédie humaine*, track recurring characters. How I wish he could, in good old novelistic fashion, receive an inheritance from a deceased foreign aunt, retire from *Harper's*, and, when not tending to his children, keep writing novels in this manner, letting souls with only minor roles in one story migrate to a new novel and become the (often falling) "stars," capturing the consequential connectedness of an apparently atomized contemporary existence.

Georges Bernanos said of Balzac that, though he has given us frightful characters, he stopped short of that secret organization of evil from within, where corrupted consciences consciously strive "against God and for the love of death." Whereas Beha's *Index* reverberates with Balzac's unflinching interrogations into the multifarious (and frequently nefarious) motives of men, his portraits of evil flower more fully in *Wilder*, even though *Index* undertakes the harder project of painting sins' panoramic effects.

But Beha's first novel excels at more than mere sin; here we behold his best imitations of the Maker's many-colored and bolded brushstrokes. The late critic D. G. Meyers describes *Wilder* as possessing "perhaps the best conversion scene in an English-language novel since [Graham Greene's] *The End of the Affair*." Although the novel is interlaced with a postmodern narrative playfulness that at times leads to an unnerving lightness of being, Beha's conversion scene is not defined by murmurs or faint hints. When Sophie (a real-deal writer among the faux literati) attends Mass, the language does not lash with vicious force: "something came over her. . . . It got closer to say that she was, for a time, occupied." And yet, recollecting the moment much later, she calls it "the shocked grace she'd felt on that day when everything had changed." Still more, the novel as a whole does not capitulate to the postmodern conceit of sacred "traces" in a deconstructed, *deus abscondis* world. Rather, its religion's archaic torso, riddling its shadow over the whole, speaks absolutely like Rilke's poem: "You must change your life."

If the aforementioned conversion already seems explicit, the religiosity of *Wilder* gets even louder. Midway through the novel's dark forest, we come upon one of the most moving, "Dostoevskian" dialogues on God found in contemporary fiction. Sophie has stubbornly committed to caring for her dying father-in-law Crane, in spite of the fact that her husband has left her for a law office intern—and in the face of her husband's refusal to countenance the now-dying man. Tom, his son, refuses to speak of him, insinuating some sort of monstrous past. ("You really are a monster," Sophie later tells Crane, with her typical Wilder call-it-like-it-is, as when, running into her husband and his fling on the streets, she introduces herself like so: "I'm Sophie . . . I'm your boyfriend's wife.")

Beha masterfully bestows on Crane that "possessed" quality Dostoevsky gives his "demons" without reducing him to a "villainous" caricature. He emanates a fearfully palpable, surefire defiance of God complicated by the possibility that he may be responsible for his pregnant wife's death. When Sophie strives to save him through Scripture, Crane cuts her short, calls it "brutal" to "read such a passage to a dying man," and proceeds to reveal that he knows the Bible "a lot better than you do. . . . And he's a fascist." Sophie is confused: which fascist—"King James?" "God. The first totalitarian. Has to control everything. Reads your mail. Bugs your phone. Watches while you take a shit. I don't see what's to admire. And death camps. Auschwitz is a beach vacation compared to the circles of hell. You get sent there for the same reason, incidentally: for not being a Christian."

She tries to do detail work on his large and startling figure of God. "You're oversimplifying," she contends, sensing her rejoinder's insufficiency even as she says it: "He isn't spying in some prurient way. He's not trying to catch anyone at anything. And he doesn't control everything. He could, but he gives us free will."

He "almost roar[s]," slumping back to the couch, unwilling to take her "free will" ticket. Sure, he says, "You're free to do what you choose, and if you don't choose to worship me, I'll send you to the flames." Crane would grant God more homage had he "just made us do whatever He wanted, instead of leaving us to guess and burning us for guessing wrong."

None of these arguments are new to Sophie. She'd "even made them occasionally to herself," to the point of admitting Crane's "case for a malevolent God was more compelling, if anything, than the case for no God at all." Beha's sensitivity to artful counterpoint is evident throughout, and yet—commodious fictionist that he is—even in this twenty-first century of Our Lord he makes real doubt and real faith doubly persuasive, growing as they do from the characters' hearts; the exchange is wholly believable, seems almost inevitable—in spite of their free will.

Beha gives full range to Wilder's own freedom. Long after her conversion to the Catholic faith, she sleeps with Charlie Blakeman, the novel's sometimes-narrator and devotee of Sophie. Charlie long keeps her religion intentionally in the dark, asking no questions, "since her answers would only mark out the distance between us." In spite of Blakeman's initial reticence and Sophie's self-destructive acts, her conversion will eventually convince him that faith can be *vital,* giving the lie to the halfway house of half-assed religion—all that he'd known until Sophie's strange turning. (Utterly frank about its own peculiarity, the novel at one point asks us, "I mean, who converts anymore, unless they're converting *away*?")

When his father died, for instance, Charlie could not stomach the Catholic Father's homiletics of comfort: "the priest said that my father had been baptized into Christ and now he had died into eternal life." Sure, Blakeman grants, the first part is "strictly true," but "he wasn't a particularly religious man." Memorialization such as this convince him of the Church's institutional inauthenticity. Or rather, initially Charlie was relatively indifferent, seeing the funeral through for the sake of his pious grandmother. But now he thinks differently, knowing "there were still people like Sophie, who took the words of faith as more than words. In light of that fact, it seemed wrong that all these others spoke for appearance's sake." This is one of the novel's great truths: *there are still people like Sophie, thoughtful souls for whom what faith reveals is the first and final page.*

And yet Sophie's story turns wilder as she suffers under Crane's last days. Frighteningly honest, she parses her motives as she watches what appears to be a soulless husk. Keeping vigil in his lonesome apartment, she is saintly in her sacrifice but poisoned by pride, which has her send "away the rest of the world"—the hospice help and all other comers, while she tries to redeem the great sinner all alone. *Why*, the awful question surfaces? "Was it for his sake or her own that she wanted to save his soul?" Despairing over self-accusations, the hero who "knelt at his side, leaning against the bed frame as against a Communion rail," "[gives] up on prayer," and Sophie feeds Crane the pills she'd previously withheld, hastening his death and her damnation, halting her zealous redemption vigil. Later she tells it as only Wilder can: "She felt herself outside of God's attention. She had trespassed in His domain—the place where life was extended or withheld."

Wolfe's whispering will surely reach some wayfarers, lost Waste Land souls who yet have ears to hear. And yet, driven by the *sensus Catholicus*, we should avoid the false binary of either "shout" or "whisper." We should opt instead for an aesthetics more voluminous, searching out both traces and freely-voiced questers whose lives are remade as they court the Catholic faith or turn against its radical demands and still more radical mercies. Beha's novel models the latter, returning to the literati what we thought was lost: "what she would learn to call the *capax Dei*, the capacity to experience God."

Freedom, wrote Flannery, "cannot be conceived simply. It is a mystery and one which a novel . . . can only be asked to deepen." *Sophie Wilder's* deepening construction consciously departs from happy endings. The last lines resist resolution: "she couldn't know until the very last page if she had been redeemed." The final section takes us back in time—places Sophie at the threshold of a nunnery, anticipating remission of her sins. The novel's defiance of chronology defers forever our arrival at this knowledge, this "very last page," and so seems to leave unanswered the question of Wilder's salvation. But perhaps Beha is anticipating and denying our penchant for the perpetual second chances. In "resurrecting" a Sophie prior to her suicide, he is shouting out the limits of fictional representation: unhinged from time, it can assert possibilities where none remain, sobering us to the irreversibility of our misdeeds and, *via negativa,* reminding us of the vastness of *Misericordia.* Bent on saving others, sure that her sins surpass forgiveness, Sophie is both too fixed and too broken to be saved. Dead in spite of the book's resistant ending, Sophie's fatal flaws sink her walk on water. Her drowning-by-doubt burdens us so badly because we saw God start to save her—we saw the goodness of grace unburden her being and charge it with beauty. We saw her resist the godlike control that tempts all artists, all co-creators. Weighed by Beha's Jamesian "central intelligence," her fall away from faith and self-authored damnation obtain the keenly-felt minor key of tragedy; the capitulated sacred lives still loudly, long after her suicide, long after you shut the door, solemnly, on this novel's haunted house of fiction, shocked with the sense that "we ourselves groan within ourselves, waiting for the adoption of the sons of God, the redemption of our body" (Rom 8:23, DV). If faith is to be forged in contemporary letters, let it be with Beha's *capax Dei.*

24

What the Catholic Novel Might Become: Randy Boyagoda's Original Prin

Towards the end of *Original Prin*, our protagonist Princely St. John Umbiligoda sifts through the Duty-Free shop in the Dragomans' airport only to find the generically-mandated crops of globalization, including "leadership books that promised to 'unleash' some things and 'conquer' others" and "books that promised all life's lessons could be learned from Homer and Virgil." Try as it might, this satirical gem cannot keep *The Odyssey* from opening up a major problem that the novel probes: who exactly *is* the center of this man bent on persuading us he's a sympathetic cancer-survivor, tolerant global citizen, and "bad Catholic," but who—with shocking quickness—morphs into a cheating, lying "suicide bomber"?

Odysseus, seer of many cities, traveler to the ends of the earth, connoisseur of many minds, is perhaps the first fictional wandering cosmopolitan, the first to practice what Ulrich Beck, in *What is Globalization?*, calls "place polygamy," the phenomenon of being "married to several places at once" and love more than one of them. Beck contends that through "globalization of biography," the world's oppositions (of continents, religions, cultures) and the world's problems occur not merely "out there" but in the center of peoples' lives. "To live in one place no longer means to live together, and living together no longer means living in the same place." Multiple locations, transnational individuals threaten the hold of the nation-state. The pressures which stretch us in this way usher in new globalized biographies and foster lives like Prin's. Here we have a protagonist who moves from multicultural Toronto to terror-ridden Dragomans, striving to "repurpose" his college into a continuing education endeavor tied to reeducation and humanitarian relocation (or so the story goes) of suffering Middle Easterners. All of the above, by the way, is underwritten by a sketchy Chinese businessman, known only as "the Nephew," who isn't afraid to exercise vague but volatile threats to seal the art of the deal. To go to Dragomans, Prin must leave behind his children and his wife Molly and knock knees, in a chillingly vacuous governmental "safe zone," with his ex-girlfriend Wende.

As he has been doing since *Governor of the Northern Province* (and *Original Prin*, by the way, is better-written than both that novel and *Beggar's Feast*, by far), Boyagoda gives the yields of globalizations comic twists; Prin, negotiating an unexpectedly shady deal concerning eldercare studies and healthcare internships, finds his devotion to literature subjugated to the dross of a woke Dragomans Minister who introduces the Canadian professor's lecture like so: "It's time to hear from our storyteller. He will be speaking to us today about just one word—metamorphosis—and how all of us can transform ourselves and our nation. Many years ago, a passionate and innovative writer, Franz Kafka, absolutely crushed a story about metamorphosis. I remember reading it as a student and being truly inspired. . . . Dragomans was once a lowly caterpillar. Right now, IMO, it's in a cocoon. In the future . . . we will all be drag racers, we will all be butterflies!"

As Boyagoda's able satire unveils, the corporatization of academe relegates literature to the cliché, the tritely and terribly "inspirational,"—the therapeutic. "Place polygamy" is the new morality of globalization, says Beck. And Prin's travels to Dragomans, the conjugal incorporation of Canadian college and Dragomans state, bear this out. But, as Boyagoda makes evident, "place polygamy" occasions awful questions concerning identity.

Through figures as distant from one another as Odysseus and Prin, fictionists have shown us that "many lives in one" makes the man of sorrows more than the acclimated pluralist of Beck's postmodern peace. Like Homer, Boyagoda shows that rootlessness can make plain a deeper rootlessness—from the self and its Source. "Why do I request you to come to me when, unless you were within me, I would have no being at all?" St. Augustine asks. *The Odyssey* is so unsettling because in a very real way Odysseus becomes his fictions; he *is* his wiliness. But though the game of self-making is as old as Homer, the Catholic novelist knows that the capacity for conversion—the shedding of deviated desire masked by manufactured deceits, kenotic self-emptying without keeping receipts—is always the measure, even when characters marvelously defy it.

Odysseus, returned in the guise of a Cretan beggar, seems disassociated from whomever he was twenty years ago. Because he arrives in stranger form, he is able to receive from his faithful swineherd a flattery-free portrait of himself. But the account that he receives of the original Odysseus, of a "good-natured lord" who treated even the lowly with justice, doesn't convince Odysseus. Wracked by much strategizing and rationalizing, "the Cretan" launches into a story of early piracy raids, his participation in the Trojan war, his raw murder of a fellow fighter over plunder, and the divine visitations that aided him on his way home. It is difficult to parse out the interconnections between what actually happened to Odysseus and the ennobling lie he tells of himself; both fought in the Trojan wars, both suffered much, but mostly the threads are too distinct to invite easy comparison. Odysseus is an excellent liar, and one wonders whether he is deceiving himself just as much as his audience, at least until the keeper of pigs peppers him with skepticism: "Yet I think some part is in no true order, and you will not persuade me in all your talk about Odysseus? Why should such a man as you are lie recklessly to me? But I myself know the whole truth."

After the Christian succumbs to infidel kisses in the Middle East, Prin narrowly evades an eruption of leveling gunfire emitted from men in "drab cloak and black balaclava." After the first rash of violence fades, shouts and shots flushing elsewhere, further away, Prin falters over children's goldfish crackers and shattered glass, stilled in terror until he sees a gunman pull a weapon from the back of his pants and point it at him. Then he utters a line his stepfather sent him as protection against fanatical Muslims: *La illah ila Allah, Muhammad Rasul Allah!* The gunman, who has been crying, asks, "Wait, bro, you're one of us." Prin, until now a bad Catholic whose guilty conscience does him a great deal of good, "makes" himself Muslim. Or at least he tries. He tries, like Odysseus, to "reinvent" himself as a radical. "If we're on the same team, bro, why are we both hiding back here instead of going out there to, er, to wage holy jihad?"

Almost immediately, his interlocutor says that "something tells me you're just pretending," not "truly fighting for *khilafah*." In the case of "the Cretan stranger," every yarn of his that bespeaks Odysseus the swineherd calls bullocks, whereas the tender of pigs (and former prince) finds arresting the rest of the spool. Prin fumbles; how can he compete with a man who claims "my sheik's the real deal, okay? I haven't met him yet but he accepted my *bay'a* after I asked for like a year online," and who cites Hadith 54, which says that "we just need to keep on telling the truth." It is easy to forget, amidst Prin's bogus and comic attempts to mimic the fanatical Muslim, that he has abandoned his faith, that his lie is not just a clever survival tactic but an act of repudiation.

How, we can't help wonder, could he abandon his Catholicity so quickly? Clues come through, especially when the gunman says, "You're going to tell the truth." A few months ago, he was diagnosed with cancer. This is true, the novel begins with Prin planning to tell his children the news at the zoo. He prayed to God "(didn't even call him Allah Peace Be Upon His Name back then, that's how far away I was)" that he would "do something important" with his life if he let him live. This is also true; before going under, "Prin vowed" that "if he survived the surgery, . . . he'd be a much better husband. . . . He would do something worthy of all that God had granted him." And he tried to.

Post-surgery, the diapered Prin played pickleball with his fanatical sportsman father on Good Friday. True, he tried to rectify this by fasting to the point of nearly fainting. Yes, as he hears the "half-dozen whiffle balls knocking against wooden paddles at long intervals—and also the gasps of men in sudden pain, stretching and lunging, hammering shots and being hammered right back," he hears, with the sacramental ears of a saint, "the sound of the soldiers hammering into Christ's hands and feet as they hung Him on the cross." Yes, he goes to confession after his father insists that they celebrate their win by indulging at a steakhouse, on that same Good Friday. (Later in the novel, when he is spinning his lies to the gunman, he seems to both unburden himself of tensions with his own irreligious father and further acknowledge his own flippancy when he feigns that his father "laughed and ate steak and Snickers bars in front of his brothers and our cousins all day during Ramadan.")

And ultimately, yes, he agreed, albeit on account of being convinced that God's own voice gave him a "Go," to travel to Dragomans in order to establish an "all sides win" way to keep U.F.U. from closing. But he doesn't seem to think much about whether what he's seeking to save *should* remain open. What defensible goods does "U, F, U" embody—this professional playground where a *professeur* can perpetuate "cutting edge research into the symbolism of the seahorse in Canadian literature"? Prin's school had at some point determined that "Holy Family College" was "becoming increasingly irrelevant and too Catholic-seeming, so they changed its name to the University of the Family Universal," or U.F.U. The university's former cress, "Jesus, Mary and Joseph living in a house made of books—had been pried off long before. In its place was a bare, bright space." (Later in the novel, Prin comes close to matching the cress; after he kisses his former girlfriend on a Dragomans rooftop, and after he phones his wife Molly to confess the mess, he tries to reply to her hang-up with a text message, but his sweaty fingers fumble and he sends her no more than "a blank message from this, the dark end of his life.")

Besides the problem of U.F.U.'s self-preserving desperation, there's a more intimate catch to Prin's quixotic quest—a catch that would strain credulity in a novel that isn't strung-through with implausibles—that is, in a novel that shows us that our terror-troubled, globalized world is in itself implausible: to find a solution, the school has hired his ex-girlfriend Wende, who "specialize[s] in identifying financially viable options for under-performing academic institutions to continue delivering content."

Once his wife gives him permission, he cannot stop "assuring" Molly that there is nothing to worry about. She finally points out that he is "constantly trying to make [her] not worry about [his] going to the Middle East with his girlfriend." Prin doth protest too much. His polygamous heart is displaced long before he takes flight. This is yet another truth that rolls from his feigned-fanatic lips: "I'm not actually married," he says, when the gunman nods suspiciously at his "fellow fanatic's" wedding ring. "I don't have a wife," he says, pulling off his wedding ring and passing it off as a way to "get past passport control" before he "tossed his wedding ring down the aisle" of the Duty-Free.

From a certain angle, he is not lying. It is true that Prin's explanations are consistently oversimplified, so that the gunman grills him with an "I don't believe you" and a "That's just too easy. No one's story is that easy." I do not wish to oversimplify here either, by contending that if his heart is not faithful to his spouse it may as well be as if they weren't—or aren't—married. When he gives in to Wende, however, he cannot help but admit that for who knows how long now his gaze has been craned away from Molly. (How carefully and masterfully he has for so long explained his late-night Google searches of his former girlfriend, their too-frequent communications kept "professional" through the "secure"—from what conscience?—messaging app called VaultTok.) He exploits the fact that his fling with Wende cannot consummate in the conjugal act; his imagination as impotent as his loins, he rationalizes a second kiss with his ex-girlfriend by concluding that "he felt nothing in his head and hips."

Besides being fodder for Wende's hermeneutic of skepticism concerning the persistence of Prin's piety, fidelity, and faith, Molly's husband has long since tried to eliminate peccadillos from the spiritual economy. When his nephew fakes a drowning accident at the pool, Prin, who saw the lifeguard's puckered, pranked face as and after she gave the young man CPR, decides not to confront his godson. Instead, he interiorly congratulates young Patrick, and then colludes with Patrick's Iraq-deployed father who confers that "the lifeguard in question was worth the collateral damage he sustained."

Of course, a considerable chasm separates a teenage prank from an extramarital affair, but the point is that the former foreshadows the latter: Prin's disposition toward both, his initial rationalization of both, prove that the two are justified by the same divorce. His conscience has long mastered Odyssean deception, except that the pleasant fictions he tells fool only the original (pre-jihadi) Prin. Earlier in the novel, his conscience pickled him after he watched Wende's lithe body walking away. He comes close to confessing the fact that he "looked at her walking away and then looked away," but in the very confessional, he rationalizes his gaze because "in none of this had he *felt* felt."

Prin's originating sin seems to be his transvaluation of the sacraments, of the Catholic faith itself, into a maneuverable system that can protect him from himself. Even though he regrets responding to the erotic selfie that Wende sent him after he initially rejected her, when Prin calls home from Dragomans, he is diverted; he puts his family on speakerphone "so he could look up the metaphysical implications of failing to do penance for a mortal sin."

This isn't to say that Prin doesn't admirably struggle to turn away from deceit; Boyagoda gives us much nuance amidst the sometimes buffoonish self-justification. But the layers of rationalizations and lies are so labyrinthine that it somehow becomes believable that Prin *could* turn himself into a Muslim in a matter of minutes. After all, this is the same man who, though convincing us and himself that he is a decent dad and husband, bent on doing better, makes haste to conclude the following while watching a terrorist gun down his ex-girlfriend at the airport: "His only thought was that Wende was dead and now Molly need never have known. Damn. Just then he felt something open up near his chest. In it. All this noise of gunfire and casings dropping on the floor—had he been shot without noticing? No. So what was this sudden blackness come into him? It was that these, his final moments, that, *that,* had been his only thought. Not for Wende's soul. Not for Molly's mercy . . . but that it was unfair he had told Moly something now that never needed to be told."

Overcome by his overwhelming self-centeredness, Prin, like the defiant Odysseus, would rather damn the divine than make a confession with compunction: "Damn you," he says to God, who has purportedly asked him to come to Dragomans "for this" incontrovertible truth. And soon thereafter, with laughable, amateurish storytelling, he remakes himself into the image of the violent God of his imagining.

"Nietzsche replaces sympathy or compassion with laughing together," writes Beck, who argues that in a globalized world, "the sacrilege of polytheism must be committed in the cause of universalism, and first of all with regard to oneself." Laughter must ring out at the foolishness of human certitude. Although the novel may induce laughter over shakiness of human certitudes, it is underpinned by faith, by "the substance of things to be hoped for, the evidence of things that appear not." Prin's many falls are only meaningfully funny or unsettlingly sad insofar as these things hoped for *are* substantial, unshakeable realities.

Catholic writers from Chaucer to J. F. Powers to Evelyn Waugh have given Boyagoda a comic vein to inherit. As John Hagopian has demonstrated, at its best, the comedy of Powers, which "is initially satiric wit—not humor, but wit—which modulates into humor and finally into a quiet seriousness and even a sombre grandeur."

The weakest parts of *Original Prin* come when Boyagoda's prose seems to be chuckling to itself, pleased with its own wittiness with a pressure that implodes the gravitas of the story's lower frequencies. But taken as a whole, the novel surpasses self-satisfied wit and leaves us instead wincing under the weight of the comic spirit's humbling capaciousness. With its comic skewering of conscientious Catholicity and fanatical Islam, *Original Prin* might seem bent on ushering in a hyper-tolerance, but Boyagoda's novel does not laugh at what each of us holds most sacred, so much as he laughs and then weeps at the self-delusions of believers. Nor does the novel present Islam and Catholicism as "equal paths" to the same shared Father.

It is precisely in his fictional-actual metamorphosis from bad Catholic to Muslim terrorist that Boyagoda enunciates how far Prin was from the precepts of his faith in the first place. Although he fools himself well enough, whenever he spins deception aloud, he fails miserably. Though this failure becomes undeniably apparent during his discussion with the gunman, it has always been there. Consider his abstracted, abstruse attempt to confess his attraction to Wende early in the novel: "No Father, it's more that any reasonable interrogation of the interior movements that informed my agreeing to serve on a particular committee in light of the external representative on the same committee." To which the priest, tapping loudly on his watch like a referee awaiting the horsemen of the apocalypse, says, "You're enjoying your professorizing too much. I've certainly heard worse language in here, but not by much."

If he seems far from salvation at the novel's brutally abrupt ending (the ending is literally filled with abrupt explosions), Boyagoda teases us, in this first of a trilogy, with the possibility that this self-made suicide bomber might just yet—through the force of his own violent self-erasure—die to his fictional self and yet find his Source, might just barely meet grace on the other side of violence, taking the same route that O'Connor's characters, in a prior century, travelled. "I'm sick of Flannery O'Connor," Boyagoda once quipped. Thankfully so, or we might not have a novel such as *Orginal Prin,* a major foray into what "the" Catholic novel—through its many metamorphoses, beyond our many wiles—might become.

Part V

HOW TO WRITE (LIKE A CATHOLIC)

25

Introduction

"I find that most people know what a story is until they sit down to write one."

—Flannery O'Connor

"In my end is my beginning."

Or, to transpose T. S. Eliot into a more colloquial key, we must finish where we started: the imagination, when it obtains the depths of Catholicity, seeks to save.

If we translate this into fiction, the Christic imagination incarnates human nature as having its final end not in the characters' self-actualization but in salvation. Say we inhabit a mundane living room scene, in a secular age—in the Midwest, no less. Say that in this miniscule room, a couple is quarreling over an exorbitant heating bill and the shoddy windows of their old house. Even *here*, however subtly, the Catholic imagination senses and suggests a vast and eternal stage that extends far beyond the seen scene: like the protagonist of Goethe's *Faust*, this couple tips the eternal scales, albeit by sometimes miniscule degrees.

True, there is no one, fool-proof, self-help, twelve-step way to write like *a* Catholic. And yet, as Dana Gioia argues in "The Catholic Writer Today," though there is no stringent Catholic aesthetic, "Catholic writers tend to see humanity struggling in a fallen world. They combine a longing for grace and redemption with a deep sense of human imperfection and sin. Evil exists, but the physical world is not evil. Nature is sacramental, shimmering with signs of sacred things. Indeed, all reality is mysteriously charged with the invisible presence of God. Catholics perceive suffering as redemptive, at least when borne in emulation of Christ's passion and death." Catholic literature will be marked by the aforementioned world without end. Amen.

However, to write like a Catholic, you must first learn how to write. According to a panel of infallible experts (also known as "parents"), the preferred starting point would seem to be recitation of the alphabet in the early years of life (putting the letters to a tune can aid and hasten memorization), followed by transposition of those sounds into written symbols penciled or chalked onto papers and sidewalks. Adult supervision required.

All that follows should be read against Flannery's only apparently discouraging insistence that a writing teacher's "work is largely negative, that is it is largely a matter of saying 'This doesn't work because . . .' or 'This does work because . . .'" The *because* is very important. Thus the problem with this book is the problem Plato, in *Phaedrus,* found in all books: they can't talk back. They can't sit across from a table with you, bent over a manuscript, red-pen wielded with love and fervor. As Maritain says in *Art and Scholasticism*, "Precisely because art is a virtue of the practical intellect, the naturally appropriate method of teaching it is education by apprenticeship, a working novitiate under a master and in face of reality, not lessons doled out by teachers." May you, dear reader, find a real reader, find such a master, a generous and exacting one, for there's always a chastening chiseling to come—a truth both harrowing and exhilarating, because the house of fiction needs many rehabilitations before it can really be lived in.

Rehabilitation is harder than the romantic rush of a first draft, however beautiful that azure-colored turret that teeters on plastic foundation; it can bring on near-despair, convince you to give up on writing entirely, especially when time lapses between fixers' visits; the electricity (style), say, cannot be worked on until the architect (plotter) does his work, but though the owners (the characters) want him to begin, the mysterious official housed in city hall will not return calls, will not grant legal permission. Everything stalls and the workers grow restless, rattle off complaints in your brain, waxing ornery in their temporary purposelessness. O'Connor was frank about the fallout: "Writing a novel is a terrible experience, during which the hair often falls out and the teeth decay," she declared. "I'm always irritated by people who imply that writing fiction is an escape from reality. It is a plunge into reality and it's very shocking to the system." Caroline Gordon touched on something similar during a Newman Center lecture: not infrequently, when you have "a dead-line to make," you suddenly find that "you can't put anything down. Nothing comes to you. The characters in your book who yesterday seemed more vivid than the members of your own family have gone away." Amidst this, you strive to get a hold of these ephemeral beings, these figments of your failing imagination. Still nothing: "Of course there are certain things you can do that may induce them to come back sooner, but the main thing you have to do, the only thing that always works, is to exercise patience. It seems to me that the writing of even a short story calls for an almost superhuman amount of patience."

Our paltry efforts, she chastens, are infinitely insignificant when compared to Christ, who "stooped low enough to lift up a whole universe." Still, the artist's end is the same as "the contemplative, the mystic—in this respect at least—his task is to imitate the patience of Christ."

Patience, death to self, a kind of ascetic commitment to the making of art—lacking these, the would-be writer will ever remain a poseur. I will never forget the days I spent half-living in a Milwaukee coffee shop from about sixteen to twenty-two; all sorts of *artistes* gathered there, but whereas a handful were bent over their tables in rapt revision and admirable abandonment to the craft, others spent their days manufacturing identities: the only things they painted were the romantic writerly aureoles encircling their heads. As Orhan Pamuk puts it, "A novelist impresses us not by his . . . romantic vision, but by his patience."

26

The Trouble with Technique and the Artistic Habit

Pending your location of a dream reader, we ought to pause and pay our respects to that most esteemed question of whether writing can be taught at all in the first place. The problem has been with us since Longinus and surely long before him too. Longinus gives voice to skeptics early in *On the Sublime*, admitting that the first question which vexes him is "whether there is any art which can teach sublimity or loftiness in writing. For some hold generally that there is mere delusion in attempting to reduce such subjects to technical rules." Such critics claim that "the Sublime is born in a man"—nor not—and is "not to be acquired by instruction; genius is the only master who can teach it. The vigorous products of nature," so they say, "are weakened and in every respect debased, when robbed of their flesh and blood by frigid technicalities."

In response to his imagined interlocutors, Longinus grants that nature itself determines whether someone has innate talent and the capacity for genius, and "yet to determine the right degree and the right moment, and to contribute the precision of practice and experience, is the peculiar province of scientific method." He cites Demosthenes's remark regarding human life more broadly: "the greatest of all blessings is to be fortunate, but next to that and equal in importance is to be well advised, for good fortune is utterly ruined by the absence of good counsel." We can apply this remark to literature, substituting *genius* for *fortune*, and *art* for *counsel.*

We moderns are inclined to mistakenly equivocate "art" and "method." In *Art and Scholasticism*, Jacques Maritain cautions us against this "leveling" impulse, bequeathing a definition of art which has influenced generations of Catholic writers and artists:

> 1. Art is before all intellectual and its activity consists in impressing an idea upon a matter: therefore it resides in the mind of the *artifex*, or, as they say, it is subject in that mind. It is a certain quality of that mind.
>
> 2. The Ancients applied the term *habitus* to qualities of a distinct and separate kind, essentially permanent conditions perfecting in the line of its own nature the subject they inform. Health and beauty are habits of the body, sanctifying grace a (supernatural) habit of the soul: other habits have for subject the faculties or powers of the soul, and as these naturally tend to action, the habits related to them perfect them in their very dynamism, are operative habits: such are the intellectual and moral virtues.
>
> Habits are, as it were, metaphysical letters patent of nobility, and just as much as inborn talents make

> for inequality among men. The man with a habit has a quality in him for the lack of which nothing can compensate, as nothing can take its place; other men are defenceless, he is armour-clad, but his armour is the living armour of the spirit.

Art is a habit of making a virtue of the practical intellect: in other words, the habit of art triumphs over the intellective faculty's original inexactness, "at once sharpening and hardening the point of its activity, raises it in respect of a definite object to a maximum of perfection, and so of operative efficiency."

Art's end is making, even though it is bound up with a habit of being that precedes the work which emerges. But the matter with which he works—in our case words and the things they signify and symbolize—is, like all matter, sometimes reluctant to be given the form we possess in the visions of our souls. As Maritain says, the "work of art has been pondered before being made, has been kneaded and prepared, formed, brooded over, and matured in a mind before emerging into matter." This brooding and maturation can come at the cost of sleepless nights when, on the deep, the writer floats aboard a single shard of wood, chiseling the infinite currents of the ocean with the marks of his little raft.

The equivocation between "art" and "method" reaches an absurd, almost satirical tenor in Edgar Allan Poe's essay "The Philosophy of Composition," where he intended to prove through an analysis of his own poetry that "no one point in the composition is referable either to accident or to intuition, that the work proceeded, step by step, to its completion with the precision and rigid consequence of a mathematical problem." Poe, says Etienne Gilson, sets out to "exclude from poetical composition what might seem completely foreign to arithmetic, namely originality." Maritain further teases out this tension between the singular potentialities of a particular soul and the reduction of artistic production to "methodism": "So method or rules, considered as a collection of self-adjusting formula and processes, an orthopedic and mechanical truss for the mind, tend throughout the modern world to take the place of habits, because a method is open to everybody whereas habits are reserved for the few."

"The modern conception of method and rules," Maritain continues, ignores the deeper essence of art, which requires "formation of a habit, a living rule." Lacking this living habit, which requires constant commitment, "rules mean nothing. Stick the consummate theoretical knowledge of all the rules of art upon an industrious graduate working fifteen hours a day but without a shoot of habit sprouting in him, and you will never make him an artist."

Because art is an "intellectual habit," at all times it presupposes the formation of the spirit in deep solitude, where the highest expressions of art must be cultivated without anyone's immediate aid or instruction. Alongside this solitary cultivation, the artist needs the discipline of education under masters, collaboration with living and dead exemplars with the ever-alert aim of absorbing techniques and styles.

27

Most Grievous Faults and Fictional Reparations

Before delving into some elements of fiction's art—and only *some*, for to cover all would require not only another book but another lifetime ("art is long, life short," wrote Goethe)—I must begin by declaring a war on clichés. I am afraid that I cannot distribute dispensations for even the most pacifistic among you. If the cliché covers our moral life in a banal funeral pall ("You only live once!"), it blanches literature of one of its duties: to make us pay attention, see things freshly, find epiphanies where we thought all was said and done. (Okay, I committed one just now. Well, it's not over till it's over, and "you can't win 'em all"—all the skirmishes of this undying war.)

One of the surest safeguards against cliché is fictional defamiliarization. We discussed "defamiliarization" earlier, watched how other authors employ it as a necessary means of bringing deadened consciousness back to life. Let's revisit it with a little more depth here in order to conceive ways by which we might make use of this device in our own writing. The cliché is a child of boredom, which, as Jean-Luc Marion explains (in "The Reverse of Vanity"), "does not have any interest in whatsoever may *be,* and hence has no more negative interest than positive: it never destroys, but always turns away; even less, boredom does not have to turn its gaze away in order to dismiss the thing from all . . . dignity."

The gaze of boredom sees somethings as nothings. This reduction of life to near-nothing is described by Tolstoy in one of his diaries. He was dusting the room, he says, and after coming full circle, he could not recall if he had dusted or not. Because his movements were "routine and not conscious," he feared he could never remember it. If he *had* dusted the sofa, it would be "as if this never happened. If somebody had watched consciously, reconstruction would have been possible. But if nobody watched, if nobody watched consciously, if the whole life of many people is lived unconsciously, it is as if this life had never been."

Viktor Shklovsky transposes Tolstoy's diary into one of his most potent insights:

> If we examine the general laws of perception, we see that as it becomes habitual, it also becomes automatic. So eventually all of our skills and experiences function unconsciously—automatically. If someone were to compare the sensation of holding a pen in his hand or speaking a foreign tongue for the very first time with the sensation of performing this same operation for the ten thousandth time, then he would no doubt agree with us. It is this process of automatization that explains the laws of our prose speech with its fragmentary phrases and half-articulated words.

> And so, in order to return sensation to our limbs, in order to make us feel objects, to make a stone feel stony, man has been given the tool of art. The purpose of art, then, is to lead us to a knowledge of a thing through the organ of sight instead of recognition. By "enstranging" objects and complicating form, the device of art makes perception long and "laborious." The perceptual process in art has a purpose all its own and ought to be extended to the fullest.

Enstrangement, defamiliarization, is but one way to war against boredom and its kissing cousins—banality and clichés. That said, it can advance the cause considerably.

Consider the way David Foster Wallace employs a Saudi medical attaché in order to achieve enstrangement in *Infinite Jest:*

> On this Wednesday night, trying buttons and abbreviations almost at random, the attaché is able to summon up only live U.S.A. professional sports—which he has always found brutish and repellent—Texaco Oil Company-sponsored opera—which the attaché has seen today more than enough of the human uvula thank you very much—a redisseminated episode of the popular afternoon InterLace children's program 'Mr. Bouncety-Bounce'—which the attaché thinks for a moment might be a documentary on bipolar mood disorders until he catches on and thumbs the selection-panel hastily—and a redisseminated session of the scantily clad variable-impact early-A.M. 'Fit Forever' home-aerobics series of the InterLace

> aerobics-guru Ms. Tawni Kondo, the scantily clad and splay-limbed immodesty of which threatens the devout medical attaché with the possibility of impure thoughts.

While a wry American, in fiction, could get away with drawing out the bizarre, mood-disorder ethos of too many children's shows, it takes a true foreigner to make strange the ubiquitous immodesty of aerobics videos that saturate our contemporary milieu—and to do so from *within* the vision of a character instead of via the heavy-handed *ressentiment* of talk show radio.

Enstrangement has affinity with what Flannery called the grotesque, a device by which "the writer has made alive some experience which we are not accustomed to observe every day, or which the ordinary man may never experience in his ordinary life." Through the grotesque, the innately freakish elements of human life—those strange things we might rather keep at bay, tamed under clichés—are drawn out and painted in large and startling figures. O'Connor concludes that "it is when the freak can be sensed as a figure for our essential displacement that he attains some depth in literature." Grotesqueries masterfully capture our fundamental fallenness. Just look at the paintings of Hieronymus Bosch.

While on a global level I'm waging a war on clichés, on the local level of Catholic fiction I'm especially concerned with rooting out another insidious corruption: the heresy of sentimentality. Hilaire Belloc helpfully defines "heresy" as "the warping of a system by 'Exception'—by 'picking out' one part of the structure." The total "scheme," the fullness of truth, is "marred by taking away one part of it, denying one part of it, and either leaving the void unfilled or filling it with some new affirmation." Sentimentality is fictionally heretical in that it dislocates affectation from action and character: it is right to seize upon the importance of emotion (prose wholly without feeling becomes cold-hearted fast) but stories cannot live on emotion alone.

In "The Church and the Fiction Writer," O'Connor argues that if we could truly locate "the average Catholic reader," we would discover that he is a sentimental sap. He has separated nature and grace as much as possible, reducing the supernatural to "pious cliché." As such, when he reads literature, he can only recognize nature's truths in two distorted forms, "the sentimental and the obscene. He would seem to prefer the former, while being more of an authority on the latter, but the similarity between the two generally escapes him. He forgets that sentimentality is an excess, a distortion of sentiment, usually in the direction of an overemphasis on innocence." Innocence, she warns, whenever it is unduly emphasized, "tends by some natural law to become its opposite."

She goes on to describe sentimentality, in Christian terms, as a shortcut from our Fall to Christ's resurrection—sans deep faith and daily participation in his holy crucifixion. Sentimentality, she says, is "a skipping of this process in its concrete reality and an early arrival at a mock state of innocence." Pornography, she continues, is "essentially sentimental" because it omits "the connection of sex with its hard purposes," bracketing procreation and framing it as a self-contained experience—not to say experiment.

The fictionist's anodyne against sentimentality is not abstracted rationality—but rather sense and sentiment. As Douglas Bauer puts it in *The Stuff of Fiction: Advice on Craft*, to guard against the minimalizing, trivializing tendencies of sentimentality, we must "suffuse our work with a quality of sentiment that does not become exaggerated." While sentimentality swoons us into submission, bidding us "surrender the intellectual, the mindful, aspect of [our] makeups" in favor of the fleeting feelings built on naïve tidiness, sentiment asks no such *surrender*. Rather, it deepens our sentiments, our *sense* of all things in the world of the story through what Bauer calls "rigorous descriptive precision"—an ingredient dispersed amidst the thick complexities that also appeal to our cranial parts. Bauer cites John Cheever's "The Cure" as a paradigm of sentiment without excess. After sustaining pages and pages of half-convincing dispassion in the wake of his divorce, the narrator at last *feels,* and his way of feeling reaches into our hearts, hearts (to paraphrase Faulkner) ever in conflict with themselves: "I took the train home, but I was too tired to go to Orpheo's and then sit through a movie. I drove from the station to the house and put the car in the garage. . . . As soon as I stepped into the living room, I noticed on the wall some dirty hand prints that had been made by the children before they went away. They were near the baseboard and I had to get down on my knees to kiss them."

Bauer praises the precision here, the restraint. The act itself is innately dramatic, but "the teller's tone is not altered."

Cheever narrates a heartbreaking scene but he rescues it from sentimentality through the "casualness reverberating, as though he were saying he got down on his knees to plug in a light." Sentiment, says Bauer, is "emotion that serves the scene." Sentimentality dominates with its feels. Sentiment "defines the dramatic instant. It adds to its dimension and refines its details. Sentimentality inflates the dramatic instant." If the perils of sentimentality are ever-present to the writer, so are the perils of safe, emotionless portraits. As George Saunders says, "So I don't think we'd want to risk sentimentality, if we define sentimentality as 'causing unearned emotion.' I think we'd want to risk earned emotion." Amen.

The risk seems greater when we tell stories that reach after revealed truths. In Chekhov's "The Student" (his own favorite among his stories), a young student, preoccupied with melancholy musings on poverty and pain, encounters a woman warming herself by a fire. Recalling that Easter would arrive in two days (thus placing the story's action on Good Friday), he retells the tale of Peter's denial. When he finishes, the woman, "still smiling . . . suddenly choked, and big, abundant tears rolled down her cheeks."

We are only three pages into a four-page story: has Chekov taken a short cut, has he committed sentimentality? No. It is evident that the primary cause of her crying is not some saccharine communion with the passing student, but rather that she deeply identifies with his gloss on the Gospel's recorded denial.

Second, Chekhov paints with care. Her tears are preceded by a smile, and even as she cries, she tries to hide how much the story has moved her: "She shielded her face from the fire with her sleeve, as if ashamed of her tears"; when she tries to do this, she ends up staring at the student with a heavy, strained look, like "someone who is trying to suppress intense pain." And here their interaction ends.

A lesser writer may have had them embrace, share their sadness verbally. Chekhov lets the Word do the speaking, lets its power pulse through them. The student is stunned by what just happened: "If she wept, it meant that everything that had happened with Peter on that dreadful night had some relation to her." He does not get lost in a proliferation of emotive expressivism. Rather, "joy" stirs his soul as he realizes that "the past . . . is connected with the present in some unbroken chain of events flowing one out of the other. And it seemed to him he had just seen both ends of that chain: he touched one end, and the other moved."

Crucially, Chekhov gives him this epiphany *after* he has departed from the woman at the fireside. It takes time for him to see what truly happened. An immediate "insight" would have had a cheapening effect. As the story stands, joy is mingled with sorrow, and, as such, Leonoid Grossman is right: "In his revelation of those evangelical elements, the atheist Chekhov is unquestionably one of the most Christian poets of world literature."

In its early drafts, my short story "Horseradish" was slipping into sentimentality, in part because I slowed things down too much—drew out, to a torturously sappy degree, the key heart-full scene. I called in the inquisition.

The story follows a father and son. The judge, a formidable cardinal dressed in silken purple, was indispensable.

No, he said, though writers have told that tale since Telemachus and Odysseus, from David and Absalom to Turgenev's *Fathers and Sons,* the theme is intrinsically eternal—not definitively cliché. No, he said, the father did not need to keep mum, forever failing to tell his son he loved him. But, given the character, the truth needed to come out with a contingency that would help restrain the scene from sentimentality. Who would have thought that a simple swear word could exercise such a salutary influence—buying him the chance to give his heart voice?: "'You're a shit, you know that,' he said. And then, gripping the steering wheel, 'Love you.'"

Good writers get us to feel by maintaining distance at the crucial moment. Narratorial distance is not the only remedy. Pacing is also—as elsewhere—key. The heresy of sentimentality preys in all sorts of ways. It can arrive at its "shortcut" by *slowing down*: staring too long into the lover's eyes; squatting too long, weak-kneed, in the narrow, crooked corridor, after the death of a child. Maestro of errors, it can also take us to legitimate ends but can do so too easily—too quickly. A mother's grief over her dead child is by all means the stuff of legitimate fiction. But sentimentality would give it to us immediately, often through clichéd objects (revealing its affinity with our other enemy). Bauer has a list: "the set of crutches uncovered in the garage, left from the time one of the children broke his leg"; kissing "the favorite doll, mutilated by love"; "the doll, the puppy, the son's baseball glove—these sorts of tokens, saccharine and generic, are sure signs that sentimentality has entered the building."

Henry James is right: "the house of fiction" has "not one window, but a million." But if you find yourself inhabiting the aforementioned, or anything proximate to the sins Bauer mentioned, please, please, please don't try to make it better by looking through a different window. Make your exit down the fire escape now and find a new house altogether. The house is on fire. A mother is breaking into the burning building, trying to save her youngest children again. You must leave anyway. Orphans are coming. Decades of their pictures will hang in the hallway. Mother is squatting there, her reddened eyes swiveling back and forth between the child she lost and the jesus who oozes comfort from his frame, smiling the smile of pious trash.

28

The Problem of Proper Proportion

"Beauty demands the fulfillment of three conditions: the first is integrity, or perfection of the thing, for what is defective is, in consequence, ugly; the second is proper proportion, or harmony; and the third is clarity—thus things which have glowing colors are said to be beautiful."

—St. Thomas Aquinas, *Summa Theologie*, I q. 39 a. 8

We must expand our sense of what *not* to do beyond the heresy of sentimentality and endless war on clichés. We can glean many *dos* and *don'ts* from the Catholic convert and capable teacher Caroline Gordon, who wrote not a few novels and also contributed two books to the art of fiction: *How to Read a Novel* and a little-known, out-of-print book edited and composed by Allen Tate and Gordon called *The House of Fiction.* The latter contains essential "faults of the amateur"—a cautionary list for the would-be-writer.

First, the amateur writer puts only part of her story on the page, maybe only half, and as the half that makes it to the page is comprised of "thin incidents" told with stilted sentences, the story makes a far greater impression on *her* than on her reader. Why? Because the unwritten portion remains "ideal and therefore not subject to the vicissitudes of actuality"; this glimmer, unseen to the rest of us, brings glee to the amateur author. As a corrective to this error, Gordon advises us to adopt the painter's practice of "stepping back from the easel to survey the work with narrowed, coldly critical, and self-excluding eyes."

As with the moral life so with fiction: beginners fail to achieve proportion. Although a story's separate parts may be very good in isolation, if the disparate many are not in accord, the reader will be like the patient at the optometrist's bench, looking at letters through a whir of dizzying lenses: things that come out small should have been larger, and gargantuan, domineering things ought to have been muted, miniscule. If the story lacks proportion, the reader may skim over actions of import and become bogged down in paltry gazings. As Gordon says, the author whose art is to imitate life is "in the position, say, of the man who attempts to make a manikin." Although the figure's legs, hands, and hair need not be as long, wide, and curled as the real thing, "they must bear the same relation to his torso as a real man's."

Pace and timing, a persistent sense of the overarching arc, are the vital constituents of proportion. Excess may here mean rushing through scenes that should be slow (or moving in an utterly linear manner through scenes better served by intriguing asides and necessary digressions), or prying from the reader a cataract of feelings about a certain character who remains as yet half-known, or granting a grandiose roundness to a character who will never appear on page again. Thoughts need homes. As O'Connor says in *Mystery and Manners,* in the stories of novices, "dialogue frequently proceeds without the assistance of any characters that you can actually see, and uncontained thought leaks out of every corner of the story. The reason is usually that the student is wholly interested in his thoughts and his emotions and not in his dramatic action, and that he is too lazy or highfalutin to descend to the concrete where fiction operates."

Key incidents must stand out. They must, Gordon says, be "furnished with slopes, either steep or gentle; a succession of minor incidents so cunningly arranged that they throw into sharp relief the peak which they support." To cite Yeats's memorable advice, a "tense line" should be preceded and followed by what he calls a "numb line." In order to write "suddenness," you need to write "delay." "We keep the reader tarrying at a particular spot by entertaining him so well that he does not notice that time is passing." It may not be a bad idea, after you've reeled the reader up into a lyrical reverie, to let them down slowly with a few softer, shorter sentences. Take this passage from Joyce's *A Portrait of the Artist as a Young Man*: "The veiled windless hour had passed and behind the panes of the naked window the morning light was gathering. A bell beat faintly very far away. A bird twittered; two birds, three. The bell and the bird ceased; and the dull white light spread itself east and west, covering the world, covering the roselight in his heart."

Notice the intensive anticipation created in the first sentence, through its absence (veiled, windless), its searching gaze, and its polysemous suggestiveness (the window is not merely open, or without drapes, it is *naked*). After this, Joyce lets us rest through a few terse sentences full of sounds—a bell and birds, both of which remain less lyrically explored. The sentences ratchet back up as he returns to the splendor that binds what he senses with his sight; it soars into the skies (literally), even as he links horizon with his own heart.

Or consider the proportionality found in a passage of Thomas Pynchon's *The Crying of Lot 49.* Oedipa Maas, protagonist of the unnerving and absurd novel-pastiche, has been searching for clues and answers to a prospective worldwide conspiracy. Chasing signs that only doubtfully signify, her longings at times extend beyond the secular realm to the world wherein meaning has a Maker, and the prose picks up its pace and grows charged with an ethereal verve: "And the voices before and after the dead man's that had phoned at random during the darkest, slowest hours, searching ceaseless among the dial's ten million possibilities for that magical Other who would reveal herself out of the roar of relays, monotone litanies of insult, filth, fantasy, love, whose brute repetition must someday call into being the trigger for the unnamable act, the recognition, the Word."

By beginning with *And,* Pynchon leaves us, as it were, catching up to the action—as if all there is to document can barely be kept up with. He waxes sonorous (searching ceaseless) and alliterative (r̲oar of r̲elays) as the burning yearning explodes, growing staccato only when the sentence dips into the most mundane and even ugly earthly things (insult, filth, fantasy, love) before it rushes to a conclusion with "the Word," appropriately giving the last word to the ultimate Other.

For a key insight to obtain its proper peak, Gordon says, a story might need to say the same thing twice—differently each time—so that the actions of a story obtain an altered meaning when measured against the epiphany, and the epiphany happens not in a vacuum but amidst a string—or sometimes a *web*—of interconnected settings and sequences and characters. Pynchon does this in *The Crying of Lot 49*, punctuating a paranoid sense of conspiracy with allusive reaches to an elusive God.

29

Dialogue, Dead or Alive

Dialogue, like Odysseus, is a metaphorical "man of twists and turns"; it can speak in the voices of serpents and doves. But before we come to its capacity for polyphony, let's start with one of its more basic purposes: dialogue quickens pace. Using it as a "device" in this way is as old as the ancient Greek playwrights Sophocles and Aeschylus. Traditionally called *stichomythia*, this extended back-and-forth of terse lines is used to show characters caught in ripening contention and to increase emotional force. Often when this device is employed, characters give voice to antithetical arguments, as in this *stichomythia* from *Oedipus Rex*. (I am citing from Robert Fitzgerald's translation. Flannery O'Connor lived with Robert Fitzgerald while he was at work on it. Do what you will with the end of *Wise Blood* now that you know this.) As Thebes suffers under a relentless plague, Oedipus seeks prophetic clarity from the blind prophet Teiresias, not knowing how awful the answers will be:

> Teiresias: How dreadful knowledge of the truth can be
> When there's no help in truth! I knew this well,
> But made myself forget. I should not have come.

Oedipus: What is troubling you? Why are your eyes
so cold?

Teiresias: Let me go home. Bear your own fate, and
I'll bear mind. It is better so: trust
what I say.

Oedipus: What you say is ungracious and unhelpful
To your own native country. Do not refuse to speak.

Teiresias: When it comes to speech, your own is neither temperate
Nor opportune. I wish to be more prudent.

Oedipus: In God's name, we all beg you—

Teiresias: You are all ignorant.
No, I will never tell you what I know.
Now it is my misery; then it would be yours.

Oedipus: What! You do know something and will not
tell us?
You would betray us all and wreck the State?

René Girard notes the "faster and more abrupt" action of the "tragic dialogue or *stichomythia*, that is, in the exchange of insults and accusations that corresponds to the exchange of blows between warriors locked in single combat." The verbal violence takes on the tenor of a duel, elevating the reader's (or watcher's) attention. Although sometimes fiction embodies this device to the point that certain scenes seem indistinguishable from theatrical drama, typically such dialogic spats are not quite so terse—and sometimes not so serious.

Take this one from early on in David Foster Wallace's *Infinite Jest*. Hal and Mario (aka Boo) are talking:

> "When I asked if you were asleep I was going to ask if you felt like you believed in God, today, out there, when you were so on, making that guy look sick."
> "This again?"
> ". . ."
> "Really don't think midnight in a totally dark room with me so tired my hair hurts and drills in six short hours is the time and place to get into this, Mario. You ask me this once a week."
> "You never say, is why."
> "So tonight to shush you how about if I say I have administrative bones to pick with God, Boo. I'll say God seems to have a kind of laid-back management style I'm not crazy about. I'm pretty much anti-death. God looks by all accounts to be pro-death. I'm not seeing how we can get together on this issue, he and I, Boo."
> "You're talking about since Himself passed away."
> "See? You never say."
> "I do too say. I just did."
> "I just didn't happen to say what you wanted to hear, Booboo, is all."
> ". . ."
> "There's a difference."

> "I don't get how you couldn't feel like you believed, today, out there. It was so right there. You moved like you totally believed."
>
> ". . ."
>
> "How do you feel inside, not?"
>
> "Mario, you and I are mysterious to each other. We countenance each other from either side of some unbridgeable difference on this issue. Let's lie very quietly and ponder this."
>
> "Hal?"
>
> ". . ."
>
> "Hey Hal?"
>
> "I'm going to propose that I tell you a joke, Boo, on the condition that afterward you shush and let me sleep."
>
> "Is it a good one?"
>
> "Mario, what do you get when you cross an insomniac, an unwilling agnostic, and a dyslexic."
>
> "I give."
>
> "You get somebody who stays up all night torturing himself mentally over the question of whether or not there's a dog."

Notice, by the way, Wallace's use of the dialogic " . . ." to indicate a kind of spoken silence—a fine device worth stealing (Eliot assures us that the greatest artists steal, and Wallace himself took it from William Gaddis), if I do say so myself.

Cormac McCarthy uses stichomythia in a manner closer to the ancient tragedians—achieving their sparsity.

In this exchange between father and son from *The Road*, you can see even more clearly how this device can help pick up a story's pace:

> "I want you to tell me. It's okay."
>
> He shook his head.
>
> "Look at me," the man said.
>
> He turned and looked. He looked like he'd been crying.
>
> "Just tell me."
>
> "We wouldn't ever eat anybody, would we?"
>
> "No. Of course not."
>
> "Even if we were starving?"
>
> "We're starving now."
>
> "You said we weren't."
>
> "I said we weren't dying. I didn't say we weren't starving."
>
> "But we wouldn't."
>
> "No. We wouldn't."
>
> "No matter what."
>
> "No. No matter what."
>
> "Because we're the good guys."
>
> "Yes."
>
> "And we're carrying the fire."
>
> "And we're carrying the fire. Yes."
>
> "Okay."

If you pass through McCarthy's novel's with a "bird's eye view," just staring at the chunks of text on the page, you'll find that he alternates between dense, infamously-lyrical paragraphs and these thin columns of dialogue; when you hone in and read what this amounts to experientially, you feel the pace quicken through these short exchanges.

We witness a dialogic dynamic that is similar to stichomythia in Ralph Ellison's *Invisible Man* when the protagonist / "scholarship recipient" is pummeled by his purported benefactors:

> "What's that word you say, boy?"
> "Social responsibility," I said.
> "What?"
> "Social . . ."
> "Louder."
> " . . . responsibility"
> "More!"
> "Respon—"
> "Repeat!"
> "—sibility."

The dramatic violence tainting the exchange is evident; Ellison captures it especially through interruption (the "—" always helps to presence disruption), which I strongly recommend making use of if one of your characters is stubborn, heedless, controlling: the kind who never lets another complete a single sent—

Dialogue is a superb source of tension and dramatic misdirection. Interruptions and misunderstandings, in literature and in life, deepen our understanding of characters' relationships and their own psychological states—and the surest way to achieve miscommunication and interruption is through dialogue.

Here's Lorrie Moore delivering a painfully "professional" spar between patient and medic:

> "The surgeon will speak to you," says the Radiologist.
> "Are you finding something?"
> "The surgeon will speak to you," the Radiologist says again. "There seems to be something there, but the surgeon will talk to you about it."
> "My uncle once had something on his kidney," says the Mother. "So they removed the kidney and it turned out the something was benign."
> The Radiologist smiles a broad, ominous smile. "That's always the way it is," he says. "You don't know exactly what it is until it's in the bucket."
> "'In the bucket,'" the mother repeats.
> The Radiologist's grin grows scarily wider—is that even possible? "That's doctor talk," he says.
> "It's very appealing," says the Mother. "It's a very appealing way to talk."

Moore is doing so much with so little, here. The awful repetition of the bureaucratic process challenged by a frantic mother, who wants to know more even as her speech betrays her knowledge that knowing more might be as bad for her as it was for Oedipus. She uses the word "something" to gamble with neutrality, even as her sense is that there's something worse. The surgeon speaks with even heavier contingency (seems, something, there) mingled with deflection. The mother openly takes refuge in her prior experience with prospective cancer—her uncle's case is safe, as it ended well. It is noteworthy that Moore has her say this aloud instead of thinking it—so that this nervous optimism would have been visible to us but not the Radiologist. By having her say it aloud, Moore provides another occasion for painful miscommunication. The Radiologist's response reveals a familiarity with this kind of self-protective wishful thinking and the smile cannot mask his interior snickering, which is in fact only amplified.

Moore is on point. His cynicism and ineptness is hard to bear—made harder because the day has already been dragging with difficulties, and this could have been one "expert" able to lend a hand.

And then the descent into colloquial, casual language so tone-deaf to the moment. The image, spoken aloud at the wrong time, in the wrong place, to the wrong person, is so shocking to her that "she imagines it all"—"Swirls of bile and blood, mustard and maroon in a pail, the colors of an African flag or some exhuberant salad bar: *in the bucket.*" The scene ends with the Radiologist repeating his now grating good news, "The Surgeon will see you soon," before patting the mother's child and proclaiming the baby a "Cute kid."

Good dialogue is difficult to write if you don't do a lot of listening to real people and, still further, if you don't relish the singularities of sound contained in idiomatic speech. As O'Connor indicates, the South is "rich in its speech." We could say the same of so many "subcultures" of the States. Ignoring the idiom, swapping the idiom for grammatically-correct idealizations: these errors lead to a stilted speech safety-pinned to an abstracted social whole. An idiom, O'Connor explains, "characterizes a society and when you ignore the idiom, you are very likely ignoring the whole social fabric that could make a meaningful character." Those who have a bad ear for dialogue might consider limiting, at least initially, the amount of talking that happens in the story—dwelling instead in third-person omniscience, for instance. That is, until they can get outside and assume the fictionist's inescapable espionage, overhearing real humans speaking and shouting, whispering and listening with all of our manifold tones.

Gordon warns of "dead dialogue"—speech blanched of *life.* In the life which writers imitate, humanoids hardly ever "succeed in emitting more than three sentences at a time." And then, if someone does, he will typically signal "his decision by taking his stand on the hearth rug." In fiction, the author would do well to "point to" the man who delivers the monologue. That is, "the fact that he is making a speech ought to be *dramatized.*"

Pending this, even if the speech seems "life-like," unless you can reincarnate yourself as a Russian writer of the nineteenth century (why hello, Dostoevsky, who in, for instance, *The Idiot* pulls off pages and pages of one man's speech in part because he counters the tubercular Ippolit's holding forth by occasional interruptions, not to mention the manifold dialogue that build most of the novel!), the long and winding monologue will be bereft of believability. And then, tempting as it is, no fictionist who wishes to escape the pains of literary purgatory should dare use dialogue to "convey to the reader . . . features of the scene or mere expository information." Here is my own attempt at that fictional sin of "dialogue-as-exposition":

> "Well, gee, here we are, Ebenezer, in our kitchen like we are every night, here, in Nowhereville, Ohio. Would you look at that Masonic pattern on the wallpaper that's been here since I been born, looks an awful lot like the symbol on our dollar bills, the floating eye on top of the triangle, you know what I mean, hon? Heh. Hark! Can you smell that fish stench leaking from the refrigerator like it always does on account of that can of anchovies that our son Harold opened two years ago and never finished but which we are also too tired or—well why exactly is it that we don't throw it away, hon, what is it about human nature that makes such a small task seem impossible or unimportant even when it would be so simple for you or I to stop talking right now and rise up and toss the galdarn tin into the gotforsaken trash? Hark! Is that little Ebeneza playing a moonlight sonata—even though there is no moon tonight, it is in fact overcast and starless to boot—on the little spinet piano that you received from your uncle Larry in 1999, the year you made valedictorian and also lost your house to the worst flood Ohio has ever seen?"

Given that they sit there every night, Mrs. Ebenezer (Evelyn, we'll call her) wouldn't go about remarking on and relating the obvious to her beloved of fifty years. Gordon rightly reminds us that "the fault can be subtly committed, but in principle" it is as bad as it is in such over-the-top examples as the one I gave above: "This is merely one way in which the author gets between us and his characters and his scene. It is well to remember that in life conversation is not logical or systematically informative but allusive, proceeding through a series of antiphonal explosions." Many of our conversations are like bullets, cooked and shaped "in the heat of our desire to communicate" and pointed at our interlocutor, who points and fires back. Or at least "conversation today" is too often like that, she concludes.

Conversations like this might "lead nowhere" in terms of reconciliation between estranged characters, might consist of each character answering another's questions with more questions—but whereas in, say, a marriage, such a dynamic would be disastrous, in fiction this is all to the good. As Bauer puts it, good dialogue might result in only "partial recognition" or "near communication," but "happily . . . one of the marks of successful dialogue" is "a pattern of give-and-take in which the characters do not answer the questions, or answer them only partially, or appropriate them to satisfy their own ends." All of these ends must be achieved as though we are "eavesdropping" on the interlocutors. In bad dialogue, we feel as though the conversation is "staged."

Dialogue, that antiphonal animal, also creates tension in that it permits the writer to contrast a character's interior with what he does. Its structure also allows us to show the antinomy between what a character says and what she truly thinks. John Updike tells us that "to write how people talk one must know how they think." This is a preliminary step to demonstrating the difference between what is thought and what is said. A Catholic writer might profit from this dissonance by, for instance, contrasting what a purportedly

Christian character *says* about her own salvation with what she *really* thinks, in secret, of her hopeless brethren or her own impeccable self. At the end of "A Good Man is Hard to Find," the grandmother has Jesus ever on her lips, while mostly her heart is a shrine to herself.

A writer can heighten this dissonance by alternating between a line of spoken dialogue, which a character—a priest, say—says, "Good to see you again," and narration of his interlocutor's psychic fallout, known only to her and the reader. Let's make something up as we go:

> "How good to run into you, Alice. Really, I've been meaning to call you. Haven't seen you in the pew for the past few months. It's—good to see your face."
>
> "And you," she said, staring over his shoulder, suddenly, at one of the waxless votive candles. Not again, God, *him.* Again and again. God.

So says and thinks a mother whose child has been abused by the priest who just greeted her. She has not yet the courage to slap him, verbally or with her palm, which has not yet been burned to ashes.

The Catholic, Christian writer can learn from Dostoevsky and O'Connor how she might turn a conversation toward supernatural things. In an initially suppressed chapter of Dostoevsky's *Demons* (translated here by Virginia Woolf!), the revolutionary Stavrogin pays a visit to Bishop Tikhon. Given the established character of each, it is only natural that their conversation would eventually turn toward ultimate questions. Notice the way that Stavrogin's skepticism is both challenged and given full, persuasive expression:

> "You believe in God?" Nikolai [Stavrogin] suddenly burst out.
>
> "I do."
>
> "It is said, if you believe and bid a mountain move, it will move . . . though, pardon me this nonsense. Yet I am curious to know: could you move a mountain or not?"
>
> "If God will, I could," Tikhon uttered quickly and calmly, again beginning to look down at the ground.
>
> "Well, it's just the same as saying that God Himself could move it. But you, you, as a reward for your belief in God?"
>
> "Perhaps I could move it."
>
> "'Perhaps.' Well, that is not bad, either. But you are still doubtful?"
>
> "Through the imperfection of my belief I have doubts."
>
> "Why, do *you* believe incompletely?"
>
> "Yes . . . perhaps; I do believe and not perfectly," Tikhon replied.
>
> "That is what I should not think, looking at you!"—he suddenly gave him a look of some surprise, a perfectly simple look which did not at all harmonize with the mocking tone of the preceding questions.
>
> . . .
>
> "And can one believe in the devil, without believing in God?" Stavrogin laughed.

> "Oh, there are such people everywhere." Tikhon raised his eyes and smiled.
>
> "And I am sure that you find such belief more respectable after all than complete unbelief. . . ." Stavrogin began to laugh.
>
> "On the contrary, complete atheism is more respectable than worldly indifference," Tikhon answered, with visible gaiety and good-nature.
>
> "Oho, that's how you get round it!"
>
> "A complete atheist stands on the last rung but one before absolute faith (he may or may not step higher), but an indifferent man has no longer any faith at all, nothing but an ugly fear, and that only on rare occasions, if he is a sentimental man."

As I've mentioned elsewhere, Christopher Beha's *What Happened to Sophie Wilder* continues this "Dostoevskian" strand of dialogue. Let's revisit that scene, one of the most intense theological snippets in contemporary fiction. Remember that the stubborn-hearted Sophie has committed to caring for her dying father-in-law Crane, in spite of her husband's estrangement from both her and his own father. Beha paints Crane with that "demonic" quality Dostoevsky often achieves, without flattening him into a "villainous" caricature. When Sophie unthinkingly reads him Scripture, he cuts her short, says it's "brutal" to "read such a passage to a dying man," and proceeds to reveal that he knows the Bible "a lot better than you do . . . And he's a fascist." Sophie is confused: which fascist—"King James?"

> "God. The first totalitarian. Has to control everything. Reads your mail. Bugs your phone. Watches while you take a shit. I don't see what's to admire. And death camps. Auschwitz is a beach vacation compared to the circles of hell. You get sent there for the same reason, incidentally: for not being a Christian."
>
> . . .
>
> "You're oversimplifying," she said, aware of how inadequate her response was. "He isn't spying in some prurient way. He's not trying to catch anyone at anything. And he doesn't control everything. He could, but he gives us free will."

He "almost roar[s]," slumping back to the couch, unwilling to take her "free will" ticket. Sure, he says, "You're free to do what you choose, and if you don't choose to worship me, I'll send you to the flames." Crane would grant God more homage had he "just made us do whatever He wanted, instead of leaving us to guess and burning us for guessing wrong."

This sort of back-and-forth continues to the novel's end. Later, in his last days, Crane commands her to stop praying in his presence. "If it's useless, what difference does it make whether I do it or not?" she presses.

He doesn't want to look at it, he says, "You can do it outside."

But she doesn't rise. Instead she says she's "sorry you're suffering," to which he stubbornly sticks up his verbal middle finger: "I'll be suffering either way. Your prayers don't do shit about it. They'll just make you feel better." His challenge prompts her to examine her conscience, weigh the ways she prays—what for. Beha gives full-throated voice to both faith and doubt, modeling the art of doing both justice.

30

The Heresy of Formlessness and Old Faithful Unity

SPEAKING OF FAITH and free will in fiction, God knows you can of course do whatever you want. It's a free country, as they say. But Flannery is entirely right when she levels the following rejoinder: "It's always wrong of course to say that you can't do this or you can't do that in fiction. You can do anything you can get away with, but nobody has ever gotten away with much."

For instance, while you are free to tackle everything but the kitchen sink in a single story, fiction lacking unity tires us with its flaccidity. Amateurs, beware the heresy of formlessness!

In his *Poetics,* Aristotle points his condemnatory finger at an already-forgotten author of "The Heracleidae." The poet, says Gordon, "included *all* the adventures of Heracles in his epic poem, thereby failing to achieve any form," whereas Homer hones in on only those of Odysseus's actions which could be formed into an intelligible unity. O'Connor puts the same point slightly differently when she says that "art is selective"; if he is "any good," the artist "selects every word for a reason."

Traditionally, unity is achieved primarily through action—all actions correlate with an overarching Action. But this unity can be tonal, too. Gordon describes this as "consistency of attitude towards the material of the story," which means "consistent use of language out of a certain core of meaning appropriate to the scene and characters." Shifts of tone can serve the story, as when Tolstoy changes voices in *War and Peace* depending on whether we are domestic or on the battlefield. But even these shifting tones must adhere to the central Action.

Take Stephen Crane's "The Open Boat," which remains nearly always in a naturalistic, sober tone, until the final sentence: "When it came night, the white waves paced to and fro in the moonlight, and the wind brought the sound of the great sea's voice to the men on the shore, and they felt that they had been interpreters." The elevation of tone, Gordon explains, is "unpredictable" but tied to resolution of the tale's prior tensions. Either every action, every bit of dialogue, is forged into the overarching form and its melded meaning or the story bloats, grows holes, is literally ripped like a canvas stretched in too many directions at once.

31

A Handful of Dust (Drop the Rest on the Floor), and a Half-Sketched Story with an Essay Woven Through it

THE WRITER MAKES meanings, her stories may make statements or arguments, but these statements will be made slowly, through the accumulation of what she chooses and what she omits. However "universal" it may be, all good fiction will bow to the commonplace. Walker Percy argues that this absorption of "the common," unique to the novel, is essentially Christian: "Something is happening in ordinary time to ordinary people, not to epic heroes in mythic time."

In Eric Auerbach's genealogy of the novel, he links the genre to a scene in the Gospel of Matthew—Peter's denial of Christ—because this drama does not fit easily into any of antiquity's extant genres. Trevor Cribben Merrill expounds that Peter's "exchanges with individual bystanders are recorded in direct speech; at one point his accent gives him away. Then the cock's crow brings him to his senses, and he weeps." Mark's Gospel, Merrill argues, "takes insignificant everyday contemporary reality seriously enough to represent it with great immediacy. It infuses the humble with sublimity, puts fishermen on an equal footing with powerful leaders, and treats ordinary life as the setting for world-historical events."

Fiction, says the ever-salient Flannery, "is about everything human and we are made out of dust, and if you scorn getting yourself dusty, then you shouldn't try to write fiction. It's not a grand enough job for you." Fictionists, especially those with philosophical bents, must be "humble in the face of what is." Hamlet, even as he praised the pinnacles of human *being*, professes this:

> What a piece of work is a man!
> How noble in reason, how infinite in faculty!
> In form and moving how express and admirable!
> In action how like an angel, in apprehension how like
> a god!
> The beauty of the world. The paragon of animals.
> And yet, to me, what is this quintessence of dust?

Beware the scribbler possessed by the hankering to make himself into the Paragon of Writers without passing through particularity. O'Connor goes so far as to say that maybe even most people "who think they want to write stories" actually pine to "write about problems, not people, about abstract issues, not concrete situations." Thrilled by an "idea" and "an overflowing ego," they bend themselves hell-bound to "Be A Writer."

Those who withhold submission to our quintessential dustiness inevitably flirt with a conflation of genres and forms. It is such writers O'Connor has in mind when she speaks of the "sketch with an essay woven through it, or an essay with a sketch woven through it." Now, there are innumerable instances of idea-driven fictions: masterful boundary-pushers from Dostoevsky to David Foster Wallace have embedded philosophical wrestlings in their novels. As Josef Skvorekcy, the Czech novelist, maintained, "Every good novel is a thesis-novel." And, of course, the degree to which ideas take root is determined in large part by the characters. Imagine how hard a novelist would need to work to excise entirely the ethos of the essay from a novel whose protagonist is a philosopher.

Granting the above, a good fictionist will still ever-remember that the thesis is mere skeleton, that in fiction ideas are like dry bones aching for muscle and flesh, wardrobed and spoken through the mouth of, say, Byron Thinkpiece. As he tells us his thoughts, we hear the nasal tone, see the cut on his chin from when he shaved in the dark. Such images need to assist in the thought's incarnation—they cannot be containers or awkward bodily cages trotted out to underwrite interesting philosophizing.

In *Christ and Apollo,* William F. Lynch puts it as follows: "images are in themselves the path to whatever the self is seeking; to insight, or beauty, or, for that matter, God." No writer can take shortcuts to these epiphanic ends. Fiction's innate thickness helps teach all of us this fundamental feature of reality: "we must go *through* the finite, the limited, the definite, omitting none of it lest we omit some of the potencies of being-in-the-flesh."

The neophyte fictionist will pass through it violently, will try to force an exit from the concrete limits of life. The master will patiently follow the contours, infectiously relishing what Hopkins named the "inscape" of "all things counter, original, *spare*, *strange*," and what Catholic theologian Duns Scotus called "thisness" (*haecceitas*)—the inner-essence and singular effervescence of details that tell the character of every, single, thing: *this* abandoned house on a gravel highway, *that* towering tenement at 777 Mott Street in New York, not just any tree but one that bears pears (which in Hopkins's hands is inherently "glassy," the fruits of which are, in the hands of young Augustine, pointlessly stolen) or a particular afternoon's particular sky (which Hopkins populates with "silk-sack clouds"), and even those oddities that don't have any apparent "significance" beyond the fact that they *are*.

32

The Duties of Details

In *How Fiction Works,* James Wood calls those fictional representations that are not bogged down with connotation, symbolic significance, or double meanings "off-duty details." These "off-duty" elements of a story may sound like lazy job-dodgers, but they comprise "the standing army of life, as it were . . . always ready to be activated." The world is full of what Wood calls "puffs of palpability," so many of which, for the Catholic writer, proclaim God's splendor.

But the Catholic writer comes bent with a proclivity to name and tell and show God too readily—to lend every detail a transcendent significance. One anecdote to this inclination is the off-duty detail.

In *Visions of Gerard,* Jack Kerouac offsets a hagiographic description of his brother as "saintly Gerard, his pure and tranquil face, the mournful look of him", with a more commonplace concretization, a detail and a gesture that grounds us in the *person* he is painting: "the piteousness of his little soft shroud of hair falling down his brow and swept aside by the hand over blue serious eyes." Kerouac conjoins "blue" and "serious." He rescues the heavy-handed halo-making with a typical, scraggly-haired child's sweep of follicles from his face.

Insights will emerge as-if-mysteriously as the "eye" of the narration passes through a three course meal of appetizers and rich dishes, a mixture of unremarkable front lawns and invigoratingly palpable noticings. Take a scene from Hemingway's *In Our Time*:

> They shot the six cabinet ministers at half-past six in the morning against the wall of a hospital. There were pools of water in the courtyard. There were wet dead leaves on the paving of the courtyard. It rained hard. All the shutters of the hospital were nailed shut. One of the ministers was sick with typhoid. Two soldiers carried him downstairs and out into the rain. They tried to hold him up against the wall but he sat down in a puddle of water. The other five stood very quietly against the wall. Finally the officer told the soldiers it was no good trying to make him stand up. When they fired the first volley he was sitting down in the water with his head on his knees.

The specificity of "six" ministers and "half-past six in the morning" is exemplary. These "off-duty" details do not allude to some larger, layered meaning, but they root us in the actuality of *this here* courtyard. As does Hemingway's important distinction between "one of the ministers" who "was sick with typhoid" and all the rest. Differentiations such as this deliver us from what Dana Gioia calls "the homogenous suburbs of the imagination." D. H. Lawrence's story "Odour of Chrysanthemums" starts like so:

"The small locomotive engine, Number 4, came clanking, stumbling down from Selston—with seven full wagons." Ford Madox Ford (who first published the story) said that the precision of "Number 4" and "seven wagons" indicated the presence of a real writer: "The ordinary careless writer," he said, "would say 'some small wagons'" instead. Other details pulse with "on-duty" significance.

In Hemingway's scene, we see more than just a minister bent over instead of standing up like all good prisoners should do when they are being shot; we have a singular man whom others have tried to elevate several times and who, failing this, leave him sitting in a puddle, head on his knees—this last touch carrying the very faint allusion or at least connotation of prayer, which suits the situation. The "dead leaves," with their familiar, moldy smell, connect us to the impending human deaths. Of all possible backdrops for this shooting, Hemingway selects a hospital, a decision that heightens the story's ironic mood: *"All the shutters of the hospital were nailed shut."*

While on a superficial level the narrator is doing no more than "painting a picture" or "setting the scene," this picture pounds with implied tension: the hospital is a site not of healing but of killing, however justified the shooting might be (and, importantly, Hemingway gives us nothing in terms of evidence or rationale or motives). With Hemingway, alluded-to ideas or multiple meanings come only when we follow the reflections emitted from the iceberg's tip. This commitment to the details is a disposition every writer can profitably study, as only habituation to such specificity can open the inner rooms of the house of fiction. As O'Connor reminds us, the fiction writer "is much less *immediately* concerned with grand ideas and bristling emotions than he is with putting list slippers on clerks."

Lynch outlines several imaginations, each of which attend to "the definite" differently. Earlier I referenced "exploiters of the real" who touch the finite "just sufficiently" to produce a profound vision which would (so say the exploiters) be undermined by the "actuality of things." The Christian imagination employs singularities—someone shouting "fire" in a smokeless street, a three a.m. knock on a dubiously-locked door, a steep gravel path trod by bare feet, an amnesiac patient narrating his past—in a manner that invites polysemantic meaning and multiple readings without losing actuality at all.

As O'Connor says of symbols in "The Nature and Aim of Fiction," although some writers eschew symbols entirely, and though the word "*symbol* scares a good many people off" (sounding to their ears like a "literary Masonic grip that is only for the initiated"), symbols are nearly-inevitably a matter of course for the fictionist. Symbols are details which accumulate meaning over time. Badly written, symbols come off as notes lightly played "in order to send the soul shooting into some kind of infinite or absolute." Well written, they "are details that, while having their essential place in the literal level of the story, operate in depth as well as on the surface, increasing the story in every direction." To borrow Lynch's phrasing, symbols "make the imagination *rise* indeed, and yet keep the tang and density of that actuality into which imagination descends."

Andrei Sinyavski's depiction of Gogol's aesthetics is especially instructive on this point. Gogol, he says, commits an "ostentation of language" flowing from the commonplace. In consequence, "the everyday and the commonplace look somehow extraordinary in Gogol"—and for no other reason than that his fictionist's eye has fixated on them: "Things seem to hide or hold something in themselves, unreal in their real aspect, so wholly familiar that you cannot imagine they are just simply and causelessly standing there without signifying anything," even as it is their very ordinariness that "constitutes their lot and their unsolved mystery."

Some writers, on the other hand, invite us into real, gritty, sonorous details, but only to either rush towards something else or rebound "into the self." We witness this in Proust's narrator, who longed to see someone because he longed to recall some flora affiliated with that "useful" other soul. Other times he is more frankly self-centered: "I drink a second mouthful," he muses. "It is plain that the object of my quest, the truth, lies not in the cup but in myself." This self, Lynch says, seeks to create an emotive, affective paradise. The density of the real is wholly lost to such skimming souls, trapped in their heads, living sometimes as if they are relatively bodiless.

33

Don't Make a Scene: Consciousness and Three Sensuous Strokes

THE FICTIONIST FACES a difficult task in responding to Lynch's judgments on these various "erroneous" imaginations. Was Proust *wrong* to portray his protagonist as "rebounding" constantly back into himself? No, for his narrator's self-bound proclivities proliferate in numerous souls, and the fiction writer is strengthened by his familiarity with a vast array of characters. At times, then, the character will determine that the author assume a narration which partakes of one of Lynch's maladjusted imaginations. Some characters will by fate occasionally "penetrate . . . our human flesh and environment" only to "recoil"—driven away by heavy emotion, or boredom, or habituation into familiar, safe abstractions—the cocoon of consciousness.

Henry James is instructive in this regard. In fiction, especially in his last three novels (*The Ambassadors*, *The Wings of the Dove*, *The Golden Bowl*), James was a pioneer who hypnotically rendered various people's penetrating consciousness. Because many of his novel's characters are entrapped in their own consciousnesses, it would be disingenuous for him to have them complete what Lynch would consider a proportionate encounter with the definite. James writes rightly when in "The Beast in the Jungle" he has the protagonist John Marcher remain caught in his own head for over fifty pages.

For much of the long short story he carries his cranial self like so:

> He had thought himself, so long as nobody knew, the most disinterested person in the world, carrying his concentrated burden, his perpetual suspense, ever so quietly, holding his tongue about it, giving others no glimpse of it nor of its effect upon his life, asking of them no allowance and only making on his side all those that were asked. He hadn't disturbed people with the queerness of their having to know a haunted man, though he had had moments of rather special temptation on hearing them say they were forsooth "unsettled." If they were as unsettled as he was—he who had never been settled for an hour in his life—they would know what it meant.

Only on the rarest occasion can he escape the blinding intensity and immediacy of his mental turnings and teasings and torments. Because we readers remain with him there, we perk up when he exits pure thought for a fleshy excursion like this:

> Her own aspect—he could scarce have said why—intensified this note. Almost as white as wax, with the marks and signs in her face as numerous and as fine as if they had been etched by a needle, with soft white

> draperies relieved by a faded green scarf on the delicate tone of which the years had further refined, she was the picture of a serene and exquisite but impenetrable sphinx, whose head, or indeed all whose person, might have been powdered with silver. She was a sphinx, yet with her white petals and green fronds she might have been a lily too—only an artificial lily, wonderfully imitated and constantly kept, without dust or stain, though not exempt from a slight droop and a complexity of faint creases, under some clear glass bell.

We cannot even really relish these rare details of what May Bartram is bodily like. Immediately, Marcher interprets them for us, ordering them into a sphinx. Of course he would mystify what may well be mundanity. And yet there is a truthfulness to this interpretation and insight: he has "plunged through, or down into the real contours of being" in order to "shoot up into insight."

But what of James's other (merely) mental meanderings and obsessions? In *How to Read a Novel,* Caroline Gordon takes to task those "who complain that nothing much happens in a James novel." She cites Joseph Warren Beach, who contends that James refuses all who would "keep constantly to the superficial levels of consciousness." Through his prose, they become "like visitors to mines, a smoky lamp is fixed to their caps and they are taken for excursions through dark subterranean galleries." A great deal *happens* in James, but the action has been transposed from exterior deeds into the inner-consciousness of the characters.

We find the same phenomenon in Dosty's (as Kerouac called him) *Crime and Punishment.* In a novel that includes the utterly external action of an ax murder, most of what happens is found on the lower frequencies of Raskolnikov's consciousness, as in this paragraph from the novel's first page. Notice that here we are not properly speaking in the first person, because Dostoevsky still gives us the tag "he thought," but we may as well be in his (anti-) hero's head:

> I want to attempt such a thing, and at the same time I'm afraid of such trifles!" he thought with a strange smile. "Hm . . . yes . . . man has it all in his hands, and it all slips through his fingers from sheer cowardice . . . That is an axiom . . . I wonder, what are people most afraid of? A new step, their own new word, that's what they're most afraid of . . . I babble too much, however. That's why I don't do anything, because I babble. However, maybe it's like this: I babble because I don't do anything. I've learned to babble over this past month, lying in a corner day in and day out, thinking about . . . cuckooland. Why on earth am I going now? Am I really capable of that? Is *that* something serious? No, not serious at all. I'm just toying with it, for the sake of fantasy. A plaything! Yes, a plaything if you like! Yes together in my den thinking . . . of Jack the Giant-killer. Why am I going there now? Am I capable of *that*? Is *that* serious? It is not serious at all. It's simply a fantasy to amuse myself; a plaything! Yes, maybe it is a plaything.

Here, as in *Notes from Underground*, the protagonist can conduct numerous contentious conversations with *himself*. Of course, *Notes* culminates in a second half that is far less cranial; the Underground Man moves, with all the weight of his unshakeable analyses, through numerous scenes and doings. Writers who wish to explore similar territory, who with Henry James and James Joyce would (to cite O'Connor) have us "floundering around in the thoughts" of various characters, would do well to remember O'Connor's warning that "a perception is not a story," for "in a story something has to happen," even if what happens is a reversal in the manner which the main character perceives, or a change in *what* he is able to absorb into his sinuous, flowing consciousness.

It is important to remember that the novel developed out of theatre, and this development corresponds with a kind of intensification of interiority, a "louder" consciousness. In the novel, Wood notes, the soliloquy goes inward. When Shakespeare's Macbeth conducts a conversation with his Lady in the presence of their guests, we have a kind of "publicized privacy," that is somewhat awkward: watching it on stage, we know it is odd that *we* can hear them talking privately, even though the other characters carry on as though oblivious.

In the case of Dostoevsky's Raskolnikov, on the other hand, we readers experience a kind of scrutinized privacy: the reader is, Wood continues, "invisible but all seeing." Because of this development, then, the novel is able to, among other things, analyze and probe unconscious motives, as the reader must look "between the lines for the *actual* motive." This point is extremely important: while access to character's consciousness may superficially suggest that we are "getting the deeper, inner truth," a careful writer can create dramatic tension not just between what a character does and what he thinks, but between why a character tells herself she is doing something and why she is *really* doing something. This would add yet another level of action to the unfurling of consciousness.

Granting the possibility of a story whose "setting" is largely a character's psyche, for most stories scene-setting is an absolute necessity. In Henry James's preface to his first novel, *Roderick Hudson*, he explains that "the centre of interest throughout 'Roderick' is in Rowland Mallet's consciousness, and the drama is the very drama of that consciousness—which I had of course to make sufficiently acute in order to enable it, like a set and lighted scene, to hold the play. By making it acute, meanwhile, one made its own movement." That is, even though Roderick is the protagonist, his patron Rowland's consciousness is the novel's *actual* center. Still, James's novel is thick with set and lighted scenes that stretch beyond Rowland's cranium—rooms that his character enter and exit. As Caroline Gordon relates, "I have a friend . . . who used to say that he would write fiction if he could only figure out some way of getting people in and out of rooms." This conclusion, Gordon concedes, is sound: "everything that happens in fiction must be represented as happening *somewhere* . . . the house has to be built before you can induce people to walk in and out of it." She goes so far as to say that when at last a writer learns to set the stage before peopling it, he has "lost his amateur standing."

Christine Flanagan points out the fact that, for Gordon, "technique and faith became synonymous." Weighing O'Connor's "A Good Man is Hard to Find," Gordon contends that "the story, on the whole, does not have enough 'composition of scene' to borrow a phrase from St. Ignatius of Loyola. Remember that the Lord made the world before he made Adam and Eve. Events take place in time and space. . . . I particularly miss the landscape after The Misfit comes on the scene."

William F. Lynch also turns to St. Ignatius's *Spiritual Exercises* as a "source of poetic as well as spiritual insight." St. Ignatius, he says, leads the person making the exercises "*proportionally* through the life of Christ . . . step by step, forbidding him again and again to take the way of magic impatience or hatred and commanding him to stay" rooted in place and time. By "composition of place," Ignatius means that the one who is praying into a passage of Scripture should "submit his mind and will completely to perfect and complete *detail,* the detail of that moment which is being separated and patiently considered."

In our contemplative advance through the mysteries of Christ, there is "no separation" between our advance through the incarnation of his humanity and time, our apprehension of the face of God; nowhere in Ignatius's exercises do we find a "pure theology" angelically severed from the concrete. In his directions for the first week of the exercises, St. Ignatius is clear:

> The first prelude is a composition of place, seeing the spot. Here it is to be observed that in contemplation or meditation on visible matters, such as the contemplation of Christ Our Lord, Who is visible, the composition will be to see with the eyes of the imagination the corporeal place where the thing I wish to contemplate is found. I say the corporeal place, such as the Temple or the mountain where Jesus Christ or our Lady is found . . . hear what people are saying on the face of the earth; how they converse together, how they blaspheme . . . likewise what the Three Divine Persons are saying . . . see with the eyes of the imagination the road from Nazareth to Bethlehem; consider its length, breadth, and whether the way be level or through valleys and hills; and likewise seeing the spot or cave of the Nativity, how large or small, how low or high, and how it is prepared.

This "application of the senses," while prescribed for spiritual exercises, can be applied in an analogous manner by the Catholic writer, who makes palpable the shabby as well as the sublime, who listens to blasphemies *and* God's own whispers and tries to saturate his stories with all of it.

If starting with setting is for the most part indispensable, the level of immersion in the scene should be proportionate to the story's larger texture: inevitably, the lines devoted to place will exist in relation to the actions that happen there. The more lines you spend on scene, the slower the pace, for instance. Some scenes should be slowed, others sped.

James Wood notes that during the nineteenth century "the novel became more *painterly*." In *La Peau de chagrin*, the great French novelist Balzac describes a tablecloth "white as a layer of newly fallen snow, upon which the place-settings rise symmetrically, crowned with blond rolls." Paul Cézanne was for a long while preoccupied with painting that "tablecloth of new snow." As Lessing demonstrates in *Laocoön*, visual art is fundamentally defined by place rather than time, whereas verbal art drives us across time more than place. When a novelist becomes more painterly, pausing to overtly notice details, she slows down the story's action.

Just before the most consequential moment in her story "Two Friends," Willa Cather pulls out the paintbrush and applies the acrylic liberally, going so far as to employ the painting metaphor as she places us in a run-down section of the city: "These abandoned buildings, an eyesore by day, melted together into a curious pile in the moonlight, became an immaterial structure of velvet-white and glossy blackness, with here and there a faint smear of blue door, or a tilted patch of sage-green that had once been a shutter."

In contrast to these decrepit buildings and environs made glorious by the narrator's brushing eye (her description is more extensive than the passage I just cited), the scene switches to an event that is intrinsically awesome, but which receives less tangibles: "Then we saw a bright wart on the other edge of the moon, but for a second only, — the machinery up there worked fast. While the two men were exclaiming and telling me to look, the planet swung clear of the golden disk, a rift of blue came between them and widened very fast. The planet did not seem to move, but that inky blue space between it and the moon seemed to spread. The thing was over."

Here it is just that the transit of Venus receives only a few quick if clarifying sensuous strokes because the narrator remembers it as happening very fast. Additionally, the diction Cather applies implies the story's underlying truth: lacking a true foundation, the friendship of the "Two Friends" is imperiled. There is a "wart" on the illumining moon. A "rift of blue" comes between these heavenly bodies, even as one character's political commitments will imminently rend what remains of their relationship.

Writers inclined to painterly prose must constantly ask themselves if they have "noticed" overmuch, and whether what they have noticed really does serve the story, even if Wood is mainly correct when he says that "from Balzac on" readers have "come to expect of narrative that it will always contain a certain superfluity, a built-in redundancy, that it will *carry more detail than it needs.*"

Gordon seems to agree. Insistent that Balzac was "one of the greatest" writers who ever lived, his sometimes-meticulous "piling up of detail is clumsy." This is not always the case. In the opening paragraphs of *Eugénie Grandet,* for instance, the purposefulness of his pausing is evident enough, and so doesn't come off as tedious. Here, you see, the *house* is a character, or, as Henry James said of Balzac's settings, they are "almost by themselves a living subject":

> There are houses in certain provincial towns whose aspect inspires melancholy, akin to that called forth by sombre cloisters, dreary moorlands, or the desolation

of ruins. Within these houses there is, perhaps, the silence of the cloister, the barrenness of moors, the skeleton of ruins; life and movement are so stagnant there that a stranger might think them uninhabited, were it not that he encounters suddenly the pale, cold glance of a motionless person, whose half-monastic face peers beyond the window-casing at the sound of an unaccustomed step. . . .

It is difficult to pass these houses without admiring the enormous oaken beams, their ends carved into fantastic figures, which crown with a black bas-relief the lower floor of most of them. In one place these transverse timbers are covered with slate and mark a bluish line along the frail wall of a dwelling covered by a roof *en colombage* which bends beneath the weight of years, and whose rotting shingles are twisted by the alternate action of sun and rain. In another place blackened, worn-out window-sills, with delicate sculptures now scarcely discernible, seem too weak to bear the brown clay pots from which springs the heart's-ease or the rose-bush of some poor working-woman. Farther on are doors studded with enormous nails, where the genius of our forefathers has traced domestic hieroglyphics, of which the meaning is now lost forever. Here a Protestant attested his belief; there a Leaguer cursed Henry IV; elsewhere some bourgeois has carved the insignia of his *noblesse de cloches*, symbols of his long-forgotten magisterial glory. The whole history of France is there.

Embedded in the matter of the house and its environs is "the whole history of France"! Here, in a sense, place *is* action carried across time. As James puts it, in Balzac's novels, "his towns, his streets, his houses" become "terms into which he saw the real as clamouring to be rendered and into which he rendered it with unequalled authority," even if, *things*, in his writer's hands, are "at once our delight and our despair; we pass from being inordinately beguiled and convinced by them to feeling that his universe smells too much of them, that the larger ether, the diviner air, is in peril of finding among them scarce room to circulate."

James's last point is especially salient for writers committed to passing through materiality into a metaphysical dimensionality; a writer can take a kind of obsessive, overmuch delight in material details, turning them into idols or worse—low-ceilinged habitations wherein the spiritual cannot breathe. Balzac's characters too, James says, can sometimes seem "enclosed in a particular artificial atmosphere, musty in quality and limited in amount, which persuades itself with a sublime sincerity that it is a very sufficient infinite." (Of course, the trouble with James's critique is this: what if Balzac's characters can't be otherwise? What if that is the whole point: Balzac is painting the dead end of materialism? That was Bob Dylan's reading of the prolific French novelist: "Balzac was pretty funny. His philosophy is plain and simple, says basically that pure materialism is a recipe for madness.") Still further, if Balzac can get too stuck in his "objects," James can at times get equally lost in the knee-deep marshes of his characters' psyches, leaving us wondering whether they have souls that transcend the hyperfine details devoted to their minds.

While certain moments might call for painterliness, then, writers need be cognizant of the proclivity to pile, writers should "compose their scene so that things move faster and in a more lifelike way." Flaubert, says Gordon, took the device of detailed noticing that he learned from Balzac "and transmut[ed] it to suit his own purposes."

In *Madame Bovary*, though the "setting plays a great part in every scene, it is so involved with the action that it takes a cunning eye to see where setting leaves off and action begins, as is evident from the novel's opening":

> We were in class when the head-master came in, followed by a "new fellow," not wearing the school uniform, and a school servant carrying a large desk. Those who had been asleep woke up, and every one rose as if just surprised at his work.
>
> The head-master made a sign to us to sit down. Then, turning to the class-master, he said to him in a low voice—
>
> "Monsieur Roger, here is a pupil whom I recommend to your care; he'll be in the second. If his work and conduct are satisfactory, he will go into one of the upper classes, as becomes his age."
>
> The "new fellow," standing in the corner behind the door so that he could hardly be seen, was a country lad of about fifteen, and taller than any of us. His hair was cut square on his forehead like a village chorister's; he looked reliable, but very ill at ease. Although he was

> not broad-shouldered, his short school jacket of green cloth with black buttons must have been tight about the arm-holes, and showed at the opening of the cuffs red wrists accustomed to being bare. His legs, in blue stockings, looked out from beneath yellow trousers, drawn tight by braces. He wore stout, ill-cleaned, hob-nailed boots.

Here, Flaubert sets the scene by granting considerable attention to the "new fellow" Charles Bovary's clothing, but these aren't just off-duty details: they establish his character as much if not more than his demonstrable awkwardness in action, which soon follows—and continues, by the way, until the novel's end.

The problem of what we should and shouldn't notice in a given scene must be mastered at the cost of failure. This concern is caught up with another: the writer's general inclination to appeal to the sense of sight more than any other. O'Connor learned from Caroline Gordon, and as Gordon learned from careful study of *Madame Bovary*, "it takes at least three activated sensuous strokes to make an object real"—at least for beings who have been given five senses. Her advice is wholly sound. However, combing through the works of even great writers only seldom do we find more than two sensuous strokes in a short space. Typically a writer will appeal to two senses, applying two strokes to one and one or two to the other. Take the following paragraph from F. Scott Fitzgerald's *The Great Gatsby*: "The caterwauling horns had reached a crescendo and I turned away and cut across the lawn toward home. I glanced back once.

A wafer of a moon was shining over Gatsby's house, making the night fine as before and surviving the laughter and the sound of his still glowing garden. A sudden emptiness seemed to flow now from the windows and the great doors, endowing with complete isolation the figure of the host who stood on the porch, his hand up in a formal gesture of farewell."

Fitzgerald really does get us "in" the scene, through his specificity (caterwauling horns; a laughing, glowing garden; a wafer of a moon; the host's silhouette, lonesome in spite of the party). Still, a half-line devoted to the peculiar scent of Gatsby's imported cigar, still clinging to Nick as he departs, would have done wonders to increase the dimensionality.

When Flannery O'Connor introduces Mount St. Scholastica in "A Temple of the Holy Ghost", she too calls on sight and sound:

> It had a high black grillework fence around it and narrow bricked walks between old trees and japonica bushes that were heavy with blooms. A big moon-faced nun came bustling to the door to let them in and embraced her mother and would have done the same to her-but that she stuck out her hand and preserved a frigid frown, looking just past the sister's shoes at the wainscoting. They had a tendency to kiss even homely children, but the nun shook her hand vigorously and even cracked her knuckles a little and said they must come to the chapel, that benediction was just beginning.

Note the specificity of "japonica bushes" and "heavy with blooms"—which grounds us much more completely than "bushes" would. Here we have not just a fence but one made of "high black grillework." And like Fitzgerald, O'Connor latches onto the moon when setting her scene. In her story, however, the moon's roundness is melded with a human face rather than the strongly-Eucharistic "wafer" we found in *Gatsby*. The lunar roundness of the nun's face draws out the fact that her body is "big"; still more, the moon could connote a bright but pale face, an association that would have been disrupted had O'Connor written of a "blood moon." We can feel the apprehension of the girl watching the nun hug her mother, reeling back at their weird charity which would have us kiss urchins and other deplorables (even this imagined kiss has a puckering presence to it, feeling it as we do from the girl's vantage). And then, finally, the "cracked knuckles" fill the space with a sound, snapping the tension that has laid latent since we arrived in it.

O'Connor's deliberate evasion of explicit explanation keeps us somewhat in the dark, unable to discern a single intended association for the moon. Here she works in contrast to a novelist like Balzac, who in *Père Goriot* writes of the "inane simplicity of the old chap's moon-like face." Many fictionists and critics see the movement from Balzac to the present as a progressive evolution away from direct expression and toward a more authentic indirection. Although beginning writers ought to take care to avoid short-cut reliance on authorial interventions and explanations that save time but create seams in the art, occasional broad strokes—especially when surrounded by thick scenes that keep the senses engaged—can achieve stunning characterizations.

Balzac regularly injects his novels with these psychological probings, some of which read like aphorisms. Take the tinted-whiskered Vautrin. Having known him for half a paragraph, we already learn that those who owed him money "would rather have died than failed to repay him, for, in spite of his good-natured appearance, his way of looking hard and searchingly at people inspired fear."

But Balzac does not doom him into one-dimensional roguery; he paints him, instead, with alluring and satisfying complexity. Although Vautrin has "erected his ostensible affability, his constant helpfulness and good humor into a barrier between himself and others," his is not a duplicitous shell hiding shallowness. Rather, he has the gaze of a "harsh judge, his eyes seem[ing] to go to the heart of every question, every conscience, every emotion." Again, such forthright psychological, spiritual, and moral portraits can become overmuch if leaned on as surrogates for the hard work of revealing character through action, but we must not slavishly heed the constant dictum of contemporary creative writing: "Show, don't tell."

Sensuous strokes can also achieve necessary discomfort—a visceral ache that advances the narrative's end. Michael Chabon's "Along the Frontage Road" begins with a deeply-sensed description of a father gutting a pumpkin: "I do remember the way [he] would go after our pumpkins, once we got them home, with the biggest knife from the kitchen drawer. He was a fastidious man who hated to dirty his hands, in particular with food, but he was also a doctor, and there was something grimly expert about the way he scraped the orange crania, excised the stringy pulp, and scraped clean the pale interior flesh, with the edge of a big metal spoon."

The account is intense, violent even, in and of itself, and then we find that an abortion ghosts the story's background. Chabon introduces this sensuous image before we learn of a "deceased girl of seventeen weeks." Bauer expounds: "We read this passage naively when we first encounter it; that is, before the narrative's deeper context has been introduced." Later we will remember the image, "this time with the added dimension of its haunting context."

For the Catholic writer, surely the "telling image" or the "on-duty detail" can signify some more natural meaning, as when Flannery's Mr. Head awakens in the moonlight at the onset of "The Artificial Nigger":

> Mr. Head awakened to discover that the room was full of moonlight. He sat up and stared at the floor boards—the color of silver—and then at the ticking on his pillow, which might have been brocade, and after a second, he saw half of the moon five feet away in his shaving mirror, paused as if it were waiting for his permission to enter. It rolled forward and cast a dignifying light on everything. The straight chair against the wall looked stiff and attentive as if it were awaiting an order and Mr. Head's trousers, hanging to the back of it, had an almost noble air, like the garment some great man had just flung to his servant.

Masterfully, O'Connor affixes the unmoving moon and the "straight chair" to the action of the story in order to expound Mr. Head's character. We are *with him* here, seeing the world as he sees it—everything in existence emerging as what Martin Heidegger would call a "standing reserve" awaiting his "order," his "permission." More suavely, from *within* her character rather than in a satirical, external manner, she achieves an end similar to Dickens's at the start of *Dombey and Son*: "The earth was made for Dombey and Son to trade in, and the sun and moon were made to give them light. Rivers and seas were formed to float their ships; rainbows gave them promise of fair weather; winds blew for or against their enterprises; stars and planets circled in their orbits, to preserve inviolate a system of which they were the centre. Common abbreviations took new meanings in his eyes, and had sole reference to them. A. D. had no concern with Anno Domini, but stood for anno Dombei—and Son."

Returning to O'Connor, she, at other times, lets details and images emerge outside of her characters—against their own penchants to reorder all reality according to their own predilections. At the end of "A Temple of the Holy Ghost," after benediction, after the girl finds out that the fair she pined to attend has been shut down through some preacher's intervention, she looks out the window towards a dark wood: "The sun was a huge red ball like an elevated Host drenched in blood and when it sank out of sight, it left a line in the sky like a red clay of road hanging over the trees."

Without neglecting the more earthy scene setting (literally, in this case, brushing clay into the heavens), O'Connor ends her story with a shockingly clarifying image of the sun as a Host—the unbloody sacrifice drenched in red. We can learn much from O'Connor's careful layering of sensuous images, her deceptively complex placement of them. Earlier the girl's thoughts fixed on a hermaphrodite she'd seen at the fair: "When the priest raised the monstrance with the Host shining ivory-colored in the center of it, she was thinking of the tent at the fair that had the freak in it. The freak was saying, "I don't dispute hit. This is the way He wanted me to be."

The ending image of the host links us back to this epiphanic moment. Still, why exactly the girl sees the Host now remains mysterious, as does the fact that the sun is setting. Analysis would reduce the richness of the author's associations, layerings, even as we can definitively say that she here exemplifies the sacramental vision of reality—the material pointing to something ultimately spiritual.

The Catholic writer can achieve this sacramental vision through the use of images far less grand than the sun. In Allen Tate's marvelous essay "The Symbolic Imagination," he hones in on Dante's use of the mirror. The mirror, says Tate, is a manmade thing—and as such is a "common thing." But in *The Divine Comedy*, the mirror is used to show us that the entire universe is a "replica *in reverse* of the supernatural world." I can't here sufficiently set the scene, but suffice it to say that the sacramental mirror reaches its peak when Dante sees in the mirror of his beloved Beatrice's eyes the sensible world turned inside out.

And living Catholic writers continue to inhabit this ordering of images. Lee Oser does so in *Oregon Confetti.*

Oser's novels blend the styles and sensibilities of Evelyn Waugh, F. Scott Fitzgerald, G. K. Chesterton, and Thomas Pynchon. *Oregon Confetti* is about an absurd quest—a life-or-death adventure that stretches from the temples of junk to the corridors of power, from the shadowy streets of gangland to the wide, wide deserts of lust. It has the backdrop of a thriller—replete with a conspiratorial plot thread—but it is deeply metaphysical and contains a number of theological twists.

Oser exemplifies a Catholic use of imagery that is especially beautiful in that it reaches into a particularly dark moment of the plot like a gentle light, a sort of Zippo-flicker of God's love. In a lesser writer's hands, the scene might have degenerated into a sentimentally sweet moment or been reduced to a weird Freudian Mother Complex, but instead Oser artfully points, sacramentally, to God the lover—an image many mystics have also employed. Knowingly or not, Lee Oser gives us a mirrored man and woman, and is so extending a symbol we saw in Dante:

> Agatha knocked on the door. She had a tortoise-shell comb in her hand and she wanted me to stand in front of the mirror, where I could study my crow's-feet, the bags under my eyes, the lines on my forehead, and other sobering effects of time and gravity. She stood very close behind me.
>
> "Where did you get your red hair?" she asked, going slowly with the comb so as not to tear the roots from the scalp.

> "My father. My mother had black hair, though now it's all gray. You know, she used to comb my hair like this."
>
> "You never talk about your father."
>
> "It's because he's been in jail my whole life. I was in the womb when they arrested him for stealing from Catholic charities. It was big-time embezzlement, years of white-collar crime, millions of dollars. He and his Bishop were busted by the FBI in a major sting operation. They had wiretaps showing the mob was involved. They nailed a couple of priests too. Then he copped a plea and perjured himself. The judge threw away the key."
>
> . . .
>
> When she finished she ran the tip of her finger along the top of my ear. I felt it as I watched her do it in the mirror. We looked at each other, reflection to reflection, one reflection to another.

As we pass through this scene, we can hear Allen Tate's insistence that though you can naturally explain a man-made mirror, "there is no natural law which explains man as a mirror reflecting the image of God."

34

Central Intelligence and Peripheral Points of View

Although we see a few rare souls writing extensively in second person, typically the fictionist looks out and in from the first or third person points of view. Gordon spells out the clear goods of the first-person position: "I saw it happen to these people," the structure seems to say. "I know what I am talking about." Because he is an "eye-witness," he can give you "the close-up," can give you the effect of the scene without committing to the "the strain of attention" which comes with a sustained attempt to create the same immediacy of *presence* in the third person perspective.

If she chooses first person, so the story goes, she must decide whether the narrator will be trustworthy or unreliable. Correcting this oversimplified conclusion, Wood contends that "even the apparently unreliable narrator is more often than not reliably unreliable." At least, careful authors let us "know that the narrator is being unreliable because [they alert us], through reliable manipulation, to that narrator's unreliability." The good fictionist includes clues and implications that teach us how to rightly read its storyteller.

By the time we come to the end of Graham Greene's *The End of the Affair*, we know that the first person is not a "voice-piece" for the author's "views." By selecting a purported atheist as a narrator, he brings readers into intimate familiarity with the soul's freedom to reject God. Still tormented in the novel's last lines, Maurice Bendrix's hatred of God manifests his emergent belief in God: "You're a devil, God, tempting us to leap. But I don't want your peace and I don't want your love . . . I hate you, God, I hate you . . ."

In (albeit) an extreme way, Greene gives the lie to the oversimplified superstition that a Catholic writer need to "tell" or "show" the world from the vantage point of a Catholic. We experience, *via negativa*, the excruciating longing for God in a way we would not were the narrator already "in the fold."

A Catholic writer is always conscious of her narrator's relation to the revelations and sacred that comprise Catholicity, even if her characters are antonymous to these truths. Christopher Beha is right to vocalize the fact that Walker Percy and Flannery O'Connor "did not dedicate themselves primarily to rendering Catholic experience." However, while they "wrote about the general human predicament," their "view" of "this predicament . . . was deeply influenced by their Catholic faith." As Flannery says in one of her letters, "The religion of the South [to which most of her characters adhere, or turn away from scoffing or in fear] is a do-it-yourself religion, something which I as a Catholic find painful and touching and grimly comic. It's full of unconscious pride that lands them in all sorts of ridiculous predicaments. They have nothing to correct their practical heresies and so they work them out dramatically. If this were merely comic to me, it would be no good, but I accept the same fundamental doctrines of sin and redemption and judgment that they do."

In my short story "Horseradish", the protagonist Blaise is not himself a firm believer. He maintains a persistent ambiguity towards even the apparently mystical experience he has while wrestling through patterns of family abuse with his father on their back porch. He wonders whether the visionary violation of mundanity—a burning bush in the backyard—was maybe nothing more than an aftershock of those psilocybin mushrooms he took so long ago. In spite of the fact that he is not a practicing Catholic, Blaise registers the loss of Slovenian Catholic traditions which his family has abandoned, incrementally but as-if inevitably, since their arrival in the States:

> But Babica was dead and Mom was sick and so who would do the harvesting, who the preparations, who the penances that seemed to me so archaic, arching as they did painfully backward to the Passover Seder—the five bitter herbs chewed in silence while some patriarch read the Haggadah. As though the Angel of Death hovered atop the copper *lestenec* that *dedek* made in the old country with his own fat and fireproof hands. As though they brought their devils with them, and their Savior too. As though they could smuggle such superstitions and expect them to take root in the New World.

Even when Blaise himself fails to see keenly what the loss of these traditions mean, I strive, through the story's central, guiding intelligence, to evoke the impoverishment of a world without transcendence.

I strive for this same dynamic in another short story—"Sacré Cœur," wherein two divorced, secularized parents are forced to confront their daughter Marie's obsession with *The Autobiography of St. Margaret Mary.* The book, which originally belonged to Marie's grandmother, serves as an unexpected thread, sewing Catholicism's sanctifying vision even into a girl whose mother gives her condoms and advises her to "try out" boys. When the troubled mother reads *The Autobiography*, "spying" on her daughter's mental state, she "couldn't put it down I was so disturbed. I even accidentally underlined some parts." Even if the story never definitively resolves whether the wounds on Marie's flesh are miracles or mere "cutting," even if neither of the parents turn towards Christ's Sacred Heart, the story strives to pulsate with the radical transcendence of the Catholic vision, made unsettling through the lives of the saints who are always "signs of contradiction."

I love St. Margaret Mary. Would I be vain to wager that I've prayed more novenas to her than the octogenarians at our parish who pass through their rosaries in a record ten minutes and rattle off novenas with the speed of Gatling guns? Whatever love remains in my soul I owe to Jesus's Sacred Heart. But let's admit it: *The Autobiography of St. Margaret Mary is* gloriously scandalous to modern sensibilities, as should be clear from even a single passage, which I encourage you, too, to underline, dear reader. Just after the saint asks Christ "What then, my God! Wilt Thou always let me live without suffering?" he gives a harrowing answer marked by a defamiliarizing combination of *caritas* and crucifixion: "Immediately a large cross was shown me, the extremity of which I could not see, but it was all covered with flowers. 'Behold the bed of my chase spouses on which I shall make thee taste all the delights of My pure Love. Little by little these flowers will drop off, and nothing will remain but thorns, which are hidden because of thy weakness. Nevertheless, thou shalt feel the pricks of these thorns so keenly that thou wilt need all the strength of My love to bear the pain.'"

It does not go without saying that these words "delighted" St. Margaret Mary. Her thrill is a thorn in the side of all Christians addicted to comfort ever after. (I won't even mention her abstention from liquids for days at a time.)

Whether he throws himself into first or third person, the Catholic writer will, in the words of O'Connor, "feel life from the standpoint of the central Christian mystery; that it has, for all its horror, been found by God to be worth dying for." Countenancing the same absurdities that unnerved Camus and the existentialists, the Catholic fictionist will prevent her story's perspective from relishing the farcical or capitulating to the cruel to the point of souring cynical. Still, a Catholic writer has no business shirking the contours of these cruelties; given that fiction is largely a record of man in rebellion, a large part of his work consists of drawing out the spiritual depths of man's refusal to serve. Georges Bernanos said of Balzac that "not a single feature is to be added to any one of those frightful characters, but he has not been down to the secret spring, to the last recess of conscience where evil organizes from within, against God and for the love of death, that part of us the harmony of which has been destroyed by original sin." Bernanos and Mauriac, Catholic writers both, were united in their efforts to add to Balzac's ingenuities. But how far can you go? As Maritain makes clear:

> The essential question is not to know whether a novelist can or cannot depict such-and-such an aspect of evil. The essential question is from what altitude he depicts it and whether his art and mind are pure enough and strong enough to depict it without connivance. The more deeply the modem novel probes human misery, the more does it require superhuman virtues in the novelist. To write Proust's work as it asked to be written would have required the inner light of a St. Augustine. Alas, it is the opposite which happens, and we see the observer and the thing observed, the novelist and his subject, rivals in a competition to degrade.

The Catholic vision is at times a corrective, exercising restraint where others would court scandal. Still, it does not solely "take away." O'Connor calls the Catholic vision an "added dimension." Contending with those who would see Catholicism as a limiting straightjacket stunting the writer's development, she insists that Catholic dogma "frees the storyteller to observe. It is not a set of rules which fixes what he sees in the world. It affects his writing primarily by guaranteeing his respect for mystery."

Here she seems to be building on Chesterton's insight that "orthodoxy is not only (as is often urged) the only safe-guardian of morality or order, but is also the only logical guardian of liberty, innovation and advance." This dogmatic commitment, O'Connor contends, "cannot fix what goes on in life or blind the believer to it," nor can it eliminate the need to exercise the habits of craft with zeal—for if the Catholic vision is an "added dimension," fiction must still be made according to its own intractable laws.

Like Catholic dogma, many of these laws are freeing rather than constraining. This is the case with point of view. As Henry James says, the "house of fiction" has many windows, and each narrating intelligence serves as a "field glass, which forms again and again, for observation, a new instrument. . . . He and his neighbors are watching the same show, but one seeing more where the other sees less, one seeing black where the other sees white." Because it is a capacious form, fiction allows us to move, within a single work, across numerous narrators' windows, teasing out the limits and depths of each's interpretation of reality. And yet, a Catholic will always be cognizant of the absolute vantage.

In his *Problem of Dostoevsky's Poetics*, Bakhtin contends that through Dostoevsky's dialogic imagination, what unfolds in his novels is not a single-voiced tract but "a world of consciousnesses mutually illuminating one another." From out of this polyphony, "Dostoevsky seeks the highest and most authoritative orientation, and . . . the image of Christ represents for him the resolution of ideological quests. This image or this highest voice must crown the world of voices, must organize and subdue it."

On the surface level, a Catholic writer need not make one voice emerge from the polyphony to point the way out of our problems. If he adopts multiple points of view within a single narrative, and none of these emerges to "organize and subdue" the crowd of voices, the whole will nonetheless be measured in Revelation's sacred scales. God, if unseen, exists behind, above, below each character, weighing what is committed and omitted, said and left unsaid.

Remember O'Connor's declaration that "all my stories are about the action of grace on a character who is not very willing to support it, but most people think of these stories as hard, hopeless, brutal, etc." One of the consequences of choosing a particular perspective is that some characters, some "omnisciences" will recognize the narrated effects of grace as gift, while others will see it as an inconvenience at best or an oppositional interruption at worst. Still other narrators will hardly register the supernatural at all; their vantage will be neither wide-eyed nor nose-plugged for things transcendent. They will be indifferent, with no explicit authorial "commentary" on that indifference. Gordon calls this the "effaced narrator," the narration that "never *tells* you what the characters feel and think, though he can *show* you. ... He is never inside their minds: he puts the reader inside."

Even when a story is told in "third person," we are not relegated to Olympian heights of narrational indifference. The story can gain spiritual and moral immediacy through "free indirect style," which James Wood describes as a third person narrative inflected by characters' internal speech freed of authorial flaggings. Traditional third person looks like so:

> He looked over at his wife. "She looks so unhappy," he thought, "almost sick." He wondered what to say.

The same scene told with free indirection is far more intimate:

> He looked at his wife. Yes, she was tiresomely unhappy again, almost sick. What the hell should he say?

Through free indirect style, we get the real live thoughts of characters, uncensored, unexplained, inviting us into their convoluted but compelling cacophony of thoughts, their psychic response to "third person reality." Wood cites an especially instructive instance in Henry James's *What Maisie Knew*, a novel that follows the "juvenile confusion" of Maisie as she weathers an ugly divorce and several subsequent love affairs. One of her governesses, the lower middle-class Mrs. Wix, had a daughter who died when she was about Maisie's age and is now buried at the Kensal Green cemetery:

> It was on account of these things that mamma got her for such low pay, really for nothing: so much, one day when Mrs. Wix had accompanied her into the drawing-room and left her, the child heard one of the ladies she found there—a lady with eyebrows arched like skipping-ropes and thick black stitching, like ruled lines for musical notes on beautiful white gloves—announce to another. She knew governesses

> were poor; Miss Overmore was unmentionably and Mrs. Wix ever so publicly so. Neither this, however, nor the old brown frock nor the diadem nor the button, made a difference for Maisie in the charm put forth through everything, the charm of Mrs. Wix's conveying that somehow, in her ugliness and her poverty, she was peculiarly and soothingly safe; safer than any one in the world, than papa, than mamma, than the lady with the arched eyebrows; safer even, though so much less beautiful, than Miss Overmore, on whose loveliness, as she supposed it, the little girl was faintly conscious that one couldn't rest with quite the same tucked-in and kissed-for-good-night feeling. Mrs. Wix was as safe as Clara Matilda, who was in heaven and yet, embarrassingly, also in Kensal Green, where they had been together to see her little huddled grave.

Wood helps us to see that James's "free indirect style allows us to inhabit at least three different perspectives at once: the official parental and adult judgment on Mrs. Wix; Maisie's version of the official view; and Maisie's view of Mrs. Wix." James filters the "official view" through the girl's half-grasping consciousness, emphasis on *half:* "James must make us feel that Maisie knows a lot but not enough." Wood reads the concentration of James's genius in one word: *embarrassingly.* "That is where all the stress comes to rest. . . . Whose word is 'embarrassingly'? It is Maisie's: it is embarrassing for a child to witness adult grief, and embarrassing that a body could be both up in heaven and solidly in the ground." If we remove words like *embarrassingly* from the cited passage, we lose free indirect style. If we remove a word like *huddled*, we lose an external eye: "when we reach the word 'huddled' we are reminded that an *author* allowed us to merge with his character," that "the sentence pulsates, moves in and out, toward the character and away from her."

Even writers of no small acumen can flail and trip over free indirection. Consider the opening of John Updike's novel *Terrorist*. The protagonist Ahmad is walking along, striving to conceive the "the streams and splashing fountains in which God, as described in the ninth sutra of the Qur'an, takes eternal good pleasure." As James Wood observes, though the phrasing and style pretend to Ahmad's, they are plainly Updike's, who is "unsure about entering Ahmad's mind, and crucially, unsure about *our* entering Ahmad's mind, and so he plants his big authorial flags all over his mental site."

In spite of its perils, free indirect style allows us to bring readers now-closer to, now-farther from a particular consciousness. This device is one way to develop what Caroline Gordon calls the "central intelligence," a manner of narrating that lets us merge the best of both first person and third person points of view. The "great virtue" of the strictly third person perspective is its innately "wide sweep." It impresses upon us "the vast scope of human life, the panorama as opposed to the minute scene." However, since the omniscient narrator knows, or, so to speak "acts as though he knows" everything, "he is tempted to tell the reader what happened and to leave the actual happening vague." The panoramic invites a sketch-like quality, and too much summary saps the story of "felt life."

A Catholic writer, incidentally, might well employ the "omniscient" vantage point in order to accentuate the difference between God's true all-seeing omnipotence (what Boethius, in *The Consolation of Philosophy*, calls the "simultaneous possession in all its perfection of endless life") and our own inherent narrowness by, for instance, bumping us up against the limits of the narrator's knowledge just when we thought "he" (whomever he is) knew it all. The all-encompassing design of panorama, which leads the reader through an experienced vastness, can serve as a necessary corrective to individualism and solipsism, the narrow Cartesian interiority of too many contemporary selves. In this way the omniscient narration gives the reader a hint of God's great and incomprehensible vision—though a hint it remains.

The device of "central intelligence," especially when carried out through free indirect style, creates a constant, fertile tension between the panoramic sweep and the narrow intensity of the eye-witness. As Gordon explains, "Through the central intelligence the author may permit us to meditate upon the state of affairs as a whole at a certain stage, and thus give us the panoramic sweep; or he may involve us in the central intelligence's immediate concerns, and thus put before us a close-up scene." In this way, the author escapes the narrowness of the effaced and first-person perspectives, which often struggle when moving from scene to scene or when trying to imply an overarching sense of meaning. A Catholic writer might adopt this technique by bestowing a Catholic sense on the "central intelligence." She might affiliate free-indirection with a Catholic character. This would mark and quietly measure the whole work with a way of being and feeling, a way of thinking and seeing that is steeped in the sacramental.

One of the most explicit manners of achieving intensification of sensation—applied to Catholic ends or not—is the selection of a protagonist with especial sensibilities, a person on whom nearly nothing is lost. As Henry James says in the preface to *The Princess Casamassima*, he made Hyacinth the main character for this reason:

> This in fact I have ever found rather terribly the point—that the figures in any picture, the agents in any drama, are interesting only in proportion as they feel their respective situations; since the consciousness, on their part, of the complication exhibited forms for us their link of connexion with it. But there are degrees of feeling—the muffled, the faint, the just sufficient, the barely intelligent, as we may say; and the acute, the intense, the complete, in a word—the power to be finely aware and richly responsible. It is those moved in this latter fashion who "get most" out of all that happens to them and who in so doing enable us, as readers of their record, as participators by a fond attention, also to get most. Their being finely aware—as Hamlet and Lear, say, are finely aware—*makes* absolutely the intensity of their adventure, gives the maximum of sense to what befalls them.

A Catholic writer might choose an acute soul like this for any number of ends: to draw out the grandeur of the world God made; to deepen our sense of the complexities and clarities of moral responsibility; to inch forth intimations of the unseen. An obvious weakness to this selection is that the rest of reality—that which falls outside of the sensitive and extraordinary soul—is at risk of "coming up pale," too pallid to solicit our attention. This is a problem because, as Gordon says, the fictionist must learn how to dramatize the whole, to "render active *everything* in the story, from the close-up scene to the large summary."

35

Complication and Resolution: Tragic, Eucatastrophic, Comic

For Tragedy is an imitation, not of men, but of an action and of life, and life consists in action. . . . Now character determines men's qualities, but it is by their actions that they are happy or the reverse. Dramatic action, therefore, is not with a view to the representation of character: character comes in as subsidiary to the actions. Hence the incidents and the plot are the end of a tragedy; and the end is the chief thing of all. Again, without action there cannot be a tragedy; there may be [action] without character.

—Aristotle, *Poetics*

ALTHOUGH IT IS true that some of us will write in a manner that makes "the main interest" less in "*what* happens than in that it happens to a certain character," a novel can only impart the sense that human beings are "richly responsible" if it rightly accentuates the importance of action—this not in the oversimplified sense of "keeping busy," or "getting work done," but in the way St. James registers it in his Epistle:

> What good is it, my brothers, if someone says he has faith but does not have works? Can that faith save him? If a brother or sister has nothing to wear and has no food for the day, and one of you says to them, "Go in peace, keep warm, and eat well," but you do not give them the necessities of the body, what good is it? So also faith of itself, if it does not have works, is dead. Indeed someone may say, "You have faith and I have works." Demonstrate your faith to me without works, and I will demonstrate my faith to you from my works. (2:14–18, NABRE)

The truths of faith and their attendant responsibilities for all souls, the implications of revelation—fiction can perhaps best restore these not simply by *perceiving them* richly and compellingly through a central intelligence on whom nothing is lost, but by paying due heed to that mysterious freedom at the heart of human life, a freedom worked out in fear and trembling through a narrative's necessary action. Remember O'Connor's reminder that truthful novels must make freedom a mystery. With characteristic hyperbole, Chesterton proclaims the liberating sanity of the unsolved: "As long as you have mystery you have health; when you destroy mystery you create morbidity. The ordinary man has always been sane because the ordinary man has always been a mystic."

Gordon roots fictional greatness in the author's attention to an old Aristotelian contention: all great narrative art falls into two parts—complication and resolution. In a masterpiece, she says, "the Resolution is always embedded in the Complication from the very start." Aristotle defines complication as "all from the beginning of the story to the point just before the change in the hero's fortunes," and resolution as "the beginning of the change to the end." For Aristotle, resolution starts with a character's "recognition," which he defines as "the change from ignorance to knowledge, and thus to either love or hate, in the personages marked for either good or evil fortune."

As any eighth grader knows (God please may it be so), the conflict of the complication typically takes one of three forms: man against nature, man against man, a man against himself. A Catholic writer might expand this list of possibilities by adding a fourth: man against God.

From Adam and Eve's Fall to Jacob's wrestlings, from Jonah's hiding to Christ's crucifixion, the biblical narrative penetrates this category. Alternately, a Catholic writer might choose as complication a matter of immediate concern to the mind of the Church. Or she might make a character's doubt—his outright atheism—the core conflict. The complication could be a moral malady, so long as she can reach it through the contours of the story without collapsing into cheap moralizing. By choosing "Catholic" complications of various shades, we are bestowing on our stories a spiritual structure. Both the complication and resolution should make one thing plain: grace and the devil make characters move just as much as their appetites and intellects, their habits of good or ill will. As Dostoevsky's Dmitri Karamazov says, "The awful thing is that beauty is mysterious as well as terrible. God and the devil are fighting there and the battlefield is the heart of man."

A writer might begin with one apparent complication only to *complicate the complication*, as Christopher Beha does in *What Happened to Sophie Wilder.* Early in the novel we learn that the narrator, Charlie, is romantically bound to the titular character. To make matters more convoluted, we realize that "she'd been gone from New York since her split with Tom," Tom being her husband. Charlie learns that she "left town" while he was deliberating "how to go about" reaching out to her after "her marriage was over."

Here, as in his novel *The Index of Self-Destructive Acts*, Beha is brilliant at building intrigue. Soon we are enthralled with Sophie too. Who wouldn't be drawn to someone who has a "habit" of "taking everything I said seriously, even small talk, so that I always wanted to be my best self around her"? Of course, it isn't that simple: "I remember too how this habit occasionally became suffocating, as the constant demand to be your best self naturally does." And it really *isn't* even that simple. What starts out as a complicated bond between the narrator Charlie and the mysterious Sophie morphs into a complication between Sophie and God, a tension brought to bear on all of her other relationships. She is, "for a time, occupied" by "something outside of herself, something real, not an idea or a conceit or a metaphor." This occupation "reshapes . . . her very outline" of her life, as well as the arcs by which the novel is resolved.

In "A Good Man is Hard to Find," O'Connor spells out the seeds of the resolution in the complication with which she begins:

> The grandmother didn't want to go to Florida. She wanted to visit some of her connections in east Tennessee and she was seizing at every chance to change Bailey's mind. Bailey was the son she lived with, her only boy. He was sitting on the edge of his chair at the table, bent over the orange sports section of the Journal. "Now look here, Bailey," she said, "see here, read this," and she stood with one hand on her thin hip and the other rattling the newspaper at his bald head. "Here this fellow that calls himself The Misfit is aloose from the Federal Pen and headed toward Florida and you read here what it says he did to these people. Just you read it. I wouldn't take my children in any direction with a criminal like that aloose in it. I couldn't answer to my conscience if I did.

The grandmother's stubbornness, stated here according to a harmless predilection, will later tip the family into crisis. The Misfit, now a two-dimensional threat contained in the newspaper, will arrive in full form and serve as the occasion of the grandmother's recognition—her departure from self-absorbed, opportunistic sophistry and her arrival at deep affinity with her enemy: "'Why you're one of my babies. You're one of my own children!' She reached out and touched him on the shoulder. The Misfit sprang back as if a snake had bitten him and shot her three times through the chest. Then he put his gun down on the ground and took off his glasses and began to clean them."

Although some Christian writers and readers reel away from explicit violence (and any representation of sex whatsoever) and condemn these things as intrinsically gratuitous or scandalous, everyone with the *sensus Catholicus* knows that there is a difference between pornographic violence (and sex) and graphic elements that are necessary for the achievement of the story's total effect. (I am sympathetic with those sensitive souls who refrain from some graphic art which, even if it is not objectively morally ill, may occasion them to sin. Literature is not necessary for salvation! I do not pretend that when painting a scene, the distinction between graphic and pornographic is easily ascertained, which sends us once again back to our knees, and also in search of that virtue *phronesis*—perfection of the practical intellect.) A character's later reticence, for instance, might only obtain sublimity if we first see him falling into several women's beds.

The shock of recognition in O'Connor's stories, helped and hastened by necessary violence, is reminiscent of those great tragedies Aristotle cites in his *Poetics.* Thomas Merton was only slightly hyperbolic when he compared her not to "Hemingway, or Katherine Anne Porter, or Sartre, but rather . . . someone like Sophocles. What more can be said of a writer? I write her name with honor, for all the truth and all the craft with which she shows man's fall and his dishonor."

Slowly, tortuously, Sophocles gives us Oedipus's descent—pinnacling with his plucked out eyes. Why? To make us all sadists, or to shock us into shirking the same fate? *Oedipus Rex*'s mournful action purges us of pity and makes us goodly sorrowful because Sophocles measures our tragic descents against our prospective magnificence. Each time I read Flannery O'Connor's harrowing story "The Lame Shall Enter First," I am a better father to my children for at least three days—this in spite of the fact that the story tracks a bad father whose son commits suicide. In this story, too, the resolution and complication are already evident in the initial paragraphs. Shepherd, the father, is a harsh, mechanical, enlightened hawk, pecking at his child's every move, striving to manipulate selflessness from him. ("Norton," he asks his son, "do you have any idea of what it means to share?") We are not surprised—though our stomachs descend into the grave—when Shepherd's recognition comes tragically too late.

On the final page, he knows at last that "he had ignored his own child to feed his vision of himself," which "shriveled until everything was black before him." Seeing Norton in his mind, love for the boy "rushed over him like a transfusion of life," and he envisions a future when he "would never let him suffer again." But when he ascends the attic to kiss his son, reeling at the top "like a man on the edge of a pit," he finds that the telescope has fallen, the tripod tumbled over. His son "hung in the jungle of shadows, just below the beam from which he had launched his flight into space."

Every time I reach that line my soul shivers at my own capacity for cruelty, harshness, sins of omission against my son. In the hands of our greatest Catholic writers, tragedy becomes prelude to the sacramental life; the self-scrutinies it fosters well prepare us to make a good confession.

To be sure, Catholic writers need to avoid relishing their often necessary representation of macabre realities.

Still, this need not mean a turn away from tragic resolution of a story. Students in my "Art of Fiction" class have frequently posed a sound question: need the Catholic writer resolve a story in a redemptive—or in a happy—key? Not infrequently they will thoughtfully cite Tolkien's "On Fairy Stories," his elucidation of eucatastrophe:

> Far more important is the Consolation of the Happy Ending. Almost I would venture to assert that all complete fairy-stories must have it. At least I would say that Tragedy is the true form of Drama, its highest function; but the opposite is true of Fairy-story. Since we do not appear to possess a word that expresses this opposite — I will call it *Eucatastrophe*. The *eucatastrophic* tale is the true form of fairy-tale, and its highest function. The consolation of fairy-stories, the joy of the happy ending: or more correctly of the good catastrophe, the sudden joyous "turn" (for there is no true end to any fairy-tale): this joy, which is one of the things which fairy-stories can produce supremely well, is not essentially "escapist", nor "fugitive". In its fairy-tale—or otherworld—setting, it is a sudden and miraculous grace: never to be counted on to recur. It does not deny the existence of *dyscatastrophe*, of sorrow and failure: the possibility of these is necessary to the joy of deliverance; it denies (in the face of much evidence, if you will) universal final defeat and in so far is *evangelium*, giving a fleeting glimpse of Joy, Joy beyond the walls of the world, poignant as grief.

Tolkien goes on to say that the resurrection of Christ is the ultimate eucatastrophe. Given that the pattern of Christ's life "concludes" with an otherworldly upward tilt, ought not Catholic fiction follow the same structure?

In *Christ and Apollo*, William F. Lynch grants that there is a "dishonest" tragedy which gloats and even guffaws over our helplessness. But when tragedy "is really achieved" through the "great tragic texts," we are brought to an "experience of deep beauty and exaltation, *but not by way of beauty and exaltation.*" Catholic writers can employ a tragic key insofar as tragedy is "rooted in mystical conquests of the human spirit over pain, in the emergence of godlike strength and qualities in man in the very midst of tragic defeat."

While all human life will ultimately be judged according to Christ, in fiction it would be dishonest to force eucatastrophe out of every complication: some genuine goods can sear through our encounter with decent but flawed people, with troubled, imperfect characters of good will whose decisions and situations draw them close to hell's gates. Artists who render this trajectory for us do us a great service—often purging us, through catharsis, of temptations which we share with their characters. Sins can lose their lure when we see characters act out immoralities we only imagined. We reel over Lear's awful actions, but we reel more over our near imitation of them.

True, on the deepest level of existence, the Christian must unite his agonies with those of the all-sufficient Master, knowing with St. Paul that we can "fill up those things that are wanting of the sufferings of Christ, in my flesh, for his body, which is the church" (Col 1:24, DRA). And yet, as fiction that tracks conversions can help us grasp, the human spirit frequently dies "in real helplessness," to use Lynch's language.

However, this "really tragic level of existence," he explains, "is the region of the soul into which Christianity descends in order to operate its unique effects. . . . There is a point to which the mind must come where it realizes it is no match for the full mystery of existence, where, therefore, it suffers a death." Often it is only fully here, from this posture, that we fully consent to put on the mind of God—to surrender to Christ's redemptive suffering—"and thus rise to a higher knowledge and insight." Here, at this point, death and life coincide in a single act, and thus "in this sense Christian faith has the tragic at its very core"; it is always "an extremely complicated mixture of dying and living; at no stage in the whole life of faith can death be screened out."

One of the tasks, then, of the truly Catholic writer, is to loosen tragedy from its inner-*ressentiment*, its prospective disgust and cynical gloating over our infinite absurdities. The Christian tragedian seeks to ransom our deep helplessness in the hope of redemption. This holds even if, in a given story, a character himself grows resentful, further fastening his own straightjacket. The Catholic writer will register, through the central intelligence, the radical insufficiency of this cynical turn—even if the protagonist turns totally cynical and spins circles around this world's absurdities. Although at the deepest level the Catholic is obsessed with his character's salvation or damnation, he does not defy his faith by following some of his characters into hell. Dante demonstrates that even told from hell the Catholic writer's story will refract the persisting promises of paradise in Christ.

But the Resurrection is eucatastrophic—is narratologically comic. As has already been mentioned (by whom, you ask, parsing the passive voice), Catholic writers have never been strangers to the comic vein. Sometimes they settle for mere satiric wit, mockery meant to morally instruct, but at its best, as Hagiopan has it, Catholic writing morphs from light chuckling or belly-laugh hilarity into muted seriousness.

The complications of comedy, resolved with more suddenness and surprises than tragedy, are only apparently superficial—we must pry into their depths. Comedy, Lynch says, "in its own unique language about man . . . turns the telescope around so that the eye looks through the greater end, and everything has become, not sea incardinate, but a disconcertingly small puddle." The comic, in this sense, is concerned with the low—the animals chomping hay, say, while Christ was being born two feet away. The comic, Lynch continues, is "the complete and funny reminding of the collapsibility of the divine man" ennobled so differently in tragedy. At its lowest, comedy laughs spitefully at man—with a hearty hatred that is gastrointestinal. At its highest, comedy teaches us to hate the man who cannot stand the sight of himself. Judas, Lynch says, is "the sinful and most serious form of the non-comic." The true comic writer strives to produce a kind of clownish sadness over our sinfulness and smallness; in a roundabout, circuitous manner of the best acts at the circus, the comic reminds us of "the desperate predicament of being human."

Take the following excerpts from Oscar Wilde's children's story "The Remarkable Rocket," which have become something of a medicine in our family's house; we cite them when one of us is inclined to be as ridiculous as the rocket:

> "I was saying," continued the Rocket, "I was saying—what was I saying?"
>
> "You were talking about yourself," replied the Roman Candle.
>
> "Of course; I knew I was discussing some interesting subject when I was so rudely interrupted."

And, a little later:

> "I am laughing because I am happy," replied the Cracker.
>
> "That is a very selfish reason," said the Rocket angrily. "What right have you to be happy? You should be thinking about others. In fact, you should be thinking about me."

The comic laughs at those who cannot laugh at themselves. It cuts the Christian life with a belly-ache laugh, loosening our idolatries and chastening (quite jollily) our pharisaical seriousness. Pseudo-comic authors, on the contrary, will revel in the buffoonish desperation that marks the human condition, drudging up diabolical hilarity that lashes out, teaching us, Lynch tells us, that "nothing is serious, everything is a parody of itself, about to laugh at itself."

David Foster Wallace had this mindset in mind when he wrote "E. Unibus Pluram: Television and U.S. Fiction": pervasive postmodern irony marks a "weary cynicism" which is essentially a mask to cover "gooey sentiment and unsophisticated naiveté. . . . What passes for hip cynical transcendence of sentiment is really some kind of fear of being really human, since to be really human is probably . . . to be in some basic interior way forever infantile." Wallace notes, though, that "irony has only emergency use. Carried over time, it is the voice of the trapped who have come to enjoy their cage." This, Wallace notes, "is because irony, entertaining as it is, serves an exclusively negative function."

Balzac also participated in and yet distanced himself from the penchant for satire: "All we can do these days is jest," he writes in the preface to *The Wild Ass's Skin.* "The whole literature of a moribund society is mockery." On the other hand, irony of the sort Socrates used so liberally is not merely negative—although it too can take on a cruel character. Romano Guardini said of Socratic irony, "Its object is not to expose, to wound, to dispatch, but to help." It aims to liberate, to serve truth. Guardini goes on, "Socrates's concern is, above all things, for an inward mobility, a living relation to being and truth, which can only with difficulty be elicited by direct speech. So irony seeks to bring the centre of a man into a state of tension from which this mobility arises."

Unlike Socratic irony, cynical satire is a means of dealing with the dissolution and fragmentation of the world, of so many people's disillusionment with the political, the religious, etc. through a wry grin that often affords no more than a momentary, and quite shallow, *laugh.* Again, instead of harnessing this irony in our favor, we should try to ask *what is behind the ironic impulse.* I would suggest that at least part of what we will find in those shadows is a sort of self-protection against the hollowness of the world, against those that T. S. Eliot called "The Hollow Men":

We are the hollow men
We are the stuffed men
Leaning together
Headpiece filled with straw. Alas!
Our dried voices, when
We whisper together
Are quiet and meaningless
As wind in dry grass
Or rats' feet over broken glass
In our dry cellar

Shape without form, shade without colour,
Paralysed force, gesture without motion;

Eliot's diagnosis of postmodernity is frustratingly perfect. The loss of hope in language's capacity to carry meaning. The loss of form and colour. What Martin Mosebach calls the heresy of formlessness. Paralysis. But amidst these falling forces, this incessant gesturing (the media saturation and celebrity culture, for instance . . . *art* as mere self-expression or *therapy*), Eliot articulates the transcendent. Not *outside* these things, mind you, but *between them:*

Between the desire
And the spasm

Between the potency
And the existence
Between the essence
And the descent
Falls the Shadow

For Thine is the Kingdom

For Thine is
Life is
For Thine is the

This is the way the world ends
This is the way the world ends
This is the way the world ends
Not with a bang but a whimper.

Do not these words resonate so deeply today? Have not the collective hopes prescribed by a secular culture been collapsing now for decades, so that if we listen closely, beneath the "bangs," between the noise, we hear that holy whimper? Yes, but we also hear that *For Thine is the Kingdom* struggling like a bug stuck in sweet but spoiled honey to fly aloft again.

Wallace confessed that he used "postmodern techniques . . . to discuss or represent very old traditional human verities that have to do with spirituality and emotion and community and ideas that the avant-garde would consider very old-fashioned." The movement he fostered is sometimes called "the new sincerity." It is true that sincerity in and of itself is no guarantee of truth or cultural excellence. As Jacques Maritain argues in *The Dream of Descartes*, "Many diverse states of mind, and of a greater or less degree of integrity, can find themselves compatible with *sincerity*." Still, this push towards sincerity helps us believe again in fiction, even to the point that it is possible to employ post-modern techniques like pastiche, passing *through* them to reach what matters; in fact this movement imitates what contemporary human beings inhabiting an inhuman, tech-nocratic world are often obliged to do in order to restore a humane sanity.

A Catholic writer, like any Christian creature, knows that love is the final measure; even the "objects" of his sat-ire should be leavened with the utmost charity of spirit. Lacking his love, they will spin into projected caricatures, gnashed in the writer's too-hateful teeth. In my younger and more vulnerable years, a writing mentor gave me some advice that I've been turning over in my mind ever since: "You need to love your characters more," she wrote. "Read Gogol." Until then my stories had that "something cruel and wounding" which Henry James found in Balzac, where irony makes "[being] ridiculous . . . appear like a crime." The targets of this irony are not to be ignored—"middle-class ignorance, narrowness" for instance—but fiction is weak-ened when we can hear through his pages an author's own "grudges and hates."

Well, *read Gogol.* I can only pass on the literary pre-scription, even if the chances of you having a greater capacity for charity than I are quite high. Notice, as you pick up Gogol's wildly bizarre "The Nose," that he does not merely "excoriate" his "enemies"; he courted our sym-pathy for them too. Frank O'Connor finds Gogol's "The

Overcoat" to be "neither satiric nor heroic, but something in between—something that perhaps transcends both." It is Gogol's Christian sense that achieves this transcendence. Gogol, to cite George Saunders, shows us how to "satirize and celebrate at once"; there is a kind of "verbal joy" in his stories that courts gratitude and sympathy even as they do the corrective work of comedy. As Saunders says of "The Overcoat", "The sensibility of that story is perfect. Gogol somehow manages to make us feel sympathy for the main character without that character needing to be a saint. It makes fun of him while loving him. He's a stinker, kind of—someone we wouldn't want to be around and yet, by the end, we feel so protective of him. So Gogol is, I think, modeling, in the prose, a form of Christian love—sort of training us in what it might feel like to really (really) believe that we are all brothers and sisters."

Gogol does this, Saunders says, by inciting love (not mere sympathy, or pity, but Christian charity) for a fumbling, often dull, foolish man who tries to hide in the bureaucratic hive, and who shows sparse kindness to those lower on the ladder than he is: Akaky Akakievich, this pathetic, reactionary protagonist, is truly "the least among us." In spite of the aforementioned, Gogol summons us to love him. Saunders sees this as "a real feat. And it never feels preachy but, is rather, spontaneous and funny and also formally very experimental—it keeps seeming to come to an end and then lurching back alive again."

The Catholic comic writer may tell stories that seem anarchic, teasing out threads full of vulgar characters who thieve and drink and play the fool. Between these sometimes bawdy lines, Lynch explains, comics are "only [defenders] of another and more human order (more muddy, more free)" than the false categories of stuffy conventions and pretentious inventions that teach us to worship our white-washed tombs. The Catholic who writes comically works to restore sanity by fixing his canons on a veritable nation of poor hopeless characters—*A Confederacy of Dunces*: those who see "all reality as simple and reduces a multitudinous creed to a single, exacerbating, crusading formula"; not to mention the "scrupulous man who reduces the overflowing life of being and the mind to a worrisome pinpoint"; or "the great conquerors," men who "have the universe under perfect control and have it forever fixed in an icy stare." Reader beware: the life you laugh towards sanctity may be your own.

But doesn't Christian revelation eliminate humors that have always lurked among the gentiles? Is life really something to be satirized, comically cauterized? What is so funny? Lynch emerges from the lurch to lighten our way once again: for the Catholic writer, "things are funny precisely because they can recall the relation between God and themselves." Whereas in tragedy the comic facts are concealed because the action's inner-logic is, well, utterly logical (movement from ignorance to knowledge), even tragedy concurs with the essential comic clue: "to recall this incredible relation between mud and God is, in its own distant, adumbrating way, the function of comedy." Perhaps precisely because its inclination is to lead hapless, hopeless cases towards happy endings, comedy calls tragedy's core teaching funny: man, with his godlike potentialities, is helpless when left to his own ornate devices.

36

Only a Mystic Can Be a Complete Novelist

THE CATHOLIC WRITER knows that our comic weakness obtains in life as in literature. When we hear Mauriac tell us that to rightly tackle sin in our fictional creations we must purify the source, we would do well to first laugh at our essential disfigurement—our fleshly vulgarity. We would do well to first see said tackling as impossible. And then fall to our knees, all sobriety, heeding O'Connor's preface to *Wise Blood.* For the Christian comic, sense is "very serious, for all comic novels that are any good must be about matters of life and death."

If Lynch is right, we writers, stubbornly bent on reconciling the irreconcilable—that is to say, representation and reality, dust and divinity—are engaged in a pursuit that is wholly comic. Given this, we must do more than mind our manners to survive and make felt life out of fiction's death to self. We must begin and end with simultaneous submission to our natural smallness and the supernatural largess of the Lord. All fictionists can perfect their higher faculties, crafting an art that is good in itself, developing forever with no knowledge of God. *Contra gentiles*, the Catholic writer can come to render a wholly Other world, but only by submission to his innate unknowing. Only sanctifying grace, says Father Garrigou-Lagrange, "introduces us into this higher order of truth and life. It is an essentially supernatural life, a participation in the intimate life of God, in the divine nature, since it even now prepares us to see God someday as He sees Himself and to love Him as He loves Himself." Only this grace, which elevates the soul's "vitality and [makes] it bear no longer merely natural fruits but supernatural ones, meritorious acts that merit eternal life for us"—only the Author of this grace (as it was in the beginning, is now, and ever shall be)—can make Catholics more vital—and their writings more vital also.

There is no artistic *habitus* without prudence, but writing Catholics need more than even this maestro among the virtues. Prudence may yet pause at the crucial moment that calls for decisiveness. "Even infused prudence," advises Father Garrigou-Lagrange (one of young Maritain's spiritual mentors), "hesitates, for example" discursively weighing "what answer to give to an indiscrete question so as to avoid a lie and keep a secret; while a special inspiration of the Holy Ghost will enable us to find a proper [superdiscursive] reply, as Christ told His disciples." Writing knotted scenes bred by immoral acts, striving to imitate the mysterious intersection of beatific grace and many-faced nature, whispering or shouting God's own glories—no Catholic writer approaching these difficulties can complete the demands of both art and faith by means of prudence alone. Solely the Holy Ghost can do that. Only he can give sufficient gifts at the artist's dire hour of room-pacing, red-eyed, head-scratching need.

One of the truest sentences in *Art and Scholasticism* is comically hidden in an academic footnote in the back of the book. If you blink, you can miss it: "Only a Christian, nay a mystic, because he has some idea of what there is in man, can be a complete novelist." Only a mystic can be a faithful fictionist, for only the mystic fictionist can write Balzac's novelistic, all-too-human comedy in the register of the Dantean divine.

Appendix A

101 Books to Read Like a Catholic

The Holy Bible

Homer, *The Iliad* and *The Odyssey*

Aeschylus, *The Oresteia* and others

Sophocles, *Oedipus Rex* and others

Vergil, *The Aeneid*

St. Augustine, *Confessions, The City of God*

St. Thomas Aquinas, *Summa Theologiae, On Evil*

St. John of the Cross, *The Dark Night of the Soul* and others

St. Teresa of Avila, *Interior Castle* and others

Geoffrey Chaucer, *The Canterbury Tales*

Miguel De Cervantes, *Don Quixote*

Shakespeare, "either for tragedy, comedy, history, pastoral, pastoral-comical, historical-pastoral, tragical-historical, tragical-comical-historical-pastoral, scene individable, or poem unlimited."

Dante Alighieri, *The Divine Comedy*

Honoré de Balzac, *The Human Comedy,* especially *Lost Illusions*

Jane Austen, *Mansfield Park* and others

Alessandro Manzoni, *The Betrothed*

Johann Wolfgang von Goethe, *Faust*

Bram Stoker, *Dracula*

Nikolai Gogol, *Dead Souls* and others

St. John Henry Newman, *Callista* and others

Baudelaire, *Flowers of Evil* and others

Gustave Flaubert, *Madame Bovary* and others

Fyodor Dostoevsky, *Notes from Underground, Demons, The Idiot, The Brothers Karamazov*, and others

Leo Tolstoi, *Master and Man* and others

Joris-Karl Huysmans, *Against Nature, En Route,* and others

Léon Bloy, *The Woman Who Was Poor, The Desperate Man,* and others

Henry James, *The Golden Bowl* and many others

Paul Bourget, *The Disciple*

Gerard Manley Hopkins, SJ, *Collected Works*

Francis Thompson, *The Hound of Heaven and Other Poems*

Robert Hugh Benson, *Lord of the World*

G. K. Chesterton, *The Complete Father Brown Mysteries*

James Joyce, *Dubliners, A Portrait of the Artist as a Young Man, Ulysses*

T. S. Eliot, *Four Quartets, The Waste Land,* and others

Charles Péguy, *The Mystery of the Charity of Joan of Arc* and others

Sigrid Undset, *Kristin Lavransdatter*

Paul Claudel, *The Satin Slipper* and others

Georges Bernanos, *Diary of a Country Priest* and others

Ernest Hemingway, *The Sun Also Rises* and others

F. Scott Fitzgerald, *Babylon Revisited* and others

Francois Mauriac, *The Viper's Tangle* and others

Myles Connolly, *Mr. Blue*

Willa Cather, *Death Comes for the Archbishop* and others

Gertrud von Le Fort, *The Song at the Scaffold*

Czesław Miłosz, *Collected Poems*

Katherine Anne Porter, *Pale Horse, Pale Rider* and others

William Faulkner, *If I Forget Thee, Jerusalem* and others

J. R. R. Tolkien, *The Lord of the Rings* and others

Albert Camus, *The Plague* and others

Herman Broch, *The Death of Virgil*

Graham Greene, *The End of the Affair, The Power and the Glory,* and others

Dorothy Day, *The Long Loneliness*

Thomas Merton, *Seven Storey Mountain*

Evelyn Waugh, *Brideshead Revisited*, *Sword of Honour,* and others

Robert Lowell, *Lord Weary's Castle*

David Jones, *In Parenthesis*

John Kennedy Toole, *A Confederacy of Dunces*

Flannery O'Connor, *Wise Blood*, *The Violent Bear it Away*, *The Complete Stories*

Jack Kerouac, *Visions of Gerard* and others

Caroline Gordon, *The Malefactors* and others

Shusaku Endo, *Silence* and others

Walter M. Miller Jr., *A Canticle for Leibowitz*

Ford Madox Ford, *The Good Soldier* and others

Edwin O'Connor, *The Edge of Sadness*

J. F. Powers, *Morte D'Urban*, *The Stories of J. F. Powers*

Anthony Burgess, *The Wanting Seed*

Rumer Godden, *In This House of Brede*

Muriel Spark, *The Prime of Miss Jean Brodie*

Toni Morrison, *Beloved*

John Updike, *Collected Stories*

Walker Percy, *The Moviegoer* and others

Brian Moore, *Catholics: A Novel*

John Finlay, *"Dense Poems and Socratic Light": The Poetry of John Martin Finlay*

Alice Thomas Ellis, *The Sin Eater* and others

Alice McDermott, *After This* and others

Oscar Hijuelos, *Mr. Ives Christmas*

Ron Hansen, *Mariette in Ecstasy*

Gene Wolfe, *The Book of the New Sun*

Tobias Wolff, *In the Garden of the North American Martyrs*

Michael D. O'Brien, *Father Elijah* and others

David Foster Wallace, *Infinite Jest* and others

Cormac McCarthy, *The Road* and others

Randy Boyagoda, *Original Prin*

Christopher Beha, *What Happened to Sophie Wilder* and others

Dana Gioia, *99 Poems* and others[1]

---

[1] Will you, dear reader, ever forgive me for the brevity of this list, for its radical incompleteness? And I haven't even touched upon the question of what books we should read to our children, even though our doing so is of utmost importance if we are to educate their souls in an expansive manner that bestows poetic knowledge, thickens the moral imagination, and bonds us in the great delight that comes when we read good books together. John Senior has compiled a very helpful initial list of 1,000 good books that children should read or have read to them before they begin to scale the great ones. You can find it via that invention, of recent fame, known as the World Wide Web, that wilderness of mirrors and wild frontier. Speaking of Wilde and children's books, Oscar Wilde's *Stories for Children* is one of those rare books that entertains, instructs, and delights both children and parents simultaneously. (And do not think that I forgot the importance of Wilde's *De Profundis* or *The Picture of Dorian Gray*. Since we are already whispering with a quietness no censors will hear, allow me to mention a handful of other titles here, off-census—below and beyond the official 101 (which was from the beginning an inaccuracy: the Bible is 73 books in one, for instance): Chekhov (!), Turgenev's *Fathers and Sons*, many novels of Virginia Woolf and Joseph Conrad, not a few poems of Ezra Pound, Jorge Luis Borges's *Collected Fictions,* the collected poems of Siegfried Sassoon and W. H. Auden and Edith Sitwell and Elizabeth Jennings and William Everson and Geoffrey Hill, the stories of Kafka and Poe, the novels of John Hassler, David Jones's *The Anathemata,* Andres Dubus's *In the Bedroom,* the novels of Piers Paul Read, and William Gaddis's *The Recollections* (the latter is a sprawling behemoth, what Henry James would call a "large, *loose, baggy monster," takes* you through some specious spiritual and philosophical territory, even as it embodies, novelistically, so many crises of modernity).

Appendix B

Reading and Writing Like a Catholic: Further Forays

Aristotle, *Poetics*

Plato, *Symposium*

Horace, *Ars Poetica*

Longinus, *On the Sublime*

François-René de Chateaubriand, *The Genius of Christianity*

Jacques Maritain, *Art and Scholasticism*, *The Situation of Poetry* (with Raïssa Maritain), *Three Reformers: Luther, Descartes, and Rousseau*

Flannery O'Connor, *Mystery and Manners*

Etienne Gilson, *The Arts of the Beautiful*

William F. Lynch, SJ, *Christ and Apollo: The Dimensions of the Literary Imagination*

Walker Percy, *Signposts in a Strange Land: Essays*, *The Message in the Bottle*

Caroline Gordon, *How to Read a Novel*

Caroline Gordon and Allen Tate, *The House of Fiction*

Dana Gioia, *The Catholic Writer Today and Other Essays*

Josef Pieper, *Only the Lover Sings, Leisure, the Basis of Culture* and others

Dietrich von Hildebrand, *Aesthetics*

Allen Tate, *Essays of Four Decades,* especially "The Angelic Imagination," and "The Symbolic Imagination"

John Finlay, *"With Constant Light": Collected Essays*

T. S. Eliot, *On Poetry and Poets, Christianity and Culture* and others

Harold C. Gardiner, SJ, *Norms for the Novel*

David Lodge, *The Art of Fiction*

Henry James, *The Art of the Novel: Critical Prefaces*

Virginia Woolf, *The Art of Fiction: A Collection of Essays*

Viktor Shklovsky, *Theory of Prose*

James Wood, *How Fiction Works*

Douglass Bauer, *The Stuff of Fiction: Advice on Craft*

Charles Baxter, *Burning Down the House: Essays on Fiction*

Percy Lubbock, *The Craft of Fiction*

Willa Cather, "On the Art of Fiction"

The Art of Fiction, ed. Dana Gioia and R. S. Gywnn

Jerome Sterne, *Making Shapely Fiction*

John Gardiner, *The Art of Fiction: Notes on Craft for Young Writers*

Anne Lamott, *Bird by Bird: Some Instructions on Writing and Life*

Ron Hansen, *A Stay Against Confusion: Essays on Faith and Fiction*

David Foster Wallace, "E. Unibus Pluram: Television and U.S. Fiction"

René Girard, *Deceit, Desire, and the Novel*

Joseph Bottum, *The Decline of the Novel*

Eric Auerbach: *Mimesis: The Representation of Reality in Western Literature*

Max Scheler, *Ressentiment*

C. S. Lewis, *The Discarded Image*

Henri de Lubac, SJ, *The Drama of Atheist Humanism*

Hans Urs von Balthasar, *The Glory of the Lord: A Theological Aesthetics*

John Milbank, Graham Ward, Edith Wyschogrod, *Theological Perspectives on God and Beauty*

Catherine Pickstock, *After Writing: On the Liturgical Consummation of Philosophy*

Timothy Steele, *Missing Measures: Modern Poetry and the Revolt Against Meter* and *All the Fun's in How You Say a Thing: An Explanation of Meter and Versification*[2]

Father Colum Power, *James Joyce's Catholic Categories*

---

2 Another caveat: as you now know, the "how to write" portion of this book focuses on fiction. Should you be a poet, aspiring or otherwise, I strongly recommend Winters's and Steele's books as foundations for learning the craft of versification. I also strongly recommend James Matthew Wilson's *The Fortunes of Poetry in an Age of Unmaking,* as well as Wilson's *The Catholic Imagination in Modern American Poetry*

J. F. Powers, *Suitable Accommodations: An Autobiographical Story of Family Life: The Letters of J. F. Powers, 1942–1963*

Christine Flanagan, *The Letters of Flannery O'Connor and Caroline Gordon*

Flannery O'Connor, *The Habit of Being*, letters of O'Connor selected and edited by Sally Fitzgerald

Paul Claudel, "Religion and the Artist: Introduction to a Poem on Dante"

Francois Mauriac, *Second Thoughts: Reflections on Literature and Life*

Fyodor Dostoevsky, *Diaries and Notebooks* (which contain notes on his novels)

Simone Weil, *Gravity and Grace, The Iliad, or the Poem of Force,* "Morality and Literature," and others

Czeslaw Milosz, *The Captive Mind*

Raïssa Maritain, *Adventures in Grace* and *We Have Been Friends Together.*

G. K. Chesterton, *The Utopia of Usurers and Other Essays, Charles Dickens* (premised on the presumption that you ought to read Dickens)

Thomas Merton, *The Literary Essays*

Nicholas Ripatrizone, *The Fine Delight: Postconciliar Catholic Literature*

Paul Elie, *The Life You Save May Be Your Own: An American Pilgrimage*

Edwin Fussell, *The Catholic Side of Henry James*

Matthew C. Nickel, *Hemingway's Dark Night: Catholic Influences and Intertextualities in the Work of Ernest Hemingway*

Joan M. Allen, *Candles and Carnival Lights: The Catholic Sensibility of F. Scott Fitzgerald*

Yvor Winters, *In Defense of Reason,* and *Forms of Discovery*

J. V. Cunningham, *The Collected Essays*

J. R. R. Tolkien, *On Fairy Stories* and others[3]

Edith Sitwell, *Taken Care of, The Queens and the Hive*

Joseph Pearce, *Poems Every Catholic Should Know*

Clemens Cavallin, *On the Edge of Infinity: A Biography of Michael O'Brien*

Romano Guardini, *The Meaning of Melancholy*, and others

Kurt F. Reinhardt, *The Theological Novel of Modern Europe*

George A. Panichas, *The Burden of Vision: Dostoevsky's Spiritual Art*

Konstantin Mochulsky, *Dostoevsky: His Life and Work*

Mikhail Bakhtin, *The Dialogic Imagination, Problems of Dostoevsky's Poetics*

Pierre Manent, *Metamorphoses of the City,* especially "The Poetic Birth of the City," and others

Russell Kirk, *Enemies of the Permanent Things: Observations of Abnormality in Literature and Politics*

---

3 Although in the chapter on *A Canticle for Leibowitz* I did broach the science fiction genre, I did not delve into fantasy in the body of this book. That is not because I want you to buy the book I wrote on J. R. R. Tolkien, which contains my thoughts on fantasy.

Alasdair MacIntyre, *After Virtue* and others

Philip Rieff, *My Life Among the Deathworks*

Albert Beguin, *Léon Bloy: A Study in Impatience*

Martin Mosebach, *The Heresy of Formlessness*

About the Author

JOSHUA HREN IS the founder and publisher of Wiseblood Books and co-founder of the low-residency Master of Fine Arts in Creative Writing at the University of St. Thomas in Houston. He has published two collections of short stories, *This Our Exile* and *In the Wine Press*, as well as *Middle-earth and the Return of the Common Good: J.R.R. Tolkien and Political Philosophy*. Joshua's poems and essays have appeared in such journals as *First Things*, *America*, and *LOGOS*. His first novel, *Infinite Regress*, is forthcoming from Angelico Press.